Behavioral Medicine

Behavioral Medicine:
A Primary Care Approach

H. Russell Searight
Deaconess Family Medicine Residency
Deaconess Hospital

Department of Psychology
St. Louis University

Department of Community and Family Medicine
St. Louis University School of Medicine
St. Louis, Missouri

USA	Publishing Office:	BRUNNER/MAZEL *A member of the Taylor & Francis Group* 325 Chestnut Street Philadelphia, PA 19106 Tel.: (215) 625-8900 Fax: (215) 625-2940
	Distribution Center:	BRUNNER/MAZEL *A member of the Taylor & Francis Group* 47 Runway Road Levitttown, PA 19057 Tel.: (215) 269-0400 Fax: (215) 269-0363
UK		BRUNNER/MAZEL *A member of the Taylor & Francis Group* 1 Gunpowder Square London EC4A 3DE Tel.: +44 171 583 0490 Fax: +44 171 583 0581

BEHAVIORAL MEDICINE: A Primary Care Approach

1 2 3 4 5 6 7 8 9 0

Printed by Edwards Brothers, Ann Arbor, MI, 1998.

A CIP catalog record for this book is available from the British Library.
⊗ The paper in this publication meets the requirements of the ANSI Standard Z39.48-1984 (Permanence of Paper)

Library of Congress Cataloging-in-Publication Data
Searight, H. Russell.
    Behavioral medicine : a primary care approach / H. Russell Searight.
      p. cm.
    Includes bibliographical references and index.
    ISBN 0-87630-981-3 (cloth : alk. paper). – ISBN 0-87630-982-1
(pbk. : alk. paper)
    1. Medicine and psychology. 2. Primary care (Medicine) I. Title.
    [DNLM: 1. Behavioral Medicine. 2. Mental Disorders. 3. Disease-psychology.
4. Primary Health Care. WB 102S439b 1999]
R726.5.S43 1999
616′.001′9 – dc21
DNLM/DLC
for Library of Congress

    98-35106
    CIP

ISBN 0-87630-981-3 (cloth)
ISBN 0-87630-982-1 (paper)

Dedication

For Barbara

Contents

Preface

Behavioral Medicine: A Primary Care Approach was written with two overall goals. First, the book was designed to assist mental health providers in addressing psychological disorders as they arise in a medical setting. The second objective was to sensitize all health care providers to psychosocial aspects of many common illnesses. With the rise in prominence of primary health care, the integration of medical and mental health treatment is occurring. However, there has been little formal training on either side of the fence—medical or mental health—in how to address common psychosocial problems as they interact with physical illnesses.

The book begins in Chapter 1 with a discussion of the unique features of the primary medical care setting. Efficiency, an emphasis on focal presenting problems, and pragmatism are all values of the primary care sector. Many mental health professionals are unaware of the extent to which mental health problems are already addressed by primary care physicians. Research in this area is reviewed. Readers are encouraged to adopt a healthy respect for the interaction and overlap between medical illness and psychiatric syndromes.

The next two chapters address adult psychiatric disorders in primary care. Many mental health professionals are unaware that depression and anxiety disorders are often treated by internists and family physicians. The symptoms of these common mental health problems among primary care patients, however, may not fit the classical patterns presented in the *Diagnostic and Statistical Manual of Mental Disorders, Fourth Edition* (American Psychiatric Association, 1994). In addition to symptom overlap between medical and psychiatric illness, there are unique variations on presenting symptoms such as "minor" mood disorders in the medical sector as compared with the classical major depression seen in the mental health sector. Chapter 3 continues the discussion of psychiatric conditions with an emphasis on longer standing and serious mental health problems. Considerable attention is devoted to somatization disorders—one of the most common conditions seen by primary care physicians, but a disorder neglected in the mental health field. While personality disorders are usually not a focus of treatment in the medical setting, these patients' pathologies will impact issues such as help-seeking behavior and compliance with medical regimens. Alcohol abuse/dependence is a major contributor to physical illness that may remain undetected. Accurate early assessment and clinical "clues" to underlying substance abuse are described in chapter 3.

Pediatricians and family physicians are often the first and only professionals consulted for children with behavioral and emotional problems. These pediatric presentations commonly involve subclinical concerns such as behavioral noncompliance and tantrums. These problems are often addressed with parent education and basic training in behavioral management. Current surveys indicate that attention-deficit/hyperactivity disorder is almost exclusively diagnosed and treated by primary care physicians. Other externalizing problems commonly seen include oppositional defiant disorder and conduct disorder. Brief protocols for addressing these two disorders are presented. Childhood depression often takes a distinct form compared with adult mood disorders. A comparative review of childhood depression is presented in chapter 4.

Family dynamics may play a major role in seeking health care. As discussed in chapter 5, families typically have explicit, unlabeled "rules" about what constitutes a significant symptom, and when outside medical care should be sought. A family's "culture" also may specify appropriate treatments. While most clinicians are familiar with individual developmental stages, families also have life cycles that include distinct phases. These are important to consider when working with families in the health care setting.

The next six chapters address psychosocial factors commonly associated with specific medical conditions. Cardiovascular disorders include hypertension and coronary heart disease. Life style factors have been implicated in heart disease. Chapter 6 reviews relevant research and practical, brief intervention. A common emergency department dilemma is differentiating an acute myocardial infarction (heart attack) from panic disorder. This differential diagnosis is discussed in some detail. While the role of psychological factors in asthma has become less pronounced in the past decade, medication compliance and the interaction of anxiety with asthma symptoms are common concerns. Chapter 7 also describes mental status and other psychological changes associated with pulmonary disease. One of the most common causes of respiratory disorders is cigarette smoking. Smoking cessation therapy is reviewed, which leads to a description of an efficient primary care protocol including pharmacotherapy and cognitive behavioral methods.

Both insulin-dependent and non-insulin-dependent diabetes are chronic diseases with a number of psychosocial implications. Diabetic patients have elevated rates of major depression. In addition, patients' coping styles influence compliance with diet and medication. Obesity, a common contributing factor to Type II diabetes, has become a significant health concern in the United States. Behavioral approaches to treating obesity are described with an emphasis on brief behavioral counseling. Chapter 8 concludes with a discussion of anorexia nervosa and bulimia with guidelines for assessment, treatment, and when necessary, referral of these patients to specialized providers. Chapter 9 focuses on Human Immunodeficiency Virus (HIV) and AIDS. Sexual behavior and drug use play a significant role in acquiring HIV. Testing for the virus is a stressful experience for many patients. Guidelines for pre- and post-test counseling are described. Psychiatric disorders frequently found among HIV-positive and AIDS patients are also discussed with attention to the virus' impact on the central nervous system. Unique ethical and legal dilemmas, including confidentiality and developing advanced directives, may arise in treating HIV/AIDS patients. Chapter 9 concludes with a discussion of chronic fatigue syndrome, a disorder with an ambiguous etiology that seriously impairs patients' daily functioning and emotional well-being.

Mental health professionals in primary care settings will frequently be consulted about suspected cases of dementia. In its early stages, Alzheimer's dementia is usually diagnosed solely on the basis of cognitive and behavioral changes. This second most common type of dementing illness, Multi-Infarct Dementia, should be considered in evaluating patients with cognitive behavioral changes. In its early stages, Alzheimer's dementia symptoms may be difficult to distinguish from geriatric depression. Chapter 10 includes a set of clinical guidelines for making the differential diagnoses. This chapter concludes with a discussion of acute mental status changes associated with delirium as well as psychosocial aspects of seizure disorders.

Chapter 11 concludes the material on psychological aspects of specific medical illnesses with a general description of psychological factors and pain. Psychological aspects of migraine and tension headaches are described. Two other common pain symptoms, temporomandibular joint pain (TMJ) and lower back pain, are briefly reviewed with an overview of psychological treatment.

Culture, sexual orientation, and gender all play a role in seeking health care. The prevalence of certain illnesses may be influenced by these cultural and demographic factors. Additionally, communication styles, acceptability of specific treatment, and the role of family/significant others are influenced by culture and gender. Chapter 12 provides a brief overview of cultural diversity with specific examples of issues arising in primary care.

Health care settings raise a unique set of ethical dilemmas. Confidentiality and informed consent are often viewed differently in medical versus mental health settings. Guidelines for ethical management of psychological issues are discussed in chapter 13. The shift in managed care presents additional dilemmas including information disclosure to patients and regulations governing duration and level of care. Psychologists and psychiatrists are frequently called upon to assess patients' decisional capacity and to aid in the legal determination of patient competence. Guidelines for these evaluations are presented. Chapter 13 concludes with a discussion of the newly evolving area of genetic testing and counseling.

The book concludes with a brief historical overview of managed care. Many managed health care programs carve out mental health treatment as distinct from medical care. The previous chapters hopefully present a significant challenge to this dichotomy. The separation of physical and mental well-being is not in patients' best interests. The integration of medical and psychological care—one of the overall objectives of this book—would best occur through collaboration between medical and mental health providers.

Acknowledgments

Ten years ago, I eagerly accepted a position as a behavioral science faculty member in a family medicine residency program; this is something I had wanted to do since my second year of graduate school. I came into my new position with a broad background in clinical psychology. I had also trained in psychiatric hospitals, specialized medical settings, and outpatient clinics serving patients of all ages. However, I rapidly came to appreciate that the primary care setting required a unique set of skills. The traditional "full battery" of psychological tests and weekly 50-minute-hour psychotherapy sessions did not fit with the fast-paced, problem-focused world of family medicine. While I also had considerable experience in college and graduate school teaching, I soon learned that my seemingly thoughtful discourses on theory and obsessive reviews of research findings were not helpful approaches to teaching family physicians and internists.

At the time I began in primary care, there was little organized information about the knowledge and skills necessary for addressing mental health problems as they uniquely presented in this setting. Many of my colleagues in psychology seemed to find my interest in effective collaboration with physicians to be an odd pursuit. Other psychologists often didn't understand what I did or why I rattled on about the benefits of pharmacotherapy, how to identify depression and substance abuse in 5–10 minutes, as well as my interest in topics such as patients' capacity to consent to surgery or counseling sessions that took place during a physical examination. Since that time, interest in primary care has risen dramatically. During the past five years, changes in health care delivery in the United States have given primary health care providers a central role.

Although I began to think about writing this book about five years ago, I could not get past the idea stage for some time. Each time that I began an outline for the book, I inevitably became frustrated and "stuck." I could not find a coherent framework for organizing what seemed to be an overwhelming and unwieldy set of topics that make up behavioral medicine in primary care. The range of content, from bedwetting in a 4-year-old to Alzheimer's disease in a geriatric patient, is an inherent part of family medicine, the primary care specialty with which I am affiliated. Yet whenever I tried to draw up a sample table of contents, I failed to find a coherent pattern that lent itself to a series of book chapters.

My problem with organization was solved when David Campbell, the chair of the Department of Family Medicine at Deaconess Hospital, developed a new framework for our monthly set of resident conferences, which focused on distinct organ systems. Preparing a lecture on psychological aspects of cardiac disease one month and behavioral issues in respiratory illness the following month helped me further integrate behavioral science with medical care. In addition, Dave's innovative lecture format provided the organization that I was searching for in a book of this type. Although the actual writing took about a year, I always felt sure where I was going during the process.

In addition to providing the organization for this book, I again need to thank Dave for his ongoing support for writing and research in the department. His encouragement for faculty development and individual initiative made this book a reality. As department chair, Dave encourages faculty to achieve meaningful professional goals and make creative, innovative contributions.

Many of the book's topic areas were originally developed through collaboration with other Deaconess Family Medicine faculty. Several of the pediatric topics and attention-deficit hyperactivity disorder (AD/HD), in particular, arose through working with James Nahlik. Several years ago, Jim developed a course on AD/HD for the American Academy of Family Physicians and kindly invited me to participate. Presenting with Jim at the conference and in several publications helped me focus on key dimensions of diagnosing and managing childhood behavior problems in primary care.

Lesley McLaren and I collaborated on an article and audiotape on psychological aspects of HIV. Some of the material resulting from our work together is referenced in the chapter on infectious disease. Lesley has also continually provided helpful editorial feedback about my writing and diplomatically pointed out when I became overly wordy, unclear, or both.

My behavioral science colleague, Susan Hubbard has undoubtedly influenced this book in many places. We have most directly collaborated on two topics addressed in this volume: primary care counseling and capacity/competence assessment.

I also wish to thank several colleagues for providing opportunities for me to test out and develop many of the ideas in this book. Scott Soerries has allowed me to present a weekly behavioral science conference to residents and students who are rotating on our inpatient service. Scott and Jack Burke stimulated helpful discussion about a range of psychosocial topics and their application to medical practice. Scott and Jack, as well as our residents, not only graciously tolerated but also even read the array of occasionally esoteric articles that I brought for discussion.

Michael Railey invited me to provide monthly lectures for his family medicine class at Saint Louis University School of Medicine. I have genuinely enjoyed the opportunity to teach in this setting as well as Mike's thoughtful feedback and ongoing support. Much of the material on psychiatric conditions in primary care was originally developed for this class.

Without blinking, Sandra Duvic, our residency administrator, obtained much of the tangible support necessary for this book's completion. Sandy's help as well as her incredible skill in keeping the department running smoothly, attention to detail, together with her warmth and good humor established a setting in which large-scale projects like this one can be completed.

One of the benefits of teaching is that I continue to learn. My primary teachers for this book have been the family medicine residents that I have worked with over the years. One of my teaching responsibilities is to observe resident physicians in their clinical encounters with patients. The objectives of these observations are to help the residents improve interviewing and other doctor–patient interaction skills. While I hope that the residents have taken something from my feedback, I am sure that I have learned far more from the privilege of observing their work with patients. I am also grateful for the many "hallway consultations" that we continue to have. These exchanges and clinic observations have been the most valuable experiences in teaching me to adapt psychological practice to the primary health care setting.

At the editorial level, I wish to thank Bernadette Capelle of Brunner/Mazel for seeing the value in this book in its early manuscript stages. Thaisa Tiglao has efficiently and professionally edited the book and moved it through production.

In St. Louis, Virginia Myrick and her staff graciously typed and patiently retyped various versions of this book in its manuscript form.

The influence of my family was always present in completing this book. My parents provided me with models of self-discipline to take on a project of this magnitude and see it through to the end. I cannot thank my wife Barbara and daughter Alicia enough for their ongoing support of my writing even though it took time away from them. Barbara has known that this project has been important to me and, as always, has been understanding, loving, and caring. My daughter prods me along by asking if I am "done with it yet" while her enthusiasm and great sense of humor continues to enrich my life.

Chapter 1

Overview of Primary Care

The primary medical setting is rapidly becoming the most common arena for patients seeking health care. Primary care includes family medicine, pediatrics, internal medicine, and frequently, gynecology. Primary medical practitioners treat a broad range of medical problems across multiple organ systems and anatomical regions. The family doctor or general practitioner treating most acute and chronic illness across the life span is the "popular" image of the primary care provider. During the 1960s and 1970s, specialty physicians, (e.g., ophthalmologists, neurologists, and cardiologists) were seen as technologically superior to the general practitioner and were sought out by many patients for specific medical problems. Many persons did not have a general or family physician.

Changes in the health care delivery system in the 1990s increased the public visibility as well as the number of patients who were seeing primary care physicians. Third-party payers, including government health insurance such as Medicare and Medicaid, required patients to have a primary care physician. One practical reason was cost containment. Many patients would self-refer conditions to more expensive specialists that could be as effectively treated by an internist or family physician. The primary care physician has recently become the gatekeeper to specialists: patients who seek specialty medical care have to be referred by their primary provider. In some insurance plans, access to mental health care follows this same guideline.

Primary care providers have increasingly devoted attention to psychosocial issues. For example, family medicine residency programs require mental health specialists (usually a psychologist, family therapist, or licensed clinical social worker) to be on their teaching faculty along with physicians. Pediatrics and internal medicine frequently include psychological aspects of patient care as part of the curriculum. In clinical practice, primary care physicians directly and indirectly evaluate and treat psychosocial problems. As will be evident in the chapters that follow, most common psychiatric disorders are treated by family physicians, pediatricians, and internists. At the same time, there is evidence that these providers fail to detect prevalent problems such as depression and alcohol abuse. Most health

1

care clinicians also recognize that medical problems like diabetes, asthma, hypertension, HIV/AIDS, and seizure disorders all have a psychological component. In addition to elevated risks of mental health problems, patients with these medical disorders often have developmental, emotional, or interpersonal issues that exacerbate their illness. Many diseases are preventable, including respiratory disorders such as emphysema, Type II diabetes, and hypertension. These illnesses are influenced by diet, exercise, and smoking. Individual cognitive, emotional, and personality dimensions as well as family and marital dynamics play an important role in habit control and life style modifications.

The goal of this book is to help mental health professionals acquire basic knowledge and skills so that they can work effectively in this new, important health care context. Much of this material is not formally taught in graduate programs in clinical psychology, psychiatry, social work, or marital/family therapy. The material covered in the remainder of this chapter is rarely addressed in mental health education. Although other topics such as psychiatric disorders, family dynamics, and psychological aspects of medical disorders have been described elsewhere, this material has not been organized in one volume to address the unique issues arising in primary care.

Many mental health professionals are unaware of the extent to which primary care providers are involved in psychiatric treatment. In addition, there is research, albeit limited, indicating that psychological treatment impacts medical service utilization—an issue of considerable importance in this era of health care cost containment. This issue will be reviewed, followed by a discussion of values and skills that are helpful to the mental health professional practicing in primary medical care.

THE "HIDDEN" MENTAL HEALTH SYSTEM

Although most mental health providers are well aware of the various disciplines specializing in psychiatric care (psychologists, social workers, family therapists, licensed professional counselors, and psychiatrists), these professionals are often unaware of the role of primary care providers in mental health service delivery.

It has been estimated that at least 30% of primary care patients have a psychiatric disorder that is the focus of treatment or a psychosocial problem that is a direct contributor to their medical illness (Ford, 1994; Leaf, 1994; Miranda, Hohmann, & Attkisson, 1994). At least half of all office visits involving a psychiatric diagnosis are to nonpsychiatric physicians (Fischer & Ransom, 1997; Schurman, Kramer, & Mitchell, 1985). Further evidence that patients with psychiatric disorders commonly present to primary care providers comes from epidemiological data. In the United States, the overall 6-month prevalence rate of psychiatric disorders, including substance abuse, is about 15% (Miranda et al., 1994). Among patients seen in primary care practices, however, rates of these disorders are close to 22% (Kessler, Cleary, & Burke, 1987). Although fewer than 30% of people with psychiatric or substance abuse problems are seen in the formal mental health sector, nearly 80% of people with mental or addictive disorders receive general health care services (Miranda et al., 1994). There is considerable evidence that patients with relatively common psychiatric disorders such as major depression or anxiety disorders are about equally likely to be treated in the primary care sector. The majority of patients with somatization disorders receive care exclusively in the primary medical care sector. Even severe psychiatric disorders such as schizophrenia and bipolar disorder are often managed by primary care physicians. Miranda and colleagues (1994) reported that 29% of patients who met diagnostic criteria for schizophrenia were treated by physicians in the general medical sector, with 14% of these patients being seen exclusively by nonpsychiatric physicians. Interestingly, patients with bipolar disorder are about equally likely to be treated in the general medical versus the mental health setting (Miranda et al., 1994). In the area of substance abuse, more than 50% of patients with alcohol or drug abuse disorders are seen exclusively by general medical practitioners with only about 10% receiving specialty mental health care (Havassy & Schmidt, 1994). Primary care providers frequently report that their patients with psychiatric problems are much more difficult to diagnose accurately than those seen by specialists. One impediment to diagnostic accuracy is a fairly high co-incidence of somatization, anxiety, and depression among primary care patients. Similarly, patients often have comorbid medical problems that are exacerbated by their psychiatric condition. Several studies have suggested that among patients who are depressed, those presenting in the psychiatric sector exhibit more "classical" depressive symptoms. In contrast, those seen in the family practice setting had a higher incidence of chronic illness, less specific complaints, and more emphasis on physical than psychological difficulties (Williamson & Yates, 1989). However, at the same time, the family practice patients appeared to be less severely depressed. Demographically, Coulehan, Schulberg, Block, and Zettler-Segal (1988) found that compared with mental health patients seen in community mental health settings, those seen in primary medical care offices were more likely to be African American, unmarried, and of lower income.

It is important to recognize that many psychiatric treatment episodes in the primary care sector do not involve an official psychiatric diagnosis. Many primary care physicians have evolved an informal policy of using a general medical diagnosis instead of a mental health diagnosis. Rost, Smith, Matthews, and Guise (1994) found that about half of a sample of primary care physicians indicated they had engaged in this practice during the two weeks prior to the interview. Reasons included uncertainty about the diagnosis but also concerns about reimbursement and the possibility that a psychiatric label would have an adverse effect on the patient's future insurability.

Seaburn, Lorenz, Gunn, Gawinski, and Mauksch (1996) note that several factors contribute to mental health treatment by primary care providers. In some areas of the country, particularly rural areas or in impoverished inner city neighborhoods, mental health providers are unavailable. Additionally, patients have often developed a relationship with their primary care physician and have come to trust them. This trust is often developed and enhanced because the provider took care of the patient while they were in a vulnerable position during an acute physical illness. Often patients view a referral to a specialist as a "cutting off" of their valued relationship with their primary care physician.

Additionally, many patients do not perceive their problems as psychological in nature. Particularly patients with somatization and panic disorder and even many depressed patients perceive their symptoms as medically based. Even though they may be treated with anxiolytic or antidepressant medication, prescribed by their primary care physician, the patient continues to perceive his or her difficulties as within the realm of their physician rather than a mental health professional. Certain ethnic groups in particular, such as Asian Americans, are more likely to experience emotional problems as somatic (Kleinman, 1988). Many patients also tend to view a referral to a mental health specialist as stigmatizing. The rise in managed care has provided economic obstacles to mental health care. Medical care is often reimbursed with fewer limits and at a greater rate than mental health services. The use of "carve outs" (separate medical and mental health insurance plans) often results in the patient going to a provider that neither they nor the physician knows. This is likely to increase anxiety and greatly reduce the likelihood of follow-up by the patient as well as reduce mental health referral by physicians.

A consistent finding is that a high proportion—between one third and one half—of primary care patients do not follow through on referrals to mental health professionals (Fisher & Ransom, 1997). These referrals are more likely to be completed if mental health providers are in the same office as the physician and also if the referral is presented as part of a continuing care including the physician. However, the reality is that many patients expect their physicians to address their mental health issues along with their physical well being.

HEALTH CARE UTILIZATION

Several studies have found that when a referral to a mental health professional does take place, there is a reduction in health care visits for the patient. Huygens' (1978) study of Dutch families seen in brief family therapy found that the number of contacts with the primary care physician declined not only for the index patient but also for family members. There was also a decline in use of overall prescriptions, as well as psychotropic medications specifically. Several other studies have consistently found reductions in outpatient and inpatient health care utilization services associated with mental health and substance abuse (Mumford, Schlesinger, Glass, Patrick, & Cuerdon, 1984).

Interestingly, in nearly all the studies reviewed by Seaburn and colleagues (1996), the major financial impact of mental health care was on inpatient hospitalization. Additionally, the majority of the patients received relatively brief to "moderate" levels of mental health intervention.

Although limited, available research suggests that patients who use a disproportionate amount of health care have both medical and mental health problems. In one sample, 30% of health services were utilized by 10% of patients. Half of these mentally ill patients had concurrent psychiatric illnesses (Katon, Von Korff, Lin, Lipscomb, Wagner, & Polik, 1990; Seaburn et al., 1996). There are certain subgroups of patients who are likely to benefit from collaborative care between a primary medical and mental health professional. Patients with somatization disorder who received a psychiatric consultation including recommendations to their primary physician had a 50% decline in health service utilization (Smith, Monson, & Ray, 1986). Other patients likely to benefit from collaborative care include those with physical distress that is not well-articulated. These patients include those with vague symptoms such as fatigue, dizziness without an established etiology, or "minor" depression. In this latter situation, patients have depressive symptoms but do not have enough of them to meet clear-cut criteria for dysthymic disorder or major depression. Chronically ill patients with compliance problems, such as those with diabetes, asthma, or hypertension, are also likely to benefit from mental health involvement. With these patients, the focus should be on the role of an undiagnosed psychiatric disorder or psychosocial conflict upon compliance. Additionally, mental health professionals may be better skilled at assessing a patient's "world view" and the complicated reasons associated with failure to follow through with medical treatment (Searight & Noce, 1988).

Given the prevalence of psychiatric problems in primary care and data suggesting that mental health care is likely to improve patients' functioning as well as decreased health service utilization, collaboration between these physicians and mental health professions would seem to be a natural partnership. Yet, the number of successful health care alliances is limited. Although economic and insurance issues play a significant role in hindering mental health care in many medical settings, mental health professionals are often not well trained for primary medicine. The formal education of psychologists, social workers, and family therapists, and to a lesser extent psychiatrists, emphasizes skills that do not transfer well to this setting. Primary care also often requires a major shift in values, priorities, and overall clinical world view (Searight, 1994). These issues will be explored in the next section.

QUALITIES AND SKILLS THAT ARE HELPFUL IN PRIMARY CARE

Tolerance for Ambiguity

Mental health professionals who are used to working in community mental health centers, outpatient private practices, or inpatient psychiatric units will experience initial frustration in primary care settings. Patients' psychological symptoms are often less clear-cut in general practice than is commonly the case in the specialty sector. For example, depression may present as chronic headache or lower back pain. Panic or acute anxiety may present as difficulty breathing or chest pain. Additionally, the provider will have to determine the relative role of medical factors and psychologic factors in the etiology of the patient's problem. For example, erectile dysfunction ("impotence") in a diabetic male may be in part attributable to the disease process but also may be associated with psychologic factors such as a perception of oneself as physically less desirable. Physical and psychological dimensions are likely to interact among these patients. Thus, it may not be an issue of either physical or psychological but of both domains operating in concert. Often, the best understanding that can be developed for a patient is a "working hypothesis." This working hypothesis may be confirmed or disconfirmed by the course of the patient's illness over time or his or her response to treatment.

Pragmatism

Mental health providers have historically devoted considerable attention to understanding the underlying causes of mental disorder. Detailed psychological evaluations including hours of specialized testing have traditionally been seen as useful for thoroughly understanding the patient. As Haley (1996) has pointed out, many mental health providers become so preoccupied with their quest for understanding patients that relatively little attention is paid to treatment. Attending case conferences in mental health settings will often underscore this value. Considerable time is spent addressing possible causes as well as complicating factors associated with the patient's, couple's or family's presenting problem. However, often the time-limited conference ends with participants still in a spirited discussion about these diagnostic issues while intervention is neglected. Primary care, on the other hand, is much more pragmatic (Searight, 1994). Although diagnosis is important, it is seen as a direct gateway to a plan of intervention. There is much less tolerance for detailed discussions of etiology and associated theoretical implications with much more emphasis on the pragmatic issues of patient care. As Seaburn and colleagues (1996) noted, one of the most helpful questions for mental health professionals to ask their medical colleagues is: "How can I help you?" "Lengthy explanation of the patient's "underlying problem" is sweeter music to the therapist's ear than the health care professional's" (p. 117). Seaburn goes on to present the example of a physician referral of a 14-year-old girl with insulin-dependent diabetes. The girl had been noncompliant with her insulin and despite considerable education, has not been taking appropriate measures to deal with her diabetes. A mental health professional with little background in primary care may respond as follows:

> Maybe compliance is not the key issue here. It sounds like the girl may need to rebel as an adolescent. This is a pretty normal thing to do. Furthermore, in all likelihood, the family may function in ways that encourage the girl not to take her insulin. Maybe the girl is caught in some marital conflict between her parents that we are unaware of. By not complying, she can draw her parents' attention to her and away from their marital discord. It could be any number of things. (Seaburn et al., 1996, p. 118)

Instead of positing multiple causal explanations for the girl's problems, the mental health professional will be more helpful to the medical staff if suggestions are practical, problem-focused and include a concrete plan:

> I would be glad to work with you to help this girl manage her diabetes better. What I would suggest we do is this: I want to meet with your patient and her parents; Since she is at such risk, they may need to be more involved until she is able to manage things on her own. You could come to that visit and emphasize the seriousness of the problem and let them know that we will be working together. (p. 118)

Efficiency

Mental health professionals are customarily used to the classic 50-minute hour. They also are customarily used to seeing a limited number of patients, with six to eight often being the maximum, per day. By contrast, primary care physicians in private practice often will see 40–60 patients per day. It is important to recognize that among primary care health providers, the average office visit is typically 10–15 minutes. For many mental health professionals, this time period is only the "warm up" to therapy—time chatting about the weather or otherwise developing rapport. One model that has been developed for psychotherapy in the primary care sector is the BATHE format. BATHE is an acronym for a brief primary care counseling approach developed by M. R. Stuart and Lieberman (1993). The model is intended to be implemented as a series of questions and statements that the provider employs in a specific order: "B" stands for background ("What is going on in your life?"); "A" for affect ("How do you feel about it?"); "T" for trouble ("What troubles you the most about it?"); "H" for handling ("How are you handling the situation?"); and "E" for empathy ("It sounds difficult.").

In mental health settings, patients are often seen on a weekly basis until problems are resolved. The primary care practitioner often will see patients when they are in distress and then may go months to years without seeing them again. Usually, after a relationship is established and with time, the medical provider better understands the personality and family dynamics of the patient and is able to predict upcoming developmental transitions that individuals or families may have that contribute to mental health problems.

Brief Symptomatic Treatment

Many mental health professionals, particularly those who are trained in long-term psychotherapy, tend to view symptom relief as superficial and incomplete treatment. The primary care setting is oriented more toward acute mental health problems such as depression or anxiety that can be addressed with relatively brief and focused psychotherapy. Although it is recognized that patients may have longer standing personality disturbance, mental health practitioners in primary care settings do not usually conduct long-term reconstructive psychotherapy. Instead, as will be discussed in a later chapter, patients with long-standing personality dysfunction are symptomatically treated with an appreciation of their underlying dynamics. These personality features are "managed" and redirected rather than significantly altered.

Similarly, it is important that the provider be able to target the most salient problems that are associated with the patient's symptoms. Addressing these issues typically requires a problem-solving focus on current job stresses or family relationships.

Knowledge of and Respect for Psychotropic Medication

Psychotropic medications are the primary modality for treating the common psychiatric disorders that present in primary care including major depression and generalized anxiety, as well as pediatric disorders such as attention-deficit/hyperactivity disorder. The majority of psychotropic prescriptions are written by primary care physicians (Sleek, 1994; Buelow, & Chafetz, 1996) whereas only 17% are ordered by psychiatrists (Manley & DeLeon, 1997). Although many nonmedical mental health professionals are uncomfortable with psychotropic medications, ("just throwing pills at patients"), most medications—when they are prescribed appropriately for a clearly diagnosable condition—have an established efficacy equivalent to psychotherapies. Nonpsychiatric practitioners should be knowledgeable about psychotropic medications as well as other nonpsychotropic drugs that may affect cognitive, emotional, or vegetative functioning. This latter category includes antihypertensive medications such as beta blockers as well as anticonvulsant medications and analgesics. Mental health professionals with an interest in this area may want to educate themselves about psychotropics so that they can be particularly helpful to providers as a consultant.

Mental health professionals should become increasingly aware of the range of psychotropic medications so that they will refer patients who would benefit from pharmacotherapy. In addition, they are likely to be in a unique position to monitor patients' behavioral, cognitive, and vegetative responses to these medications. Helpful feedback can be provided to the prescribing physician about the symptomatic effectiveness of pharmacotherapy. While the issue of prescribing privileges for psychologists continues to be debated, mental health professionals who are knowledgeable about psychotropic medications will be highly valued in the primary care setting. Primary care physicians, because of the breadth of medical problems they address, may not be as current with psychotropic medications as a mental health provider who keeps abreast of the literature in this specialized area.

Appreciation of the Role of Medical Illness

With the exception of psychiatrists and nursing staff, most mental health professionals have relatively little medical training. Those who work in primary care settings for extended periods of time will often acquire medical knowledge through their ongoing involvement in patient care and interaction with physicians. Because of their limited knowledge of the physiological aspects of disease, nonmedical providers may minimize the impact of medical problems or pharmacotherapy regimens on the patient's daily functioning and well-being. In addition, nonmedical providers may mistakenly attribute medical symptoms to psychological causes. R. O. Taylor (1990) has discussed in some detail the problem of "psychological masquerade." He notes that many medical problems present with primarily emotional or cognitive symptoms and that nonmedical providers in particular may not adequately attend to their physiological basis. Hypothyroidism may contribute to depressive symptoms. Hyperthyroid patients may present with symptoms resembling an anxiety disorder. Similarly, fatigue and apathy secondary to a myocardial infarction ("heart attack") with cardiac patients, may be misdiagnosed as depression. In working in the medical setting, it is important that nonphysician providers recognize that traditional "mental health symptoms" may be caused by biomedical illness. Most physicians and other medical providers are certainly willing to explain medical diagnoses and procedures if interest is demonstrated.

CONCLUSION

Almost overnight the primary care sector has become the focal point of health services in the United States. Fueled in part by third-party payers, many individuals are centering their medical care around family physicians, internists, and pediatricians. These providers will be able to manage the vast majority of patient concerns. However, primary care clinicians are also the source of referrals to specialists—often including mental health providers. In many health plans, the primary care office has become a required "first step" before a patient can access a specialist. Family physicians, pediatricians, and internists also treat many psychiatric conditions in the United States. While recognizing that there is a huge potential for collaboration, mental health professionals will need to develop an efficient, problem-focused pragmatic approach that includes a serious appreciation of patient's medical problems. The chapters that follow will hopefully provide the knowledge and skills necessary to collaborate successfully in this rapidly expanding health setting.

Chapter 2

Psychiatric Disorders in the Medical Setting I: Mood and Anxiety Disorders

As noted in chapter 1, mood and anxiety disorders are commonly diagnosed and treated exclusively in the primary care sector. While most mental health professionals are familiar with these disorders, depression and anxiety symptoms often are more difficult to detect in the medical setting. Patients may not clearly emphasize dysphoric or anxious mood, and the symptoms are likely to be intertwined with the patient's medical complaints. Additionally, nonpsychiatric illnesses often include symptoms that overlap with the disorders discussed in this chapter. In this chapter, considerable attention will be devoted to major depression because of its high prevalence in medical settings. Dysthymic disorder, minor depression, and bipolar disorder will also be briefly discussed. Among anxiety disorders, panic disorder and generalized anxiety disorder are commonly seen in primary medical settings.

MAJOR DEPRESSION

Background

While the overall prevalence rate of depression is about one to two percent in the general population, depression is one of the top ten conditions seen in family practice settings (Kavan, Pace, Ponterotto, & Barone, 1990). It is estimated that at least 16 million depressed patients seek treatment from physicians each year in the United States and up to a third of patients presenting to family physicians exhibit significant depressive symptoms on self-report instruments (Kavan et al., 1990).

The peak ages for the onset of depressive symptoms are ages 15–19 for women and 25–29 for men. In the general population, about three percent of women and one and one-half percent of men are clinically depressed (*DSM–IV*, 1994). Although women are about two to three times as likely to be depressed as men, this gender difference appears to be less pronounced among very young and older patients. Among pre-adolescent children, the gender ratio is less well established but may include greater representation of boys (Pfeffer, 1986; Rutter, 1986).

Although major depressive illness is consistently among the top ten most common presenting problems in primary medical care, many mental health professionals are unaware that the majority of patients with depression are treated by family physicians and internists. However, there is a growing body of evidence that primary care physicians under-diagnose depression (Nielsen & Williams, 1980; Perez-Stable, Miranda, Munoz, & Ying, 1990). While the symptoms of depression are well-known, the evaluation of these symptoms and their varied presentations—particularly in primary medical care settings—are likely to be major contributors to under-diagnosis. A misconception about depression is that it is synonymous with dysphoric mood alone. While dysphoric mood is evident in most depressed patients, four additional symptoms need to be present to meet clear *DSM–IV* (1994) criteria for a major depressive episode. In the section below, the individual symptoms of depression will be examined in some detail with particular attention to variations that are often seen in primary care settings. It is important to recognize that the prototype of depression that is often conveyed in psychiatric texts is not the representative presentation of many primary care patients. In general practice, patients' medical problems are likely to be intertwined with depressive symptoms. This interaction may play a role in the difficulty detecting depression noted above.

Symptoms of Depression

DSM–IV (1994) indicates that pervasive dysphoric mood or anhedonia are core symptoms of major depression. Although depressed mood is relatively easy to detect through observation and interview, the clinician should be aware of other variations in mood found among patients with major depression. Increased anger and irritability is not uncommon—particularly among men. The high comorbidity of major depression with anxiety and somatization may make it difficult to evaluate the patient's mood. Patients with somatic concerns may deny dysphoria, but instead focus on their physical complaints. Anhedonia may be more common than dysphoria among patients with major depression and comorbid medical illness (Cohen-Cole, Brown, & McDaniel, 1993).

As noted above, if dysphoric mood is not present, the patient must have anhedonia (loss of interest or pleasure in usual activities) to qualify for the diagnosis. Patients typically report that activities that were previously pleasurable—eating favorite foods, sexual intercourse, sports, hobbies, recreation—no longer provide much satisfaction. Patients will say things like: "I used to really enjoy going out to bingo, but it just doesn't interest me any more, and I can't summon up the energy to go."

Appetite or weight disturbance is commonly found among depressed patients. While weight gain does occur in some depressed patients, the more common change is a decline in appetite and weight. *DSM–IV* (1994) defines significant weight loss as a change of 5% or more of body weight in the course of a month. With respect to appetite, patients should report a decline or significant increase in appetite every day for a one-month period. Refusal to eat and weight loss are common depressive symptoms in geriatric patients. It is also very common among patients in rehabilitation settings and nursing homes. Among these patients, failure to receive adequate nutrition can create a life threatening situation. The dilemma often arises as to whether these patients should be fed intravenously or through a feeding tube if they refuse to eat. As noted above, weight gain is not nearly as common; however, among patients with seasonal affective disorder (SAD) weight gain does occur. Among SADS patients, there is often extensive consumption of carbohydrates, particularly during the winter months.

The fourth criterion, sleep disturbance, is clinically a particularly sensitive indicator of the syndrome. While hypersomnia (excessive sleeping) is found periodically, particularly among young adults and adolescents who are depressed, insomnia is far more common. Insomnia is often further specified by the segment of the sleep cycle that is disrupted. Initial insomnia refers to difficulty falling asleep. While this does occur among depressed patients, it is probably more common among patients with significant levels of anxiety. Intermittent insomnia refers to waking up throughout the night and not being able to return to sleep. This is sometimes difficult to evaluate, particularly with elderly patients. Nondepressed older adults will often report disrupted sleep. Clinically, the sleep cycle of older adults is often reported as more disrupted than that of younger adults. In evaluating this sleep pattern, it is important for the clinician to determine whether the patient feels fatigued during the day and in particular whether they can readily get back to sleep when they do awaken during the night. Finally, terminal insomnia typically involves awakening one to two hours before it is necessary to awaken and not being able to return to sleep. Typically, these patients report that while they do not have to wake up until seven in the morning, they usually go to bed at midnight, awaken at 4:00 a.m. and then lay in bed, unable to return to sleep. Terminal insomnia, when present in the context of the other symptoms that have been described, is a particularly sensitive indicator of major depressive illness.

Psychomotor agitation or retardation is a somewhat nonspecific symptom of depression. When retardation is present, the patient will seem overcome by fatigue. Physical movements are very slow, posture is stooped, and the patient often will also slump over when seated (*DSM–IV*, 1994). However, there are also individuals who have agitated depression. Among these persons, there is often a comorbid anxiety disorder. In cases of agitation, the individual will also wring their hands, pace the floor, tap their fingers, and be very obviously agitated. *DSM–IV* (1994) notes that the psychomotor agitation or retardation should be observable from an external perspective and is not determined to be present simply by the patient's self-report.

Decline in energy level is also commonly reported among depressed patients. Diminished energy level, usually described by patients as a subjective sense of fatigue, by itself, is relatively nonspecific and not unique to depression. However, among patients who have a number of other depressive symptoms, decline in energy level is often relevant in assessing suicide risk. For example, in inquiries about suicidal behavior, many patients will report: "You know, I've thought about it, but I just don't have the energy to carry it out." A common "clinical pearl" in psychiatric inpatient work is that staff should become concerned when a patient who previously verbalized suicidal thoughts reports or exhibits rapidly improved energy. It has been suggested that these patients may now experience the energy to end their distress through suicide.

Depressed patients also report intense feelings of worthlessness, guilt, or both. They may be very preoccupied with having wronged or insulted loved ones even when there is no objective evidence. This self-reproach is often very common among terminally ill patients who are concerned that they will die before making amends to others. In addition, life review is a common process among many older patients and may result in substantial self-criticism over perceived moral failures. In geriatric patients, these feelings of worthlessness or guilt may reach delusional proportions.

Severely depressed patients typically report problems with attention, concentration, and goal-directed thought processes. Subjective reports of diminished attention, concentration, and memory are often difficult to evaluate. Formal psychological or mental status testing may be necessary to determine whether these deficits are objective or subjective. In addition, impaired short-term memory is often an early indicator of dementia. A difficulty with discriminating dementia from depression is that in early stages of dementia there are often no positive neurological findings through radiographic studies (e.g., CT scan or MRI). The differential diagnosis of dementia versus depression is discussed in further detail in Chapter 10. In patients who have impaired attention because of depression, there is often greater variability. These patients will have periods where their attention and concentration are quite good but will later have episodes where they "blank out." In cases of dementia, while there may be some minor fluctuation in attentional capacities, the level of impairment is much more consistent and severe.

The final criterion for depression centers around recurrent thoughts of death or suicide. Depression is probably the most common diagnosis among people who attempt and effect suicide. In the general population, about 1 out of 100 suicide attempters actually succeed. However, in certain subgroups such as the elderly, the ratio of attempters to effectors is lower. In evaluating suicide risk, it is important to distinguish between passive periodic thoughts ("Sometimes I would just like to go to sleep and not wake up the next morning.") and active suicidal plans; a definite desire to end one's life and a realistic means to do so obviously should be taken more seriously.

Depression Screening Tools

Because of their brevity and because they require very little direct time on the part of the provider, self-report measures of depression have been particularly popular in primary care settings. The value of these instruments in general medical practice has included clarification or diagnostic confirmation with patients presenting with confusing sets of physical symptoms (Kavan et al., 1990). In these instances, a positive finding on a depression instrument may direct the clinician to the possibility that depression is being expressed through somatic means. The results can also be used to initiate discussions with the patient about possible depressive symptoms. Repeated administration of these scales has been used to evaluate treatment response. Lastly, most of these instruments include an array of cognitive, mood, and vegetative symptoms. The particular pattern of items endorsed by the patient will help guide the clinician to focus on particular depressive dimensions (Kavan et al., 1990). Commonly used depression scales include the Beck Depression Inventory (A. T. Beck, Ward, Mendelson, Mock, & Erbaugh, 1961), The Self-Rating Depression Scale (Zung, 1965), the Geriatric Depression Scale (Yesavage, Brink, & Rose, 1983), and the Children's Depression Inventory (Kovacs, 1983). All of these instruments generally have acceptable reliability and validity. These instruments do appear to have a potential problem with false positives. Although their sensitivity is generally fairly good, their specificity is limited.

Coyne and Schwenk (1997) have recently emphasized that although screening instruments such as the Beck Depression Inventory are often very convenient for use in primary care, they may not be very helpful with specific diagnosis. They correctly note that complaints such as sleep problems, fatigue, and appetite disturbance are very common in medically ill patients. These symptoms alone are not associated with substantial impairment or risk of depression unless there has been enduring dysphoric mood for two weeks. It was found that among nonpsychiatric medical patients, fewer than half of those meeting criteria for clinically elevated distress also met interview-based criteria for depression. Their research refutes the assumption that self-reported distress on questionnaires represents true depressive symptomatology. Overall, nonpsychiatric medical patients who scored in the distressed range on self-report measures were less distressed than psychiatric patients with similar scores. These self-report instruments are more likely valid in psychiatric outpatient populations where elevated scores are much more strongly associated with a diagnosis of depression through a structured *DSM–IV* clinical interview. Coyne and Schwenk's (1997) study relied upon the Center for Epidemiologic Studies—Depression Scale, a 20-item self-report instrument developed by the National Institute of Mental Health. The general format and scoring is similar to the Beck Depression Inventory. Even the developers of the Beck Depression Inventory have cautioned against using the term "depressed" to refer to patients who have elevated scores on self-report inventories (Kendall, Hollon, Beck, Hammen, & Ingram, 1993).

It is important to recognize that these instruments have limited value in differential diagnosis. A positive score on a screening tool does not by itself rule out the possibility of organic illness, bereavement, or other common psychiatric disorders such as an anxiety disorder. Symptoms of childhood depression such as those assessed with the Children's Depression Inventory have significant overlap with other pediatric mental health disorders such as conduct disorder and attention-deficit hyperactivity disorder (Kashani et al., 1981). Thus, the appropriate use of these instruments is as a guide to further interview-oriented assessment. The individual items will suggest topics for inquiry.

Course of Depression

Patients who have a positive family history for depression usually have an early onset of depressive symptoms in adolescence or young adulthood. These patients are at particular risk of having recurrent depressive episodes. About 50% of people who have a depressive episode will never have another one. However, by implication, 50% of those having one episode will have recurrences. Among elderly patients who have initial onset of depression in later life, there appears to be a generally better outcome. About 10–30% of these patients will remain continuously depressed, with about 40–60% recovering (Murphy, 1994). The remaining group typically has depressive symptoms that do not meet clear criteria for major depressive episode. Patients who are at risk for relapse tend to have physical illness, endogenous symptoms including marked sleep and appetite disturbance, and declining energy level as well as diurnal variation in mood (Gurland, 1994). This pattern of mood disturbance refers to a pattern in which dysphoria is significantly greater in the morning and improves somewhat during the course of the day. Male gender and the absence of a confiding relationship with low levels of social involvement are also risk factors for further depressive episodes (Berkman, 1986; Gurland, 1994).

Depression and Medical Illness

There is often considerable overlap between the symptoms of nonpsychiatric medical disorders and major depression. Providers need to consider the possibility of hormonal, metabolic, and other physiological abnormalities in evaluating depression. This is particularly problematic in the primary medical care setting in which depressed patients often do not emphasize mood and cognitive symptoms because they experience depression as a physical condition with a presumed biomedical etiology. Physiological conditions that may present as depression include hypothyroidism, viral illness, and drug reactions such as the beta blocker "blues" (R. O. Taylor, 1990).

From a practical perspective, there are several issues that emerge with the interaction of depression and medical symptoms. Among many health care providers there may be an opinion that depression is a "natural" reaction to a serious illness such as cancer. Because it is seen as "normal," depressive illness will not be thoroughly evaluated or aggressively treated. Again, given the growing data that indicates that recovery from medical illness is significantly hindered by the presence of untreated depression, this "trivalizing" of depressive symptoms impedes patient progress.

The second common concern from a diagnostic perspective is that many medical symptoms overlap to varying degrees with depression. Because of this overlap of depressive symptoms and symptoms of medical illness, several clinicians and investigators have suggested using substituted criteria when evaluating depression in patients with significant comorbid medical illness (Endicott, 1984; Cohen-Cole et al., 1993). In particular, vegetative symptoms such as sleep disturbance, appetite disturbance, and diminished energy level should be replaced with cognitive or social symptoms. Thus, sleep disturbance may be replaced with social isolation and appetite disturbance may be replaced with hopelessness about the future (Endicott, 1984). If it is difficult to determine whether diminished energy is attributable to a physical illness, low energy as a symptom should be replaced with pessimism or undue worry about the future (Endicott, 1984). When compared with an inclusive set of *DSM* criteria, the substituted symptoms diagnosed an equal number of medically ill patients (Kathol, Mutgi, & William, 1990) as depressed.

Among medical patients, prevalence rates of depression may be two to ten times as high as in the general population. Patients with various chronic illnesses including diabetes, rheumatoid arthritis, chronic obstructive pulmonary disease, and cardiac conditions appear to have significantly elevated rates of depression. Among patients with Type I diabetes, several studies have found prevalence rates of depression at about 30% (Cox, Gonder-Frederick, & Saunders, 1991). Among persons experiencing a significant cardiac event such as a heart attack, the prevalence of depression may be as high as 20% in the year to year and a half following the myocardial infarction (Cohen-Cole et al., 1993; Levenson, 1993). Depression also appears to interact with other factors to influence treatment success rates with medical illnesses. Patients who are recovering from a hip fracture are less likely to become ambulatory if depression is present (Mossey, Knott, & Craik, 1990).

Robinson (1989) found that among patients over age 75 who were currently receiving mental health services, half of those with depression had died within five years. The majority of these deaths were due to cardiovascular causes or cerebrovascular accidents (Robinson, 1989).

Depression is a fairly high frequency diagnosis in nursing home settings. A recent study found that 13% of patients in six urban nursing homes met criteria for a current depressive disorder with an additional 18% of patients having depressive symptoms (Rovner et al., 1990, 1991). In nursing home settings, depression is an independent risk factor for mortality that increases the likelihood of death by 60% in the year following diagnosis (Rovner et al., 1991).

Masks of Major Depression

As noted above, depression does not often present with the classical *DSM–IV* (1994) symptoms in the primary care physician's office. As Talley (1986) notes, the "alert, expressive patient ... who complains of chronic headache and fatigue rarely arouses suspicions that he may be depressed" (p. 16). Talley notes that presenting problems such as fatigue, chronic pain, gastrointestinal symptoms, insomnia, and irritability oftentimes represent underlying depression. In the case of pain, patients with arthritis who continue to experience fatigue and pain despite a course of anti-inflammatory therapy may report improvement if underlying depression is treated. Myofascial pain syndrome often responds very well to antidepressant medication rather than to analgesics (Talley, 1986). Among GI symptoms, weight loss, constipation, and diarrhea often are associated with depression. Diarrhea in particular may be associated with irritable bowel. Irritable bowel syndrome is often comorbid with depression or anxiety disorder.

> Ms. Bond is a 39-year-old White woman who has a history of headaches. She states that the headaches occur fairly suddenly and they feel like "a tight band around my forehead." Ms. Bond states that they are not associated with vomiting and they last for an hour up to all day. She states they began about one year ago but have increased in frequency over the past six months. Ms. Bond reports that she may have three or four headache episodes per week. Review of her medical record indicates that she was treated several times for "lower back pain" and "back spasms" over an 18-month period.
>
> Ms. Bond has been married for about 12 years. She has two sons ages 11 and 9. She says that her marriage is "okay" but reports feeling resentful that she has to manage all of the household responsibilities. She works 50–60 hours per week as a grocery store clerk where she has been employed for 3 years. She said she "needs the overtime money." Ms. Bond states that her father died 2 years ago and her mother died 1 year ago. She said she "still has not gotten over" her mother's death. Ms. Bond explains she is the oldest of six siblings and "mom held the family together."

Mental status examination reveals a well-dressed and groomed White female. Ms. Bond is pleasant but appears "controlled." She states she has been crying two to three times per week for the past several months. Ms. Bond describes her mood as "angry, irritated, and sad all in one." She describes gaining 30 pounds over the past 4 months. Ms. Bond says when she is not working she just wants to sleep—"to get away from it all." On the weekends, she says she sleeps 14 to 16 hours a day.

Ms. Bond describes herself as a "worrier." She explains that since her mother's death, her siblings have been asking her for child care, money, and advice. "Last night my brother called me from a bar at two in the morning asking me for a ride home."

Clinically, some physicians suggest that when physical symptoms cannot be attributed to an organic basis after thorough evaluation, they should be presumptively treated as depression. There is a reasonable amount of clinical evidence that many low back pain and tension or atypical headache patients demonstrate significant improvement in their functioning and report reduced pain when they are treated with antidepressant medication (Portenoy, 1993).

DEPRESSION VERSUS BEREAVEMENT

The symptom picture of patients who have recently lost a loved one and those who are experiencing clinical depression may be very similar. Bereavement is usually not considered to be a condition warranting significant clinical intervention such as pharmacotherapy. Instead, it is seen as a common stressor that most people will experience at some point in their lives. In contrasting bereavement with depression, the clinician will note that the degree of impairment with depression is much greater than with a normal grieving process. Those who have recently lost a loved one will commonly report sleep disturbance and reduced appetite, and will most likely experience significant sadness including crying episodes. However, as a general rule, bereaved individuals do not experience suicidal ideation, significant guilt, self-reproach, or hopelessness and helplessness. When an adult has lost their spouse or parent, there should be improvement in functioning and reduction in symptoms between four and six months from the loss. Typically, bereaved individuals report that they are beginning to sleep somewhat better and have become gradually re-engaged in social activities. This time frame may be somewhat longer in situations in which a loved one died very suddenly or tragically. It is possible, with the passage of time, for bereavement to develop into clinical depression. This issue should be considered when a patient's functioning has not begin to improve approximately six months after the loss has occurred. Depression should be seriously considered if symptoms remain unabated at one year after the loss (Gallagher & Thompson, 1989).

DYSTHYMIC DISORDER

Dysthymic disorder is characterized by the presence of mild to moderate depressive symptoms for a period of at least 2 years (*DSM–IV*, 1994). In addition to depressed mood, two of the following symptoms must be present: appetite disturbance, sleep disturbance, diminished energy or fatigue, poor self-esteem, impaired concentration or decision-making abilities, and a sense of hopelessness. In the general population, it is estimated that dysthymia occurs in about 3% of adults. Among primary care patients, prevalence rates have been estimated to be between 5% and 15% (Sansone & Sansone, 1996).

The symptoms of dysthymia are insidious and often do not appear to arise from a specific stressor. Clinically, mood disturbance tends to predominate but mild to moderate vegetative symptoms may be present. Both major depression as well as personality disorders appear to be commonly found among patients with dysthymia. Up to 70% of dysthymic patients have had episodes of major depression. Personality disorders appear to occur in up to half of dysthymic patients (Sansone & Sansone, 1996). It is likely that dysthymia is under-diagnosed because the symptoms are less apparent. There are suggestions that patients with early onset dysthymia (before age 21) are much more likely to develop personality disorders. Dysthymic patients are at a much higher risk for a major depressive episode, a syndrome called "double depression."

MINOR DEPRESSION

There is increased attention to the meaning of subclinical levels of depressive symptoms, particularly in primary care patients. One definition of minor depression is sustained dysphoric mood with at least two other depressive symptoms present. These should be present for at least two weeks (Beck & Koenig, 1996). Minor depression appears to be particularly common among the elderly as well as those with physical illness. Diagnostic subgroups at particular risk for minor depression include diabetic, stroke, and myocardial infarction patients. In all of these patients, it appears that while 20–30% develop major depressive disorder, an additional 30% will develop symptoms of minor depression. Other surveys indicate that up to two thirds of hospitalized medical patients have symptoms suggestive of minor depression. Among the elderly, up to 25% to 50% of patients of elderly individuals in nursing home settings experience these symptoms. The course of minor depression is not entirely clear. Figures for spontaneous remission have ranged from 70% down to under 30% (Beck and Koenig, 1996).

There is considerable evidence that subclinical depressive symptoms interact with medical conditions to produce significantly poorer medical outcomes. This pattern has been found for patients with hypertension, diabetes, arthritis, or GI problems. In addition, there may be greater susceptibility to pain (Wells et al., 1989).

Subsyndromal depressive disorders appear to be fairly common in primary care. In particular, they appear to affect the elderly. At present, neither psychotherapy nor antidepressant medication have been well-established for patients with these subclinical symptoms (Callahan, Hendrie, & Tierney, 1996). Beck and Koenig's (1996) review suggested that these patients exhibit marginal responses to antidepressant medication. It is likely that minor depression may develop into dysthymia or major depression or be a later stage of adjustment disorder or bereavement in other individuals. *How to dx ?*

TREATMENT OF DEPRESSION

The majority of cases of major depression will respond well to medication. Up until recently, the primary drugs used for treating depression were the tricyclics and heterocyclic antidepressants. Three commonly employed medications were desipramine (Norpramin), nortriptyline (Pamelor), and imipramine (Tofranil). Another common medication, particularly for those patients with some degree of anxiety, was doxepin (Sinequan). Patients on these medications often reported such adverse experiences as somnolence, dry mouth, and urinary retention. Constipation as well as sexual dysfunction were frequent but less pronounced. The tricyclics were also associated with hypotension, particularly among elderly patients. When these patients would get up out of bed or rise from a seated position, they would feel light-headed and dizzy, which contributed to falls and subsequent hip fractures. There was also concern about the cardiac effects of these medications. In some patients, tricyclics were associated with cardiac arrhythmias.

A very practical problem with these medications is that they are toxic in overdose. Historically, one of the most common forms of effected suicide was with tricyclic antidepressants. While newer medications have been developed, tricyclic and heterocyclic antidepressant medications are still employed, particularly among patients who exhibit agitation and sleeplessness and who may benefit from sedation. These older drugs are also usually significantly less expensive than the newer antidepressants. In patients who have limited health insurance coverage, these medications are still prescribed. Imipramine also appears to be useful in treating panic attacks (DeGruy, 1994). One other beneficial effect of tricyclics is that they are often associated with weight gain. While the majority of outpatients complain of this side effect and it is a common reason for discontinuing medication, patients who are seriously ill often can benefit from increased weight. Weight loss is particularly common among cancer patients (Rakel, 1996). The newer antidepressants may simply exacerbate nausea and further contribute to weight loss. The older tricyclic antidepressants such as trazodone may be helpful in treating depression while increasing weight gain among these patients.

The selective serotonin re-uptake inhibitors (SSRIs) have rapidly become the medications of choice for treating depression. The best known of these drugs, fluoxetine (Prozac) is one of the most commonly prescribed medications in the United States. Prozac, Zoloft, and Paxil inhibit re-uptake of serotonin at the synapse. There is considerable support for the role of serotonin in major depression.

The major advantage of the SSRIs is that they have fewer side effects than the tricyclic antidepressants. Fluoxetine (Prozac) is typically started as one 20-mg dose per day. This straightforward once-a-day dose is an attractive aspect of Prozac—particularly given the high rates of medication noncompliance among depressed patients.

Sertraline (Zoloft) is started at 50 mg and typically increased to 100–150 mg and occasionally up to 200 mg. Paroxetine (Paxil) is administered in initial doses of about 10–20 mg per day, with a regular dose of 20–50 mg being common. Like fluoxetine, paroxetine is typically taken once per day.

Although side effects are less pronounced with SSRIs as compared with the older tricyclics, they do occur. Common SSRI side effects include nausea, diarrhea, "jumpiness," and difficulty with sleep onset. These reactions usually are tolerated or disappear with time. However, one fairly common and enduring SSRI side effect is sexual dysfunction. Men may have delayed or no ejaculation and women report anorgasmia. Subjectively, some patients on these medications report decreased sexual interest.

SSRIs do not have pronounced anticholinergic effects and as such are not usually associated with sedation, dry mouth, constipation, and weight gain. At present they do not appear to have marked adverse cardiac effects. However, SSRIs may contribute to increased nausea and nonspecific GI upset as well as sexual dysfunction. In some patients they also may produce nonspecific agitation. Most of these symptoms diminish after several weeks. SSRIs seem to be helpful with patients who have minor depression and also in patients who have dysthymic disorder. As will be discussed in a later section, these medications also appear to benefit patients who have significant anxiety symptoms. In particular, the SSRIs are a treatment of choice for panic disorder.

Reponse to antidepressant therapy follows a fairly predictable sequence. After the first week, patients with sleep problems usually report some improvement in their sleeping and experience more energy. Individuals who were excessively somnolent prior to pharmacotherapy usually report somewhat less fatigue. After about two to three weeks of medication treatment, patients become more engaged with their environment and exhibit consistently increased activity levels. At around four to six weeks, others (family members, friends) often note that the patient seems to be significantly improved, but the patient may have not yet perceive changes. At around eight to 12 weeks, symptoms have significantly improved or may have remitted completely. One question that is commonly posed by patients is the length of time required for antidepressant medication. The general "rule of thumb" is about 6 to 12 months following an initial depressive episode. For patients who have had multiple depressive episodes—particularly those beginning early in life—the second or third episode should prompt consideration of life-long antidepressant treatment.

About 65% of patients respond to an initial trial of antidepressant medication (D. A. Casey, 1994). After three to four months of a particular medication without a response, it is reasonable to consider switching to a different drug.

Monoamine oxidase (MAO) inhibitors are sometimes used in patients who "fail" with other antidepressants. These patients, however, require dietary restrictions since the medication will adversely interact with the amino acid, tyramine. Tyramine is an amino acid found in certain foods such as cheese or wine. The MAO inhibitors also have adverse interactions with other medications including SSRIs as well as some narcotics.

An additional pharmacological treatment that has been employed with geriatric patients and medically ill patients is psychostimulants. These would include dextroamphetamine (Dexedrine) or methylphenidate (Ritalin). Most clinicians are familiar with methylphenidate as a treatment for attention-deficit hyperactivity disorder. However, the stimulants appear also to be useful for medically ill patients who have pronounced neurovegetative symptoms including psychomotor retardation, hypersomnia, and diminished activity level (Friedson, Wey, & Tabler, 1991).

These medications are particularly useful with patients who are not participating in rehabilitation or who are not eating. Of interest is that the stimulants seem to increase appetite and food consumption among medically ill patients or geriatric patients who are losing weight. At times, particularly in hospitalized patients, the failure to eat can lead to life-threatening conditions. Psychostimulants have been used alone as well as in conjunction with more traditional antidepressant pharmacotherapy.

There are few specific treatments for dysthymia. These patients do appear to demonstrate some responsiveness to antidepressant medications, particularly the newer SSRIs (Sansone & Sansone, 1996).

Specifically, sertraline (Zoloft), fluoxetine (Prozac), and paroxetine (Paxil) are preferred because of their favorable side effect profile. The dosages used with dysthymic patients may be somewhat less that those employed in a major depressive episode. The clinician should also be aware that dysthymic patients demonstrate more variable response to pharmacotherapy than patients with major depression.

Rates of noncompliance with antidepressant medications appear to be particularly high. In one study in which 80% of patients were on tricyclics or heterocyclics, approximately 28% stopped taking their medication during the first month, with

44% having ceased their medication on their own by the third treatment month (Linn et al., 1995).

One of the primary reasons for noncompliance with these medications appears to be inadequate education (Linn et al., 1995). Patients may be discouraged with the absence of a rapid amelioration of symptoms. In addition, many of the side effects are most pronounced during the first weeks of antidepressant therapy and become more tolerable with time. Patients, however, are often unaware of the time limited nature of these unpleasant effects and believe them to be an ongoing part of the medication. Additionally, patients often do not understand the need to take the medication on a daily or twice daily basis in order to achieve optimal levels. Again, patients may have the expectation that they need to take their medicine only when they "feel bad" and do not need to take it otherwise. It is likely that the poor compliance noted above can be greatly reduced if the provider engages in appropriate education around the nature of antidepressant therapy and the course of response to it.

Psychotherapy is very helpful for depression, although it is less likely to be employed in primary care. There is considerable evidence that cognitive behavioral therapy (A. T. Beck, Rush, Shaw, & Emery, 1979) of relatively brief duration (8 to 12 sessions) is associated with considerable improvement among depressed patients. Cognitive therapy is a very practical approach that targets patients' erroneous and unhealthy thought processes. Cognitive errors such as catastrophizing, minimization, and magnification are pointed out, and the patient is engaged in a Socratic process of disconfirming these erroneous beliefs (A. T. Beck et al., 1989).

In addition to educating the patient about the role of these patterns, they are also taught to monitor negative thoughts and the relationship between thoughts and adverse mood states. Additionally, they are encouraged to identify these cognitive patterns as they come up in daily interactions and engage in an ongoing process of disconfirming these beliefs. Importantly, patients are also directed to engage in structured tasks outside of session. It is often helpful, particularly early in the course of treatment, to help depressed patients structure their day and assist them in developing a schedule so that they will maintain an appropriate level of activity including recreational and social events. Depressed patients will often report that they cannot carry out these activities because they do not feel like it. It is important for the practitioner to emphasize the cyclical nature of depression and social withdrawal and point out that the patient should try some of these activities anyway. The result will usually be that they feel better as a result of engaging in them. Another activity that is particularly helpful with depressed patients is regular exercise (Hillman, Kripke, & Gillin, 1990). Regular physical activity appears to be associated with increased noradrenergic activity in the central nervous system. Patients who are sedentary should be encouraged to begin to walk on a regular basis, simply for 5–10 minutes a day. Again, patients will complain that often they do not feel like it, but should be encouraged to do so anyway.

Among medically ill depressed patients, group therapy has been found to be helpful (Spira & Spiegel, 1993). The socially supportive interaction that occurs in group treatment helps reduce the sense of isolation that many chronically ill patients experience.

Life review has been recommended for geriatric patients. Elderly individuals often reflect on their life course (Lewis & Butler, 1974). By helping the patient to engage in a focused review process, it will give their life more significance and meaning. This therapy may reduce guilt and fears as well as help the patient be more accepting of the present. Life review therapy may include trips to geographic places that have had significance in the patient's life, recontacting family members and friends, or reviewing memorabilia and photos.

BIPOLAR MOOD DISORDER

In bipolar disorder, episodes of depression alternate with bouts of mania. Classically, mania presents as a syndrome featuring decreased need for sleep, distractibility, and a very high level of energy. Patients may also exhibit delusions, most commonly of grandiosity (*DSM–IV*, 1994). Although depression is sometimes difficult to detect, mania is very distinct and the clinician should have no difficulty determining its presence.

The prevalence rate of bipolar disorder in the general population is about one percent (Robins et al., 1994). Many patients will have the onset of the disorder in mid to late adolescence. As patients continue to age, the "cycling" between depression and mania occurs with increased frequency and there is less elapsed time between episodes. Mood, in the manic state, may be elevated, irritable, or labile.

A different form of bipolar disorder involves hypomania, in which the patient does not become as agitated or floridly psychotic as in mania. They do sleep, but are able to function quite well on about four to five hours of sleep. These patients tend to have a fairly high activity level and may initiate projects, but not complete them. However, their degree of behavioral disturbance is often not so great, and they do not receive medical attention.

> Mr. Ford, a new patient, is seen at the clinic because of insomnia and a cough. Mr. Ford is 32 years old and currently resides with his girlfriend. He describes the cough as getting worse over the past two months. Upon inquiry, he notes that he is smoking three and a half to four packs of cigarettes per day. He states that his cigarette smoking increased gradually over the past several months and that previously he usually only smoked a pack per day. Mr. Ford describes sleeping only three to four hours per night for the past few weeks and states that he is generally feeling okay, although, "a bit crabby." The clinician notices that Mr. Ford seems to speak rather rapidly and

his description of his symptoms seem rather disjointed. He has no ongoing medical problems.

It is somewhat difficult to obtain a coherent narrative history from Mr. Ford. He explains that he got married upon graduating from high school and then joined the National Guard. Mr. Ford was in the National Guard for about six months. He was discharged after a fist fight with his commanding officer. He indicates that he divorced his wife and "bummed around the country" working in carnivals and as a farm worker. He met his second wife at this time and had two children before getting divorced. He is currently living with a woman he met a year ago. He is working in a factory where he has been for the past two years. Mr. Ford reports a psychiatric admission about three years ago. He says, "I went wild, I thought I had the answer to all the world's problems. I was always calling those radio talk shows and I stayed up all night. Then, I crashed; I tried to hang myself and they put me in the hospital. The doctor tried me on Prozac but it made me hyper ... he switched me over to lithium and I mellowed out. I was in the hospital for about three weeks and they gave me lithium when I left the hospital but I quit taking it after about six months. I didn't see any need for it."

Mr. Ford is dressed in a Hawaiian shirt and spandex shorts. During the interview he speaks very rapidly and occasionally jumps from his chair for emphasis. His flow of thought is at times hard to follow. He says he has not been sleeping more than three to four hours per night for the past few weeks but "feels fine." He says that his girlfriend has been complaining because he has been wanting to have sex three to four times per day. Mr. Ford explains that his job had been okay until last week—he was asked to stuff 20 envelopes but actually stuffed 2000.

The treatment for bipolar disorder is lithium carbonate. Patients who do not respond to lithium often do respond to carbamazepine, an anticonvulsant medication. Response to lithium may require up to two weeks. Compliance with lithium is often a problem because many bipolar patients complain that it robs them of their creativity and they will stop taking it.

Bipolar patients should usually be managed in the specialty psychiatric sector. Data reviewed in the first chapter suggest that these patients are, however, often managed in primary care settings. This is particularly likely in rural areas where psychiatrists are often not readily available.

ANXIETY DISORDERS: OVERVIEW

Similar to depression, the majority of patients with anxiety disorders are treated in the primary care sector. In addition, many patients with anxiety disorders focus on physical symptoms that overlap with those of other nonpsychiatric medical illnesses such as irregular heart rate and hyperventilation (D. M. Clark et al., 1997). Therefore, accurate diagnosis of anxiety disorders is often difficult in primary care settings. As compared with depression, the diagnostic criteria for anxiety disorders are less specific and require that the patient be able to recall symptoms over extended time periods. For example, in the case of generalized anxiety disorder (GAD), the time period required for symptoms to be clinically significant is six months. The most common anxiety disorders presenting in primary care are panic disorder and GAD. There is growing evidence that obsessive–compulsive disorder is a fairly common, yet undetected, psychiatric problem in primary care.

Panic Disorder

Panic disorder is characterized by episodes of panic attacks. There should be four such episodes within a four-week period or at least one attack followed by a fear of having another attack for a period of at least one month (*DSM–IV*, 1994). The subjective experience of panic is very vivid:

> I was driving my car home from work ... I began to feel kind of strange—a bit like the flu. I began feeling like everybody in the other cars was staring at me ... the noise got terrible, everyone was blowing their horns at once. Then, it all faded, like I was in my own world.
>
> I started getting the chills, but just as suddenly I felt like a fever had just come on ... I was burning up. I felt dizzy; I was afraid I was going to pass out so I pulled over to the side of the road.
>
> I noticed my heart beating fast. Then it would slow down, then fast again. I felt like my chest would explode! I suddenly felt like I was choking, I couldn't catch my breath, I was terrified! I thought I was having a heart attack, my chest started aching.
>
> After about 15 minutes, it all went away. I was back to normal. I went to my doctor the next day. He couldn't find anything wrong. A week later I had another episode—twice as bad.

With the changes included in *DSM–IV* (1994), panic disorder is no longer diagnosed independently but always with reference to agoraphobia. Thus, the formal diagnosis is Panic Disorder with or without a history of agoraphobia. This change occurred because of a view that in agoraphobia, a disorder in which patients become extremely anxious when out in public, the fundamental fear is having a panic episode in public (*DSM–IV*, 1994). Patients with panic disorders with agoraphobia may become increasingly confined to their homes, and if they go out, will only do so with a trusted family member. Panic disorder's current population prevalence is 1–2% (Horwath & Weissman, 1997).

In panic attacks, the individual experiences shortness of breath, dizziness, un-steadiness, and may feel as if they are going to faint. Patients also experience heart palpitations or accelerated heart rate. Subjectively, patients will feel that their heart is beating irregularly or abnormally loudly. In addition, patients often experience trembling, shaking, or sweating. At times, a choking sensation as if something is caught in their throat is also present. Nausea or GI distress also occurs. Patients often report a sense of depersonalization—things going on around them do not seem to be real. Paresthesias or tingling sensations, particularly in the hands or feet are also common, as are hot flashes, chills, and chest pain. Subjectively, patients often report that they are fearful of either "going crazy" or dying. One of the most consistent symptoms that panic disorder patients report is a sense of impending doom—something terrible is about to happen (Welkowitz & Gorman, 1997).

As will be more thoroughly discussed in the chapter on cardiovascular disorders, the majority of patients with panic attacks do seek care for an early episode of the disorder. A high percentage of these patients experience either pronounced chest pain or difficulty breathing and present in the medical emergency room. The panic disordered patient in the emergency room usually harbors fears that they are having a heart attack. Support for the view that atypical chest pain is often a presentation of panic comes from several studies finding that among patients undergoing cardiac catheterization, up to 30% have no evidence of cardiac pathology (Katon, 1990). In addition to asthma, other medical illnesses that present with panic symptoms include chronic obstructive pulmonary disease, sleep apnea, and esophageal motility disorder.

There is evidence that patients with panic disorder have a higher incidence of cardiovascular disease and cerebrovascular events. The exact mechanism here is unclear; however, it may be that patients who have long-term panic disorder have a higher level of physiological reactivity that in turn increases the likelihood of a myocardial infarction and/or stroke. One hypothesized intervening mechanism is hypertension, which is more common among patients with anxiety disorders, particularly African Americans (Neal, Nagle-Rich, & Smucker, 1994). Although medical illnesses do appear to occur with greater frequency among panic disorder patients, there is also considerable evidence that people who have frequent panic episodes misinterpret bodily sensations. There appears to be a feedback loop in which these individuals misinterpret relatively benign autonomic sensations which, in turn, amplifies these sensations and results in a full blown panic attack. There is considerable evidence that patients who have recurrent panic episodes tend to be preoccupied with heart attack, fainting, inability to breathe, and seizures, as well as fear of loss of control. (D. M. Clark et al., 1997).

The tendency to misinterpret bodily sensations appears to be particularly unique to panic disorder patients when compared with patients with other anxiety disorders. The high sensitivity to internal sensations may also be a factor in these patients seeking out higher levels of medical care and repeatedly presenting in the emergency room. It may be that among patients with panic disorder, their actual autonomic reactivity is not appreciably more pronounced than non–panic disorder patients. However, a key difference may be these patients' lower threshold for these sensations and their tendency to interpret them in a catastrophic manner (D. M. Clark et al., 1997).

There are several other issues that complicate accurate diagnosis of panic disorder. First, panic disorder with or without agoraphobia often does not occur in isolation. Major depressive episodes appear to occur in up to one-quarter of patients with panic disorder (Otto & Gould, 1996). In addition to a past history of depression, comorbid generalized anxiety disorder also elevates the risk of depression with panic disorder. Self-report questionnaire data suggest that treatment of panic disorders is further complicated by a very high prevalence of personality disorders among these patients (Otto & Gould, 1996). Otto & Gould (1996) suggest that 40–70% of patients with panic disorder have Axis II diagnoses, with avoidant, dependent, histrionic, and borderline personality disorders being among the more common. Age of onset of panic disorder also appears to effect recovery rates. Panic disorder with onset after age 55 generally appears to be less severe and appears to have better treatment outcome. Earlier onset panic disorder often takes a chronic course in which panic symptoms frequently wax and wane throughout the life span.

Generalized Anxiety Disorder

Generalized anxiety disorder (GAD) is also a very common presenting problem in primary care. In the general population, GAD has a prevalence rate of 6–7% (Horwath & Weissmann, 1997). Generalized anxiety disorder is characterized by excessive worry and apprehension about two or more areas of life. Topics of concern commonly include personal health and that of family members, finances, and job security. Although these are issues typically of concern to many people, the degree of distress is significantly greater among persons with GAD and should be present for a minimum of six months.

In addition to exaggerated worry, individuals should have three of the following six symptoms that are more often than not present during a six-month period: a sense of restlessness or feeling on edge, easy fatiguability, difficulty concentrating, irritability, muscle tension, and sleep disturbance (most commonly, difficulties with sleep onset;) (*DSM–IV*, 1994). GAD is a difficult disorder to accurately diagnose because of the nonspecific nature of the symptoms as well as the extended time duration. The majority of individuals have had experiences similar to generalized anxiety disorder, such as during the course of a geographic move or during final exam time in college. However, the key differentiating factor is the degree of distress as well as duration of the symptoms. The "worry" component must cause functional impairment and is subjectively experienced as outside of the patient's control (Smoller & Pollack, 1996).

Nonpsychiatric medical conditions that should be considered in evaluating patients with generalized anxiety symptoms include hyperthyroidism, excessive caffeine use, and excessive use of over-the-counter cold remedies containing pseudoephedrine. Comorbidity appears to be more the rule than the exception with generalized anxiety disorder, with depression the most common co-existing disorder (Smoller & Pollack, 1996).

Obsessive–Compulsive Disorder

Obsessive–compulsive disorder (OCD) occurs in about 1–2% of the general population (Greist, 1995). The disorder is characterized by repeated intrusive thoughts (obsessions) corresponding with ritualistic behaviors that temporarily reduce anxiety-associated thoughts (compulsions). Obsessions often center around impulses such as harming others or oneself, engaging in socially embarrassing activities, or being concerned about contamination. Fears of dirt or contamination are somewhat more common than those centering around aggression or orderliness. Persons with this disorder recognize that their thought processes are irrational but experience little control over them. Compulsions typically include behavior such as hand washing or checking door locks. However, compulsions may also not be directly observable and may include covert acts such as silently counting or repeating words (Greist, 1995). Although cognitive and operant learning patterns play a strong role in maintaining the OCD pattern, there is some evidence of a genetic predisposition to the disorder. The course of OCD is characterized by symptoms that wax and wane throughout the life span. There are suggestions that obsessive–compulsive patients may be embarrassed about their symptoms and therefore less likely to report them than patients with panic disorder or major depression. In addition, there are a number of suggestions that although primary care physicians may readily detect depression, the comorbid obsessive–compulsive symptoms are missed (Nymberg & Van Noppen, 1994).

Treatment of Anxiety Disorders

In medical settings, pharmacotherapy is the most commonly employed treatment approach for anxiety disorders. Historically, benzodiazepines (minor tranquilizers) have been the most common treatment for anxiety disorders (R. J. Goldberg & Posner, 1994). Over the years, however, it has become increasingly apparent that many of these medications are at least psychologically if not physiologically addictive, and long-term use of them is increasingly discouraged. Panic disorder appears to respond fairly well to antidepressant medications. In the past, fairly high doses of tricyclic antidepressants such as imipramine or nortriptyline were commonly used for panic disorder. Clinical observation suggests that panic disorder patients respond fairly well to the newer SSRIs. However, these medications have been less well studied for treatment of panic (Pollack & Smoller, 1996). Alprazolam (Xanax), a benzodiazepine, has been used in treating panic disorder. A concern about alprazolam is that patients with panic disorder tend to have a chronic condition and may require long-term pharmacotherapy in high doses. An additional concern is that in using alprazolam (Xanax) and diazepam (Valium) with elderly patients, the half-life becomes significantly longer and may contribute to cognitive impairment. One alternative that has been proposed is buspirone (Buspar), a nonbenzodiazepine anxiolytic that does not appear to have pronounced sedation or cognitive side effects (R. J. Goldberg & Posner, 1994). In using buspirone to treat panic disorder, it is important to recognize that it often will take several weeks to have a significant effect. The medication also must be taken on a regular basis, similar to an antidepressant, for therapy to be effective.

As noted above, panic disorder is often a chronic condition. T. A. Brown and Barlow (1992) suggested that 15–20% of panic patients are not completely free of core symptoms by the end of an acute treatment episode. A larger patient group of at least 40% do not return to a high level of functioning after treatment. In addition to comorbid psychiatric disorders that are likely to place lower limits on recovery rates, comorbid nonpsychiatric medical disorders are associated with significantly less improvement in the treatment of panic disorder. It has also been noted that patients with panic disorder are often very preoccupied with and worried about their health. There is some suggestion that panic disorder may be associated with hypochondriasis (T. A. Brown, Antony, & Barlow, 1995). This preoccupation with health concerns also tends to complicate treatment of panic disorder. These patients frequently have difficulty accepting a psychological explanation for their symptoms and continue to believe that there is an undiagnosed illness that accounts for their distress.

With generalized anxiety, buspirone may be particularly helpful. In contrast to those patients with panic disorder, GAD patients can often tolerate the symptoms for the time period for buspirone to have therapeutic effects. Unlike other benzodiazepines, buspirone also appears to have very little abuse potential. The antidepressants, particularly the newer SSRIs, should also be given serious consideration. As noted above, there is a very high comorbidity of depression with anxiety disorders. The antidepressants are often very effective in reducing generalized anxiety and panic symptoms while simultaneously addressing shared mood disorder symptoms.

Progressive relaxation including deep breathing and alternately tensing and relaxing specific muscle groups has been useful in reducing anxiety. The addition of cognitive therapy to progressive relaxation appears to be helpful in generalizing and maintaining gains. Cognitive treatment includes such components as rehearsal of anxiety-arousing situations through visual imagery, critical examination of belief systems that may exacerbate and maintain excessive worry, and actual behavioral "testing out" of irrational beliefs. Cognitive treatments that included applied relaxation were found to be somewhat superior to applied relaxation alone (Borkovec & Costello, 1993).

For patients with obsessive–compulsive disorder, the pharmacotherapy of choice is clomipramine, as well as several of the SSRIs (fluoxetine, sertraline, and paroxetine). Fluvoxamine (Luvox) and clomipramine (Anafranil) are also commonly used in treating obsessive–compulsive disorder (Greist, 1995). The SSRIs, including fluvoxamine, appear to have a lower side effect profile than the anti-obsessional drug, clomipramine. Clomipramine, a tricyclic antidepressant, has been associated with constipation, weight gain, and dry mouth (Nymberg & Van Noppen, 1994). For OCD, behavioral therapies and cognitive behavioral therapies are also very useful in conjunction with medication. Systematic desensitization and relaxation training are useful in reducing physiological arousal levels. OCD responds particularly well to exposure therapy. Exposure involves having the patient actually confront situations associated with obsessive thoughts and ritualistic behavior (Rauch, Baer, & Jenike, 1996). This exposure, however, needs to occur together with "response prevention." Response prevention involves having the patient deliberately avoiding engaging in rituals that they have used in the past to reduce anxiety. The patient may be asked deliberately not to check the gas on the stove for an hour after returning home from work.

Cognitive therapies that emphasize cognitive distortions, such as catastrophization and personalization of life events, also appear to be helpful. A recent review found that cognitive therapy was about equally as effective as the behavioral approach of exposure with response prevention (Abramowitz, 1997).

CONCLUSION

Mood and anxiety disorders are among the most common problems diagnosed and treated in primary care. Accurate diagnosis is confounded by the overlap of depressive and anxiety symptoms with those of many medical illnesses. Additionally, generalized anxiety, panic, and depression often occur among patients with both acute and chronic medical conditions. These disorders all respond well to pharmacotherapy. Cognitive–behavioral treatment is a useful adjunct to medication.

Chapter 3

Psychiatric Disorders in the Medical Setting II: Somatization, Alcohol Abuse, Personality Disorders, and Schizophrenia

Somatoform and personality disorders as well as substance abuse will be commonly encountered in the primary care setting. In many respects, these problems are not as amenable to treatment as mood and anxiety disorders. Somatizing patients, as well as those with personality dysfunction, are usually "managed" rather than "cured." Given recent changes in our health care system that constrain referrals to specialists, somatization disorders are likely to be an increased concern in primary care. Alcohol abuse and personality disorders are often not a presenting problem, nor are they readily apparent until the provider has seen the patient over a period of time. However, both categories are associated with increased health care utilization. This chapter concludes with a brief discussion of schizophrenia. While psychotic disorders are usually treated by psychiatrists, the primary care mental health provider may become involved with these patients around specific issues such as capacity to consent to treatment, pregnancy, and medical compliance.

SOMATIZATION DISORDER

Somatization involves a diverse pattern of somatic symptoms that do not have an organic etiology despite thorough medical evaluation. The current *DSM–IV* (1994) criteria for somatization disorder include four distinct pain sites (e.g., head, abdomen, back), two gastrointestinal symptoms (e.g., nausea, diarrhea, vomiting), one sexual symptom (loss of interest in sex or erectile dysfunction), and one pseudoneurologic symptom (commonly weakness or tingling, a lump in the throat, or loss of sensation in an arm or leg). The onset of somatization is usually before the age of 30. Patients often have had various symptoms for multiple years and have seen multiple physicians. These patients are often frustrating to physicians who will frequently refer to them as "hysterics" or "crocks" (Rasmussen & Avant, 1989).

Somatization is a very common presenting problem in primary care. It is estimated that between 5% and 10% of ambulatory primary care patients meet the criteria for somatization disorder (S. W. Brown & Smith, 1991). The general population prevalence of somatization is estimated to be 1–2% for women and probably less than 0.5% for men (Folks & Houck, 1993). Although the absolute population prevalence of somatization disorder is relatively low, patients with this disorder consume substantial quantities of health care dollars and providers' time. It is estimated that 10% of medical care is devoted to somatoform patients (Smith et al., 1986). Between 5% and 25% of visits to primary care physicians are for somatization (Ford, 1983; Othmer & DeSouza, 1985). In one family doctor's office, nearly half of the providers' clinical time was spent with somatizing patients (Collyer, 1979).

One major contributing factor to the demand on health care resources is that somatizing patients are usually not psychologically minded and persistently view their symptoms as organically based. This perspective is usually not consciously held. However, physicians often become frustrated with these patients' tenacity in viewing their symptoms as medically based as well as their reluctance to acknowledge psychosocial factors as contributors to the physical complaints.

Assessing Somatization

Othmer and DeSouza (1985) developed a seven-question screening test for somatization disorder: (1) Have you ever had trouble breathing? (2) Have you ever had trouble with menstrual cramps? (3) Have you ever had burning sensations in your sexual organs, mouth, or rectum? (4) Have you ever had difficulty swallowing or had an uncomfortable lump in your throat that stayed with you for at least an hour? (5) Have you ever found that you could not remember what you had been doing for hours or days at a time (If yes, did this happen even though you had not been drinking or taking drugs)? (6) Have you ever had trouble with frequent vomiting? (7) Have you ever had frequent pain in your fingers or toes?

Somatization disorder is likely to emerge in one of two patterns. Patients with high-frequency somatoform problems exhibit a stable symptom pattern. These patients will report consistent somatic symptoms over time such as pains in their chest, tingling sensations in their fingers, or consistent nausea. In the second pattern, diversiform, the symptoms will move to various body sites over time. Diversiform patients will present one month with headaches, the next month with a lump in their throat, and the following month with gastrointestinal distress.

Although somatization often co-exists with depression and anxiety disorder, somatic symptoms make it significantly more difficult for the physician to recognize underlying depression and anxiety. Kirmayer and colleagues (1993) found that among inpatients who met criteria for somatization disorder, physicians were only able to detect one out of four patients with clinically significant levels of depression. Somatization patients are more likely to abuse alcohol than the general population (Folks, Ford, & Houck, 1990). In addition, they are much more likely to be depressed and have comorbid personality disorders (Folks et al., 1990). The diagnostic picture is further confounded by the relationship between alexithymia and somatization. Alexithymia refers to a condition in which patients have difficulty articulating mood states and often appear to have difficulty experiencing pleasure or sadness, but exhibit very little evidence of other depressive symptoms. Recent research suggests that somatizing patients are more likely to be alexithymic. This personality style, in which affective states are not recognized, is compatible with psychodynamic descriptions of these patients as unreflective and not psychologically minded (Taylor, Ryan, & Bagby, 1985).

Ms. Connor is a 25-year-old single African American female who was initially seen in the clinic with several complaints. These include "low body temperature," tingling sensations in her hands, and an ache in her left foot. The symptoms are all completely evaluated, including radiographic studies of her hands and foot. All physical findings are negative. In taking a social history, it is noted that Ms. Connor is the youngest of two children. Her parents have been married for 30 years. Ms. Connor moved out of her parents' home about six months ago. She works 15 hours a week in a fast food restaurant and is taking nine hours at a community college. She reports living at home after graduating from high school and working part-time. She says she began having chronic headaches and abdominal pains while in elementary school. She also reports having a history of "elevated body temperatures" and her symptoms frequently caused her to miss school. Ms. Connor required an extra three years to complete her high school credits because of absence.

Ms. Connor's father went on disability in his early 40s because of a "bad back." Her mother has had dizzy spells and "chronic indigestion" and works 10–20 hours a week doing typing at home. Ms. Connor's family lives in a duplex, with Ms. Connor's sister living on the ground floor and her parents on the second floor. Ms. Connor's sister has been involved in assisting her mother with her typing business and does most of the housework and shopping. Ms. Connor says that about six months ago, she moved out of the family home and into an apartment to "establish independence" for more college financial aid. She lives about a mile from her parents and sees them at least three times a week and calls them daily. She says she has become worried because her sister has begun "dating some jerk" and is "letting her parents down." Three weeks after the last encounter with Ms. Connor, the provider is paged to the emergency department. Ms. Connor is in the ER reporting that she is so dizzy that she feels she will fall over. The emergency room physician cannot find anything wrong and seems puzzled because her balance and her gait are normal. He wonders about anxiety and sends her home with a week's worth of alprazolam (Xanax) and an appointment to see a mental health specialist. The mental health specialist sees her in the office again. Ms. Connor says the dizziness is better but she is missing school because of being distracted by a chronic ringing sensation in her ears and a "lump in her throat." Ms. Connor reports that her mother is worried about her falling in her apartment because of the dizziness and Ms. Connor expresses concern that she may have to move back to her parents' home. The primary care physician sees her again and refers her to an ear, nose, and throat specialist as well as a neurologist. Both specialists report no positive findings.

The mental health provider has no contact with Ms. Connor for about six weeks when she appears in the office as a "walk-in." Ms. Connor reports that she is having fainting spells. She says that her "spells" consist of trembling in her arms and legs and light headedness. She says that she believes she is generally conscious during these episodes because they last for up to several hours. Ms. Connor reports that she only took the Xanax once because it made her feel "light-headed." She interrupts the psychologist to say that she is having a "spell" right then. She continues to converse but says she feels dizzy.

Research also suggests that certain patients do focus more on benign bodily symptoms and appraise their health status negatively. For example, patients who were both highly sensitive to physical sensations and who experienced a higher number of minor daily life events reported more persistent heart palpitations. Of note, there was no relationship between palpitations and documented cardiac arrhythmias (Barsky, Ahern, Bailey, & Delamater, 1996).

Somatization may be more common among ethnic groups that tend to under-report psychological distress. Depression among African Americans, for example, as well as patients of Middle Eastern and Asian background, may take the form of physical distress rather than psychological symptoms (Kleinman, 1980).

Childhood Somatization

Somatization is a very common presenting problem in pediatric settings. Health care providers should be alerted to the possibility of somatization in children who have multiple medical visits, a number of urgent calls from parents for medical advice about benign concerns, and repeated medical visits for vague unsubstantiated conditions or self-limiting conditions such as colds. Other "red flags" that should alert the provider to consider somatization include a history of poor school attendance, parental overprotectiveness, and marital conflict (Mullins & Olson, 1990). In cases of school nonattendance, the clinician will often be struck by the absence of concern about missing school by both the child and parents. When these children do attend school, they often frequently miss classes because of aches and pains that bring them to the school nurse. Family interactions have been described as characterized by intense symbiotic relationships between one parent (usually the mother) and the child. In addition, there is a general climate of overprotec-tiveness. The clinician may learn that the 10-year-old continues to sleep with the parents. A family history of somatization is a salient predictor of the adult disorder. It has been suggested that up to 80% of children with somatization disorder have an adult family member with the disorder (Mullins & Olson, 1990). As children, adult somatoform patients are inducted into the illness role through a process simi-lar to hypnotic induction. Developmentally, children are often highly suggestible. Furthermore, somatoform patients are raised in an emotionally charged family en-vironment where at least one parent (if not both parents) are constantly monitoring and often overreacting to their own physical sensations (Mullins & Olson, 1990). In these families, the child is likely to become acculturated to an unconscious norm of heightened sensitivity to bodily sensations. Once somatization behavior is emitted, there are often secondary gains associated with it. In the case of chil-dren, they are often allowed to stay home from school and receive extra attention from parents.

Sociological Aspects of Somatization

It has been recently noted that somatization is linked to the trend toward pro-gressive medicalization of physical and psychosocial distress. Barsky and Borus (1995) defined medicalization as the "invocation of a medical diagnosis to explain physical discomfort that is not caused by disease and the application of a medi-cal intervention to treat it" (p. 1931). They noted that in up to 60% of primary care visits, the patient's chief complaints center around symptoms that have no significant organic basis. Given the increased technological focus of our society, there is a growing view that science can "stamp out" all distress. Survey data suggests that the typical adult has at least one somatic symptom every four to six days with the majority of these episodes being "treated or addressed" outside of the formal health care network (Barsky & Borus, 1995). Given this prevalence, "the lexicon for expressing somatization is almost always at hand since there is a constant backdrop of somatic symptoms available on which to focus, amplify, and become concerned" (Barsky & Borus, 1995, p. 1932). Medicalization is likely to be contributing to increased somatization.

In industrialized society, minor distress and physical problems that are un-desirable have become increasingly reclassified as diseases. Examples of these new ailments include jet lag, baldness, minor mood disorders, and indigestion. Barsky and Borus (1995) have described a growing number of "functional somatic syndromes" that have arisen in the past 10–20 years including chronic fatigue syn-drome, food hypersensitivity, systemic yeast infection, gulf war syndrome, sick building syndrome, and fibromyalgia. These problems are frequently accompanied by considerable media attention and the rapid development of consumer oriented self-help groups. Another factor contributing to a social climate of medicalization is direct marketing to the public by medical specialists and pharmaceutical companies. These social and economic factors have contributed to a public perception of medicine as a force that can alleviate all form of distress. The rise in medicalization may contribute to a reduced sensory threshold for physical symptoms (Barsky & Borus, 1995) and certainly makes it more likely that physical discomfort will be brought the to health care provider's attention.

Treatment

Somatization disorder presents a particularly difficult set of treatment issues that should be strategically addressed. First, as noted earlier, somatoform patients are not very open to psychological explanations or intervention for their problems. The mental health professional who sees these patients should work in very close contact with a primary care physician. It is important that the clinician refrain from even remotely implying that the patient's symptoms are psychosocially based. In the early contacts, the provider should allocate significant amounts of time to hearing the patient's "story" of their illness. Somatoform patients, in particular, are particularly well versed in describing and understanding their complaints from a medical model. In addition, these patients frequently have strong views about a treatment plan for their condition. This may include radical procedures such as surgery. In may respects, the somatizing patient has embraced a biomedical model and excluded a psychosocial one—a perspective not dissimilar from many physicians (Salmon & May, 1995).

Changes in the provision of medical care in the United States also present significant challenges in managing these patients. The new emphasis on primary care may make these patients more visible. This increased awareness of somatization may be partially attributable to financial disincentives for referring patient to specialists (Barsky & Borus, 1995). In the past, somatizing patients would have many of their psychological needs met through multiple medical specialty referrals for ongoing detailed evaluations of their symptoms. The current emphasis on assigning patients to a primary care provider will eliminate "doctor shopping" and also places more severe restrictions on the use of specialists.

Although mental health professionals may be helpful as consultants in managing these patients, the optimal provider for these patients is their primary care physician. These patients should be seen regularly by their family physician or internist—ideally once every two to three weeks (Rasmussen & Avant, 1989). At each visit, it is important that the patient focus on one or two bodily regions or complaints. The physician should ask: "What is bothering you the most at this particular visit?" The patient should be briefly examined and reassured. Physicians presented with this management model may object on several grounds. First, they often complain that it is a waste of time. However, it is likely to be far more efficient than having to begin anew with this patient on multiple occasions when they switch physicians. In addition, if they are not seen on a regular basis, their periodic "crisis" presentations to their physician are likely to be dramatic with long "laundry lists" of complaints. Even if physicians agree with this rationale, they often will respond that they are not "doing anything" for the patient. It is important to recognize that supportive psychotherapy is actually the treatment of choice for somatization disorder. As noted earlier, research has found that limited mental health consultation decreased their health care utilization by approximately 50% (Smith et al., 1986).

Over time, the provider may want to gradually introduce the subject of the relationship between the patient's physical symptoms and psychosocial issues. However, the basic style of inquiry should include a reversal of the usual causal connection of psychosomatic medicine. Rather than asking the patient, "How does your marriage/job/relationship with your children affect your dizziness or abdominal pain?" asking "How does your pain affect your family life or work?" (DeGood, 1983). This line of inquiry reduces the patient's defensiveness. It is extremely important that the provider not participate in a discussion about the functional or organic status of the symptoms. DeGood (1983) has noted that these patients have an "organic mythology" that is not readily surrendered. It is also important that all health care providers recognize that somatization disorder is a chronic condition. It requires a shift in thinking from a goal of cure to one of improvement. A realistic outcome for these patients is not relief from all distress. Instead, a realistic endpoint may include reports of subjective decline in physical symptoms as well as increased activity level and decreased utilization of health care resources.

Conversion Disorder

Conversion disorder is characterized by a sudden loss of sensory function or mobility. Patients commonly exhibit paralysis of an arm or leg, blindness, or deafness. The symptoms have sudden onset—typically in close temporal proximity to a significant stressor (Sarason & Sarason, 1993).

Conversion disorder is relatively rare. Sometimes the term "conversion" has been inappropriately applied to patients who have psychogenic pain or somatization disorder. Conversion disorder, in its precise definition, includes only 0.01% to 0.03% of the general United States population (*DSM–IV*, 1994). There are suggestions that the prevalence may be higher among certain ethnic groups. For example, there were reports of significant cases of "conversion blindness" among Cambodian refugees. Conversion disorder patients exhibit little concern about their condition as well as fail to recognize the relationship between the traumatic event and symptom onset ("la belle indifference"; Sarason & Sarason, 1993). The absence of emotional distress surrounding physical symptoms is not unique to conversion disorder and may be seen in patients with somatization disorder as well as certain personality disorders (e.g., histrionic). Patients may have different conversion symptoms in distinct body sites that wax and wane with external stressors (Sarason & Sarason, 1993).

Ideally, psychological intervention for conversion should be initiated as soon after symptom onset as possible. The longer the sensory or motor loss persists, the more difficult it is to alleviate. With the passage of time, conversion patients obtain increased secondary gain for their symptoms in the form of attention and reduced work and/or family responsibilities. Because of the absence of insight, conversion patients are generally not responsive to traditional verbally oriented psychotherapy. Hypnosis has been successfully employed with these patients. The hypnotic induction centers around removing the focal symptom. Oral or injectable placebo medications have also been used with the accompanying instruction that "this is a special medication that will cure your symptoms" (Reid, 1989). There is a degree of deception involved in these interventions, which may raise ethical concerns for some practitioners.

MALINGERING

Malingering is defined as the voluntary production or reporting of symptoms that is crudely motivated by external factors such as release from work, financial compensation, or avoiding prosecution (Folks & Houck, 1993). Unlike somatization disorder or conversion disorder, malingering patients are consciously aware of the relationship between their "symptoms" and psychosocial factors.

> Mr. Jones is a 28-year-old White male who was admitted to a hospital via ambulance. Mr. Jones reports that he slipped on a floor in a restaurant and hit his back. Mr. Jones states he has no sensation in his legs. Emergency medical technicians noted that at the scene of the accident, Mr. Jones did spontaneously move his left leg when it was caught on the stretcher. However, he repeatedly stated that he was "paralyzed below the waist" in the ambulance on the way to the hospital.
>
> In the interview, Mr. Jones states that he is not sure if he is married and does not recall his address. He states that he was employed at a laundromat until about six months ago when he was laid off. On mental status testing, Mr. Jones is inconsistent. There are long pauses before he begins answering questions. He reports that the current president is Lincoln and that a recent president was "Bill Reagan." He says that the year is 1812. During the sensory examination, Mr. Jones' performance is unusual and does not fit any consistent pattern. When asked about the accident,

Mr. Jones said it occurred at a specific restaurant and provides a correct address. When asked when it occurred, he responds immediately, "yesterday, March 15, 1997 ... at 3:30 p.m." Later, he is again asked today's date and says "September 5, 1892." On a forced choice task, Mr. Jones obtains a correctness score of about 20%. Radiographic studies of his back are normal. One of the nurses reports that she saw him walking over to change the channel on the television. The evaluation was interrupted when a personal injury attorney appears and says that he spoke with Mr. Jones by phone about two hours earlier.

Folks & Houck (1993) suggest that malingering should be considered in these situations: (1) A medical–legal context overshadows the presentation, (2) A marked discrepancy exists between the clinical presentation and the objective findings, (3) A lack of cooperation is experienced with diagnostic efforts where in compliance with medical regimen, or (4) The psychosocial history suggests the presence of an antisocial personality disorder (Folks & Houck, 1993, p. 283). While antisocial personality should be considered as a underlying diagnosis, malingering may also exist on a continuum with somatization disorder. This continuum may be more apparent in children who may be reporting symptoms to avoid going to school or other settings in which they may be anxious about separation from parents or evaluation. In addressing the malingerer, a direct discussion of the patient's symptoms as well as an open-minded explanation of possible of life stressors should be included (Folks & Houck, 1993).

PERSONALITY DISORDERS

Patients with personality disorders exhibit an enduring maladaptive pattern of perceiving the world and others. This pattern is characterized by rigidity, repetitiveness, and absence of insight. In addition, the personality pattern directly contributes to problems in work, social, and family relationships (*DSM–IV*, 1994).

In medical contexts, personality disorders are a difficult set of syndromes to grasp intuitively. This is because these diagnoses do not "fit" well into a medical model consisting of a clear set of symptoms deviating from normal and for which there is a specific treatment. Confounding the picture further is that personality disordered patients themselves typically do not recognize their maladaptive pattern and do not focus upon it the mental health or medical encounter.

It is estimated that about 10% of the U.S. population meets criteria for a personalty disorder (Fogel, 1993; Merikangas & Weissman, 1986). These disorders are particularly common in psychiatric settings. It is estimated that at least a third of patients in psychiatric inpatient settings exhibit evidence of personality disorder (Fogel, 1993; Koenigsberg, Kaplan, & Gilmore 1985).

Diagnosis of Personality Disorders in Primary Care

In primary care settings, a personality disorder diagnosis may not be immediately obvious. This difficulty is, in part, attributable to the continuity of personality disorder symptoms. Many of these "symptoms" exist in non-personality-disordered individuals. Personality disorders have often been conceptualized as traits that exist on a continuum between clinical and nonclinical populations (Millon, 1981).

The dividing line between a variation on normalcy and pathology may not always be clear. In primary care settings, the possibility of a personality disorder should be considered with patients who exhibit a chronic, chaotic, and disruptive life style. These patients cannot maintain employment or relationships with others. This pattern also includes disruptive relationships with physicians, mental health professionals, and other health care providers. These patients often report "firing" multiple doctors after becoming intensely dissatisfied with them. Further confounding the picture is that these patients often are likely to present with comorbid psychiatric Axis I diagnoses of depression, anxiety disorder, or substance abuse. However, standard treatments such as pharmacotherapy for mood or anxiety disorders do not appear to be as effective as is usually the case. It is estimated that up to 50% of patients with a personality disorder have a concurrent diagnosis of major depression and between 25% and 40% have a concurrent anxiety disorder. Among anxiety-disordered patients with Axis II pathology, panic disorder is particularly common (Fogel, 1993). The comorbidity of panic disorder and personality disorder is about 50%, with generalized anxiety disorders comorbidity being around 25% (Fogel, 1993; Noyes, Reich, & Christensen, 1990). The possibility of a personality disorder should be considered with patients who have intractable somatic complaints without a clear etiology or among patients with ongoing histories of noncompliance with medical regimens such as antihypertensive medications or diabetic diet.

These patients are associated with considerable distress among health care providers. Providers often experience them as disruptive and demanding. They oftentimes become very prominent when they are hospitalized on a medical floor. These patients may make repeated unnecessary requests of nursing staff and house officers and may also engage in "splitting" of providers (Groves, 1975). In the case of "splitting," a consultant may be viewed as an idealized figure who can do no wrong while the patient's primary nurse or physician may be viewed very negatively and be the subject of considerable anger and derision. Medical personnel without mental health training frequently have considerable difficulty with these patients because they do not recognize these behaviors as part of a psychiatric syndrome. As a result, these providers are often confused and experience strong resentment, frustration, and anger. Unfortunately, these adverse feelings may be "acted out" on the patient by the practitioner who is not familiar with personality disorders.

Medically trained clinicians also find personality disorders difficult in that most of these disorders are not readily treatable. The author has attended many psychiatric case conferences on inpatient settings in which the physician in charge typically reads through the patient diagnoses and closely monitors the treatment associated with each condition. A patient may have an Axis I disorder of major depression and be on 150 mg of sertraline (Zoloft). The nursing staff reports that the patient's sleep, appetite, and mood have improved. The physician then moves to the next diagnosis, an Axis II syndrome of paranoid personality disorder and requests how treatment is progressing for that illness. Typically, little progress will have been made with these symptoms. Research on the "dose response effect" in psychotherapy has concluded that only about 60% of personality disordered patients have made significant therapeutic gains after fifty sessions of psychotherapy (Howard, Kopta, Krause, & Orlinsky, 1986). In the primary care setting, the emphasis is on being able to accurately detect and manage these disorders rather than treat them. In particular, successful management of medical problems among personality disordered patients is more likely to occur if the personality style is adequately understood. These skills are particularly relevant in that there is data suggesting that personality disordered patients are much more likely to use both inpatient and outpatient medical care (Fogel, 1993). Additionally, there is some data suggesting that nonpsychiatric physicians are likely to miss a very high percentage of these patients. In one British study, general practitioners detected only about one out of five patients who were determined by psychiatrists to meet criteria for personality disorder (Casey & Tyrer, 1990).

Fogel (1993) notes that there are several practical issues in diagnosing personality disorders in medical settings. First, there is evidence that as a function of their personality disorder, these patients are less likely to be reliable and may distort and even deliberately lie about historical information. Additionally, particularly among patients who are hospitalized, acute illness together with the "normal" dependency associated with hospital care may provoke demanding or "regressive" behavior in many patients. In acute settings, the provider should be cautioned to avoid diagnosis of a personality disorder based on maladaptive behavior observed for only a week to several days. The diagnosis "personality disorder" is only appropriate when the current pattern is also associated with a long-term pattern of similar maladaptive behavior. In the section that follows, several personality disorders that commonly present in the primary care setting will be discussed.

Histrionic Personality Disorder

The major characteristics of histrionic personality are dramatic and intense emotional expression as well as efforts to be the center of attention (*DSM–IV*, 1994).

Relationships are often described as shallow and insincere and emotional expression has a very dramatic quality. These patients are often emotionally labile. Lastly, they are very concerned with their appearance and may dress in ways to draw attention to themselves. Because of their self focus and minimal capacity for reflection, these patients tend to have a rather "impressionistic" world view. When asked to describe important people in their lives, the often can only provide one-word descriptions such as, "He was great," or "My mother was outstanding!" (Shapiro, 1965). When the interviewer asks for more in-depth information, the patient typically continues to respond with these one- to two-word adjectives.

The presence of poor coping strategies is likely to lead these patients to several patterns when they are seen in the primary care setting. First, they may be particularly prone to somatic expressions of psychological distress. The patient typically does not recognize any link between psychosocial issues and physical symptoms. However, a careful history will often reveal these associations to the clinician. These patients' emotional intensity is such that their description of physical distress will seem very extreme. Depressive symptoms are likely to occur when these patients do not feel they are obtaining significant attention from significant others and will be expressed dramatically. The histrionic patient who is depressed will also often have predominant mood and affective symptoms with acute onset and less evidence of changes in vegetative functioning:

> Ms. Ball is a 32-year-old White female with a presenting problem of frequent headaches ("My head is about ready to explode ... it's just *awful*, doctor," she laments and sobs uncontrollably). Ms. Ball has a history of insulin-dependent diabetes that is poorly controlled. She has a history of changing doctors frequently and has used numerous self-help books and organizations for brief time periods. Ms. Ball's headaches have an unusual pattern. She says them come on "all at once" and "surround my whole head—it's like my head is in a huge vise." She denies any nausea or vomiting. Ms. Ball states that they "last all day ... for weeks sometimes!" Ms. Ball states that the headaches began about six months ago, but have recently gotten worse. She states that her husband has been less understanding lately and that he was recently irritated when he had to do all of the child care for a two-week period.
>
> Ms. Ball's mental status examination is somewhat unusual. Although she reports being unable to do anything at all ("I'm just a vegetable!") because of the headaches, the interviewer notices that she has rather extensive facial make-up and painted purple fingernails. She is dressed in a flowing pink caftan. When the interviewer walked into the room, Ms. Ball began writhing in pain and sobbing. She denied significant depressive moods, reported generally normal sleeping and eating, and denied suicidal ideation: "If I died, my babies would miss me so!" Ms. Ball describes one

prior psychiatric contact for "an attack of nerves" during her second divorce. Her responses to the examiner's questions often seem vague and overly lengthy so that he often find himself interrupting and redirecting her.

By way of social history, Ms. Ball has been married three times and has two children. She is currently employed as a receptionist in a large law practice. She states that she has little contact with her parents and her three siblings. She states that there was a big argument at a family gathering about six months ago that precipitated the cessation of contact. When queried about this, Ms. Ball felt that family members were being critical of her children at a family fathering and she abruptly left. She describes her husband as a "great guy, but he gets on my nerves." When asked about her children, Ms. Ball brightens considerably and shows the clinician photographs of them in "glamour shot" poses.

Antisocial Personality Disorder

The major characteristics of antisocial personality disorder include consistent violation of social norms and laws, inability to maintain enduring attachments, failure to follow through or honor agreements, lying or conning others, failure to plan ahead, and inability to function consistently as a parent or in a work setting. Patients have a history of antisocial behavior (compatible with conduct disorder) prior to the age of 15 (*DSM–IV*, 1994). When they present in the primary care setting, antisocial patients frequently have an ulterior motive. They may be attempting to obtain a release from work, immediate hospitalization to avoid jail, or prescription narcotics from a physician. Cleckley's (1978) classical description of antisocial behavior in *The Mask of Sanity* underscored how these patients may outwardly appear "normal." Antisocial-personality-disordered patients are often very skilled at presenting an outward presentation of seeming sincerity. As is the case with many people with personality disorder traits, individuals with milder forms of antisocial personality may be quite successful in different arenas of life such as sales, the military, or even police work. Their well-developed social skills, high tolerance for risk taking, and need for external stimulation are often a good "fit" with certain occupations.

In addition to heredity, there is evidence that early childhood experiences and family environment play a role in the development of antisocial behavior. Family environments of antisocial personalities are usually characterized by significant neglect, extreme abuse, and the presence of one or more parents who also have antisocial features (McCord & McCord, 1964; Robins, 1979).

Primary care providers should be cognizant of these patients in group practices and communicate their concerns to other providers in their network, as these patients often go from physician to physician or emergency room to emergency room seeking drugs or other concrete gain:

> Mr. Cass is a 25-year-old White male who reports back pain of about three weeks duration. He states that the pain has been so bad that he did not go to work for the past three days. Mr. Cass explains that he hurt his back about three years ago in an auto accident: "I was laid up in the hospital for two months—I had major back surgery." He insists that most medications don't help: "I'm allergic to nearly all of them, the only thing that works is Darvocet. I take them along with Valium." Mr. Cass's physical examination is essentially normal. He does report pain when light pressure is applied anywhere on his back. Of note, however, there appears to be no physical evidence of surgery.
>
> Mr. Cass states that he has been at his present job for about six months. He explains that he was not formally employed for a two-year period previously, but "hustled some part-time jobs" and "did some time on a mistaken identity." Mr. Cass explains that he was mistakenly arrested for a drug possession with intent to sell while "watching some crack for a friend" and spent 18 months in jail. He denies any other psychiatric contact. Mr. Cass indicates that he does not have a permanent address, but has been living in a motel for the past month.
>
> The clinician asks Mr. Cass to fill out a release for records from previous physicians and the hospital in which he was treated after his accident. Mr. Cass states that he cannot remember any of these by name, but that he will get the information later.
>
> He insists, however, that he needs his medication. In addition, Mr. Cass states that based on his experience with his back, he won't be able to return to work for another week and demands a work release for the current and the following week. Mr. Cass also asks if there would be any way that he could receive some medication samples. He explains "I'm really low on cash; I lost my paycheck at the black jack table."

Borderline Personality Disorder

Because patients with borderline personality often present to the emergency room and also because they often receive some form of mental health treatment, a fair amount is known about this disorder. Patients with borderline personality disorder are characterized by instability. This instability extends to identity, mood, and relationships (Searight, 1992b). Identity disturbance often takes the form of difficulty formulating clear life goals and rapid shifts in job and educational plans. Their self-concept is also likely to shift rapidly and may alternate between "all good" and "all bad" (Goldstein, 1990). Borderline patients also have difficulty tolerating being alone and much of their energy is devoted to maintenance of relationships. At the same time, these patients often may discharge considerable hostility toward someone that they idealize, but still anxiously persist in maintaining that relationship (Searight, 1992b). It is very common for both therapist and physician to leave an encounter with an angry borderline personality patient with an apparent understanding that the patient will seek their care elsewhere. However, the provider is frequently more likely to be surprised by the fact that the patient will want to return to their care (Searight, 1992b). Impulse control problems in terms of substance use, overspending, and overeating are common. In addition, these may also include self-injurious actions such as cutting on themselves or burning themselves:

> Ms. Zelen is a 34-year-old White female with a history of poorly controlled insulin-dependent diabetes and hypertension. She states that she is at the clinic today because of muscle tension and pain in the back of her neck.
>
> By way of social history, Ms. Zelen indicates that she has been married for 12 years. During this time she and her husband have separated multiple times ("...more than I can count"). The couple has two children ages 13 and 5. Ms. Zelen indicates that she graduated from a community college about ten years ago. Since that time she has held about 15 jobs—the briefest was for three days and the longest was for eight months. She describes her childhood as a "nightmare" and alludes to several episodes of sexual and physical abuse.
>
> During the interview, Ms. Zelen exhibits considerable lability and alternates from anger to laughter to tearfulness within a matter of minutes. She states that her mood is "a mess," but denies current suicidal ideation. She stated that she cut her wrist in the past on at least ten occasions. Scarring was visible on the inside of her arms. Ms. Zelen describes a period of drinking to the point of intoxication twice per month for the past eight to ten years. She reports smoking marijuana two to three times per week for the past five years. Ms. Zelen indicates that she and her husband frequently get into intense arguments. When they argued or she felt lonely, Ms. Zelen stated she would go to bars and leave with various men. This pattern has been present for about ten years. Ms. Zelen indicates she has not taken her insulin for the past three weeks and has not taken her antihypertensive medications for the past month. When asked about her noncompliance, she states, "I don't care ... when my time is up, it's up."

Management of Personality Disordered Patients in Primary Care

In primary care settings, formal diagnosis of personality disorders is probably not so important as understanding the interpersonal behavior pattern that creates problems for the patient. In discussing borderline personality in the medical setting, Fogel (1993) notes that a sophisticated diagnostic workup is less important than understanding the intense quality of the interpersonal relationships and use of splitting and projective identification. It is also important that the provider recognize that patients with multiple suicide attempts as well as significant childhood sexual trauma are often likely to exhibit the interpersonal dynamics of borderline personality (Herman, Perry, & Vander Kolk, 1989). In many cases, the presence of personality disorder features may not be apparent until the patient has failed a reasonable trial of therapy for an Axis I anxiety or major depressive disorder.

As noted at the outset of this section, it is unlikely that personality disordered patients will be "cured" in the primary care setting. The general focus is on successfully addressing Axis I pathology as well as minimizing the harmful impact of the patient's maladaptive personality style on their ongoing medical care. It is useful to consider providing the patient with a sense of control. This may involve negotiating with them around appointment setting, medication dosages, or discharge dates from the hospital (Fogel, 1993). Consistency on the part of health care givers is essential. This aspect includes clear documentation in the record; regular, consistent appointments; and clear guidelines for the patient about taking medication and keeping mental health appointments. Formal contracts are often useful in maintaining this degree of structure (Fogel, 1993).

Setting limits will also often be necessary with these patients. In ambulatory primary care, it is very common for borderline personality patients to become extremely angry and discharge their rage inappropriately on nursing staff or receptionists. The provider should set limits around this behavior in a firm, yet nonpunitive, manner. As Fogel (1993) notes, there may be good reasons for the patient's behavior, but the provider should communicate that the behavior itself is unacceptable. The style of communicating these limits should be a somewhat detached impersonal manner such as "verbally aggressive outbursts are not permitted in this clinic" (Fogel, 1993).

There is some evidence that pharmacotherapy has some efficacy with personality disorders. In particular, selective serotonin re-uptake inhibitors may be useful with borderline personality disorder (Searight, 1992b). Additionally, for those borderline personality disordered patients as well as schizotypal patients who have periods of transient psychotic activity, low dose neuroleptic medication may be of value.

Practical issues for the care giver also include concern about possible litigation (Fogel, 1993; Searight, 1992b). While many of these patients threaten litigation as a form of manipulation or as a means of expressing hostility indirectly to the provider, it is difficult for health care professionals to function under these threats even when they appear to be ill founded. Appropriate use of consultants as well as regular supervision from peers is also helpful in dealing with these patients. These consultative activities should be clearly documented in the patient's record. In teaching family medicine residents, the author always stresses the necessity of having a chaperon during an office visit involving genital or breast examinations with these patients. Although chaperons (e.g., nurses) are always a good idea in these situations, it is particularly important with borderline or histrionic patients who may misinterpret the examination and may make accusations toward the physician.

ALCOHOL ABUSE

Alcohol abuse is a common contributor to poor health status but is frequently unrecognized. Prevalence rates of alcohol abuse among ambulatory primary care patients have ranged from 4% to 18% (Searight, 1992c). There is evidence that alcohol involvement is even higher among hospitalized general medical and surgical patients. A study in a general hospital found that close to 25% of medical–surgical patients exhibited significant alcohol involvement (Moore, Bone, Geller, Mamon, Stokes, & Levine, 1989). These rates compare with an estimated 10% of Americans in the general population who have demonstrated alcohol-related problems such as loss of control, with 5% of those experiencing serious adverse social consequences of drinking such as arrest (Clark & Midanik, 1981).

Persons who use alcohol are particularly likely to use ambulatory medical care. One study found that 70% of persons who abused alcohol made at least one ambulatory care visit within a six-month period (Hansel, 1990). It is estimated that physicians detect between 8% and 50% of alcohol-involved patients, with most data suggesting detection rates of around 20% (Searight, 1992c). It is unusual for alcohol abusing patients to describe substance abuse as their presenting problem. Most patients who abuse alcohol present with conditions that are indirectly related to their alcohol use such as gastrointestinal disturbance, headaches, or sleep difficulties (Malla & Merskey, 1987). Several reports have documented that physicians tend to have relatively little training in substance abuse (Delbanco & Barnes, 1987). The majority of medical training centers around assessment with very little attention paid to treatment (Havassy & Schmidt, 1994; Searight, 1992c).

Assessment of Alcohol Use

Direct questioning of patients about alcohol use is likely to result in substantial underestimates. Although there are suggestions that patients may accurately report the number of episodes of drinking, they are likely to underestimate the amount of alcohol consumed by up to three and a half times (Magruder-Habib, Durand, & Frey, 1991).

Assessment tools that have proven helpful include the CAGE questionnaire and the Michigan Alcohol Screening Test (MAST). The CAGE has been used both in self-report and interview formats: CAGE is an acronym that stands for four questions: Do you feel the need to cut down on your drinking? Do you feel annoyed by people complaining about your drinking? Do you ever feel guilty about your drinking? Do you ever drink an eye-opener in the morning to relieve the "shakes"? The CAGE has fairly good sensitivity and specificity when two affirmative responses are used as the cut-off (Searight, 1992c). In a British sample,

King (1986) reported a sensitivity of 84% and a specificity of 95%. In King's (1986) study, the criterion for defining alcohol abuse/dependence was eight drinks per day.

The MAST (Selzer, 1971) is usually administered in a written self-report format. The original scale consists of 25 items that are endorsed *yes* or *no*. The content includes alcohol-related events and consequences such as fighting or arrests as well as self-evaluation of drinking habits. The MAST has been subject to a number of investigations. The MAST's sensitivity and specificity varies according to population parameters such as gender or whether patients have comorbid psychiatric condition. Sensitivity is usually in the .80 range, and specificity is in the .75 to .80 range (Searight, 1992c). A briefer version of the MAST, comprised of 13 items, has been employed in primary care research. However, the classification rate of the reduced inventory varies considerably from the longer version (Jacobson, 1983). Similar to self-report depression inventories, the MAST has also been used in primary care research as the "gold standard" for evaluating physician's ability to detect alcohol involved patients.

Laboratory data is more commonly employed in in-patient medical settings to detect problem drinking. Gamma Glutamyl Transpeptidase (GGT) and Mean Corpuscular Volume (MCV) are elevated among those with relatively lengthy histories of moderate to heavy drinking (Holt, Skinner, & Israel, 1981). GGT elevations in particular do not tend to occur until later stages of drinking (Holt et al., 1981; Searight, 1992c). Additionally, both GGT and MCV elevations may occur because of other medical conditions. For example, GGT levels may be higher in patients with any form of liver disease involving hepatocellular damage and also may be elevated in reponse to a number of medications. MCV tends to be elevated more commonly in women versus men, among older patients, and also among tobacco users (Holt et al., 1981).

A more profitable approach for early detection has been suggested by primary care physicians who have studied common physical concerns among ambulatory patients. Common complaints among heavy drinkers include dyspepsia, recurrent diarrhea, nausea and vomiting, polyuria, heart palpitations, insomnia, and memory deficits (Searight, 1992c). Malla and Mersky (1987) suggest that vomiting, stomach pain, chest pain, and tremors are particularly sensitive physical indicators associated with heavy drinking. In their study, Malla and Mersky (1987) found that one quarter of patients with more than three GI symptoms (vomiting, stomach pain, diarrhea, reduced appetite) demonstrated definite evidence of alcoholism. Thirteen percent of these patients demonstrated "probable alcoholism." This less direct approach appears to be particularly useful because the majority of heavy drinkers do not describe alcohol consumption as their presenting problem to their physician, but are instead likely to report physical distress related to alcohol consumption.

One issue that is often not addressed in primary care is assessment for other illicit substances. R. O. Brown, Leonard, Saunders, and Papasouliotis (1997) recently developed a nine-item screening interview that included attention to alcohol as well as other illicit drugs. For example, the presence of blackouts was addressed through the question, In the last year, how many times have you not remembered things that happened while you were drinking or using drugs? The investigators suggested that conjoint questions might prompt more valid reporting because respondents may perceive the need to reduce substances in general rather than decrease use of any one drug. Brown and colleagues (1997) found that in their sample of family practice patients, one in four had a current substance abuse problem, with about 22% abusing alcohol, 6% using cannabis, and 2% using cocaine. Two questions were most useful in detecting patients with substance abuse problems. These were: In the last year have you ever drank or used drugs more than you meant to? and Have you ever wanted to cut down on your drinking or drug use? The sensitivity and specificity of both these items were slightly above .80 (Brown et al., 1997).

Alcohol Withdrawal

Patients who are chronic alcohol abusers show a fairly consistent pattern as their alcohol blood level drops. In the first 3–12 hours, the patient may demonstrate significant tremulousness. Visual hallucinations may also occur within this period. Seizures often begin somewhat later, beginning at 12 and up to 48 hours after the last drink. Delirium tremens (DTs) is probably the most severe form of alcohol withdrawal. Symptoms include hallucinations, delusions, tremor, agitation, and insomnia (Knight & Longmore, 1994). DTs may endure for up to three days. Mortality rates during this period can be up to 5%. Patients who succumb usually do so because of cardiovascular problems, deliberate self-harm, hypothermia, or infection. The visual hallucinations that occur with DTs are very striking and often include small animals or people. Paranoia commonly occurs. A frequent source of injury stems from patients who inadvertently harm themselves while responding to hallucinations (Lishman, 1987).

DTs and related symptoms occur among patients who have long-term histories of substantial alcohol abuse (Knight & Longmore, 1994). These are patients who typically consume large quantities consistently on a daily basis. Possible alcohol withdrawal is a practical issue among patients with suspected alcohol histories who are hospitalized for medical reasons. Individuals with known long-term patterns of alcohol use are often placed on tranquilizing medication such as diazepam or lorazepam at hospital admission to manage the symptoms of alcohol withdrawal (Cross & Hennessey, 1993).

Neuropsychological Sequelae of Alcohol Abuse

Patients with long-term patterns of heavy alcohol use will often exhibit cognitive deficits (Knight & Longmore, 1994). In acutely ill patients, it is often difficult to determine whether cognitive deficits are secondary to long-term alcohol use or other problems. A practical question arising in this context is whether the patient is safe to be at home alone and can manage their own affairs. Psychologists may be consulted to determine whether the patient's pattern of neuropsychological impairment is consistent with long-term alcohol abuse or acute cognitive disorganization associated with hospitalization or depression.

Patients who have cognitive impairment secondary to alcohol abuse tend to show a fairly consistent pattern. Orientation to person, place, and time is generally intact. Tasks that are sensitive to disruptions in attention such as saying the ABCs or digits forward are usually performed adequately. Tasks requiring more demanding levels of concentration such as serial sevens or counting by threes may be significantly more difficult. On short-term or immediate recall tasks, in which the patient is provided with some information and then asked to state it back immediately, impairment may be evident. The most pronounced deficits, however, occur on delayed recall items. Examples of these tasks include asking the patient to remember a short passage or four or five words for a 10- to 30-minute interval. Long-term recall is also usually intact with alcohol-involved patients. In particular, information that is *least* recently encoded (e.g., childhood memories) is likely to be retained. Lastly, there does seem to be some disruption in general intellectual functioning. Thus, patients may demonstrate subtle difficulties with abstraction, calculation, verbal fluency, or shifting cognitive sets. An example of this skill is the Trail Making Test—Part B, in which the patient is asked to use a pencil to connect a series of numbers and letters in a sequential yet alternating manner (Knight & Longmore, 1994).

There are three general neuropsychological syndromes that may arise from long-term alcohol use. These include Wernicke's encephalopathy, Korsakoff's syndrome, and Alcohol-related dementia. In cases of Wernicke's encephalopathy, there is usually an acute process of confusion, disorientation, ocular palsy, and gaze paralysis. This will gradually develop into more stable Korsakoff's syndrome. However, patients also may return to their premorbid level of functioning with less pronounced cognitive deficits. Patients with Korsakoff's dementia demonstrate a pronounced anterograde amnesia. They are unable to acquire new material, and they have pronounced memory deficits for recent events. In cases of alcohol-related dementia, there is usually a symptom complement consistent with Korsakoff's. However, there are additional deficits in higher cognitive functions (Knight & Longmore, 1994).

SCHIZOPHRENIA

Schizophrenia, a psychotic disorder involving formal thought disturbance, hallucinations, delusions, and impaired social and vocational functioning, is usually treated by psychiatrists. However, the primary care physician may seek consultation when schizophrenic patients develop medical problems. Dickson and Neill (1987) have described complications arising when schizophrenic patients require medical care. When patients with histories of schizophrenia are seen on medical floors, their psychotic symptomatology may make them misinterpret medical procedures. As a result, they may refuse oxygen and sputum samples and remove intravenous lines. These behaviors may be attributable in part to paranoid ideation or significant thought disturbance and confusion. The author has often consulted on cases in which the patient has become physically ill and stopped taking their antipsychotic medication. As a result, when the patient is admitted for pneumonia or some other medical problem, their psychotic symptoms are under very poor control.

> Mr. K is a 39-year-old White single man who is currently hospitalized because of severe gangrene of the left leg associated with diabetes. Mr. K has undergone multiple transfusions in the past. He was diagnosed with insulin dependent diabetes, 20 years ago, but has not been compliant with insulin injections. He has a history of schizophrenia dating back to his early 20's and a ten year history of alcohol abuse. He currently receives Haldol Deconate on a monthly basis from a public health clinic. Mr. K's current physician as well as previous physicians have recommended amputation of his leg. Mr. K continues to refuse the procedure. The physician is concerned about Mr. K's decisional capacity, because he appears to be experiencing auditory hallucinations and is "paranoid and hostile."
>
> Mr. K is interviewed at his bedside. He states that he came to the hospital because he "felt weak." Mr. K appears to be oriented in all spheres but is not very communicative. He explains that he has been hearing voices "laughing, talking, and telling me to do dope." Mr. K describes a 10-year period of psychiatric treatment, names his current psychiatrist, and states that he currently takes Haldol. He states that his last Haldol injection was about a month ago. When asked about his medical condition, Mr. K states that he has "bad sugar in the blood" because of "problems with my pancreas." He explains that diabetes means that "I get too much sugar in my body." Mr. K describes the Haldol as causing the diabetes and making him weak. When asked about surgery, Mr. K states that "I want to keep my leg." Mr. K expresses a wish for a medicine to save his leg. Mr. K states that he does not trust doctors and does not believe that an amputation is an appropriate treatment. "They can cut the stuff out of there and my leg will be good as new." He again reiterates this belief that the Haldol is causing his weakness and explains that he takes it only because his father requires it.

A particularly difficult problem arises when schizophrenic patients become pregnant. Because of concern for the developing fetus, neuroleptic medication may be discontinued. However, the patient's psychotic symptomatology will then emerge and may prevent the patient from becoming appropriately involved in their prenatal care. In addition, they may become particularly frightened and disorganized during the stress of delivery. It may be necessary to maintain these patients in an acute psychiatric hospital or have a visiting nurse actively involved in their treatment if they are at home to ensure compliance with medical care as well as to attempt to structure their environment.

It is extremely important in managing these patients that the primary care provider be direct while avoiding a highly confrontational style. In particular, explaining the role of medication in treating both medical and psychiatric symptoms should be included. In cases in which surgery or emergent treatment is required, it may be necessary to have the patient temporarily declared incompetent if they are refusing care. In these cases, a relative or other guardian should be appointed to make these decisions. If possible, appointment of a surrogate should be deferred until psychotic symptoms are aggressively treated.

CONCLUSION

Successful treatment and clinical management models for somatizing patients are likely to become a focus of primary care providers over the next decade. Mental health professionals familiar with somatoform dynamics can make extremely valuable contributions to their primary physician colleagues who typically are frustrated by these patients. A similar description of personality disordered patients will also be invaluable to health care providers who are confused and occasionally frightened by these patients. Early detection and brief intervention with alcohol-abusing patients will likely result in lower medical health care costs associated with neurological, gastrointestinal, and cardiovascular disease among these patients. Compliance and medical decision making commonly arise among schizophrenic patients with medical conditions.

Chapter 4

Pediatric Disorders

In primary care, the clinician will commonly encounter childhood psychiatric disorders including attention-deficit hyperactivity disorder, conduct disorder, oppositional defiant disorder, childhood depression, and learning disabilities. However, providers will also see variations on normal development as well as behavioral problems that are not formal psychiatric diagnoses. Examples of this latter category include temper tantrums, poor school achievement, and argumentativeness. Mental health professionals who work in settings such as family practice or pediatrics should be knowledgeable about normal childhood development as well as common deviations. Although formal family therapy and individual psychotherapy skills are certainly helpful, much primary care with pediatric problems centers around providing advice and developing strategies for specific behavioral concerns. This chapter will begin with a discussion of some common problems encountered with pediatric patients and will conclude with more significant *DSM–IV* childhood disorders.

NONCOMPLIANCE AND TANTRUMS

The majority of behavioral problems encountered in primary care are not diagnosable *DSM–IV* disorders, but often center around difficulty with compliance. Most childhood behavioral problems, such as failure to follow through with parental requests including picking up toys, remaining seated during dinner, or fighting with parents or siblings, can be addressed through fairly straightforward behavioral methods. The most helpful parental response is first to describe the behavior desired from the child. Second, the consequence for inappropriate behavior should be described. Parents should also attempt to reinforce the child for prosocial behavior by giving a reward for periods of a day or days in which the child is compliant. When the problem behavior occurs, parents should be encouraged to give one or two reminders. At the second reminder, the child should be told of the consequence for continued noncompliance. For example, if the child refuses to get out of bed in the morning to go to school, the parents should awaken the child and then if the child is still in bed five minutes later, say "If you are not out of bed in the next 30 seconds, I will have to give you a consequence; there will no television this evening. If you are out of bed, there will be an extra treat packed with your lunch." Importantly, parents must follow through with both rewards and consequences and use them on a daily basis. Usually parents cannot address more than about two problem behaviors at a time. The author's usual advice is to target two problem behaviors until there is about 80% success before moving on to address other concerns.

With young children, time-out is a very helpful way of reducing problem behavior. With this method, a child is given a warning and told they will go to time-out unless they stop being aggressive or disruptive. The time-out area should be situated such that it is adjacent to the parents' location in the house, but ideally should not be in the same room. Parents should go on with their usual activities while the child is in time-out, but at the same time be able to monitor them. Some children will not remain seated for the time-out period. In this case, the child can be held by the parent in a basket-hold. The parent should be seated on the floor cross-legged and the child should be held on their lap. A parent can put their arms around the child's arms and legs to prevent them from lashing out, kicking, or hitting. The child should be held this way until they regain adequate physical control. Importantly, the parent should not have eye contact nor should they verbally interact with the child during this period. Once the child has regained self-control through physical restraint and it is no longer necessary, the child should serve the rest of their time-out. Additionally, some children will get up from a time-out and need to be reminded to sit for the full time period. After they have done this once and a warning is given, the child should have an extra minute added to their time-out. A kitchen timer is often a useful aid for this process.

Parents often use spanking or other forms of corporal punishment with children. Physical punishment is usually unhelpful for several reasons. First, it does not specify the desired behavior to the child. Second, it may produce side effects such as increased anxiety or fearfulness. Third, aggressive behavior tends to beget aggressive behavior. Thus, the child who is frequently spanked is often aggressive toward other children.

The child should also be rewarded for desirable behavior. Rewards may consist of stickers on a calendar, treats such as cookies, or tokens that they may trade in for a larger reward at the end of a time period such as a week. Young children, six or seven and under, will usually need some form of immediate reward. Preschool age children and kindergarten age children will usually require reinforcement at least twice a day, particularly for reducing high-frequency behavior. With older children who are exhibiting behavioral problems in school, a useful strategy is the "note home." In the note home, the teacher will indicate whether the child had a good day (i.e., without significant behavioral problems). For these days, the child should receive some sort of reward that evening (i.e., ice cream bar, extra TV time). In addition, a calendar should be used to keep a record of the child's school behavior over the course of one to two weeks. At the end of a week, if the child meets specified criteria, they should be allowed a more substantial reward such as going to a fast-food restaurant or renting a videotape.

In developing a reward system of this type for older children, it is important to have a thorough understanding of the baseline frequency of the problem behavior. For example, for a child who is having significant school behavior problems and is disruptive every day, it is unlikely that they will achieve a "perfect week" for some time in the future. If this "perfect" standard is used, the child will never receive a reward and the system will not be operative. Thus, for a child who is exhibiting a high-frequency problem behavior, two or three good days may be the initial standard for receiving a reward at the end of the week.

With older children, time-out is often not as effective a strategy for reducing problem behavior as it is with younger children. Rewards are likely to be somewhat more effective. Removal of privileges such as access to TV, computer, or video games can also be used to reduce the frequency of problem behavior. In addition, chores around the house, which are to be completed before any recreational activity begins, are also useful consequences. In dealing with older children, it is important that parents not participate in extended arguments. The consequence should be announced and parents indicate that they will be happy to discuss the issue further once the chores are completed. Although it may be helpful to the family to evaluate and negotiate consequences, this should be done after the consequence has been served (Novak, 1996).

ACADEMIC/LEARNING PROBLEMS

A large proportion of children are referred to physicians as well as mental health professionals because of school performance problems. In cases of a long-standing academic difficulty, the provider should consider the possibility of a learning disability. It is estimated that about 3–5% of U.S. school children have a diagnosable learning disability (*DSM–IV*, 1994). Definitions of learning disability vary according to different specialties as well as school districts. However, a frequently employed criterion is standardized academic test scores in a particular skill area that are 1–2 standard deviations below the child's measured IQ. If the child has not been evaluated by his or her physician, a physical examination should be conducted. In particular, attention to hearing and visual acuity should be included in the physician's screening (Nahlik & Searight, 1996). It is also important that the child have adequate exposure to academic material. Thus, particularly in children who have not had kindergarten or preschool, diagnosis may be deferred until at least second grade. Although school systems commonly define learning disabilities with respect to an academic skill area (reading, arithmetic), most of these children exhibit deficits in neuropsychological functions that underlie these academic subjects. For example, children with reading disabilities often will have underlying weaknesses in receptive or expressive language or possibly in visual/spatial skills. Arithmetic disabilities similarly may be attributable to memory deficits or visual/spatial organizational problems such that the child has difficulty keeping numbers lined up in the appropriate columns (Nahlik & Searight, 1996).

Children with higher levels of intellectual functioning or more subtle learning disabilities, may not be detected until the upper elementary school grades. The upper grade levels also have greater demands for independent work, and the absence of external structure may make an underlying learning problem more apparent.

Although learning disabilities should always be considered in situations in which grades and other objective indicators of school performance are below average, there are a number of other factors that may contribute to poor school performance. Emotional difficulties or family conflicts should always be considered, particularly in cases in which there is a sudden drop in grades. Additionally, clinical problems such as attention-deficit hyperactivity disorder are frequently associated with learning disabilities (Barkley, 1991).

However, poor school performance may become a content area for "power struggles" between the parent and child or between the parents themselves. Conflicts around homework completion, in particular, may arise because of inconsistent parental standards or parental ambivalence about academic success. For example, in the later grades, in which good academic performance may lead to greater independence through honors and college scholarships, parents may "sabotage" the adolescent's academic work to prevent autonomy.

In order to formally evaluate a learning disability, standardized psychometric testing is required. This traditionally includes intellectual testing such as a Wechsler Intelligence Scale for Children—Third Edition (WISC–III) as well as educational testing such as the Woodcock–Johnson Battery. The health care provider can serve as an advocate for the child and family for appropriate special services. Under federal guidelines and state law, children with learning disabilities are entitled to appropriate special education resources. Because of the increased number of children diagnosed with learning disabilities, these available resources are increasingly taxed. Thus, the provider and parents may need to be somewhat aggressive in order to obtain the optimal level of services for the learning-disabled child (Nahlik & Searight, 1996).

ENURESIS

Functional enuresis involves repeated episodes of urination into bed or clothes during the day or night. There should be at least two enuretic episodes per week for three consecutive months. The child should be at least five years of age. Functional enuresis is not diagnosed in children younger than five. Importantly, physical problems such as diabetes or urinary tract infection should be ruled out before a diagnosis of functional enuresis is given. (Walker, 1995) Prevalence rates of enuresis suggest that this is a fairly frequent condition. It is estimated that about 15–20% of five-year-olds, 5% of ten-year-olds, and 2% of 12- to 14-year-olds have nocturnal enuresis (Oppel, Harper, & Rider, 1968). Nocturnal enuresis is the most common form of the disorder. This disorder may persist into adulthood, with about 1–2% of adults demonstrating enuresis. While girls have a higher incidence of combined diurnal and nocturnal enuresis (Walker, 1995), boys are about twice as likely to have pure nocturnal enuresis (Walker, 1995).

Exact causes of nocturnal enuresis are not well specified. There does appear to be some evidence of genetic predisposition as well as possible developmental delays. Hormonal factors have also been implicated. It has been suggested that children with the disorder secrete decreased levels of antidiuretic hormone, which may contribute to increased urine output and wetting the bed (Walker, 1995). Although older clinical writing suggested that enuresis represented underlying child psychopathology, there does not appear to be any consistent evidence of other psychiatric disturbances that predispose children or coexists with enuresis.

There are several established treatments for functional enuresis. Medication treatment most commonly includes the tricyclic antidepressant Imipramine. This seems to be effective in about 50% of treated children. Desmopressin (DDAVP) is a synthetic hormone associated with increased urine concentration and thus decreases overall urine volume. DDAVP appears to be somewhat effective. However, it is expensive and enuresis resumes when the drug is discontinued. The primary behavioral method for treating enuresis is the bell and pad. This is a device on which the child sleeps. An alarm is sounded when urine touches the pad and the child in theory will go to the bathroom at this point. Another alternative is a timer so that the child is awakened on an hourly basis and then uses the toilet.

A recent survey suggested that among pediatricians, the most commonly held etiology for enuresis was "slow maturation of bladder control." In terms of methods used for treatment, a high percentage of primary care physicians reported using a parental reinforcement system as well as the bell and pad. Only about half (52%) recommended use of medication. The primary care physicians surveyed reported that 38% of their patients exhibited complete remission with 41% exhibiting partial remission (Vogel, Young, & Primack, 1996).

ENCOPRESIS

Children who are encopretic have bowel movements in their clothes or in inappropriate places such as the floor, bed, or wastebasket (Walker, 1995). The child should be at least four years old and episodes of bowel movements should occur at least once a month for a three-month period to meet criteria for formal diagnosis (*DSM–IV*, 1994). In evaluating these children, a confounding disorder that should be ruled out is Hirschprung's disease. In Hirschsprung's disease, the child becomes impacted and has a deficiency in nerve sensitivity of the colon such that digestive material is not appropriately moved through the gastrointestinal tract. In addition, some encopretic children may have developed constipation.

Walker (1978, 1995) suggests that there are three subtypes of encopresis. First, chronic constipation may be precipitated by heredity or diet, as well as a consistent pattern of withholding bowel movements. This often happens during the course of toilet training and the child may become impacted. Because of the impaction, fecal material and liquid may seep out. Children are usually unaware when this happens. In the second form, children tend to have frequent bowel movements and diarrhea. There is often an association between abdominal pain and bowel movements as well as life stress in these patients. The final type that Walker (1995) describes are children that he terms "manipulative soilers." In these instances, children are often expressing anger, usually toward parents. "Manipulative soilers" are typically in families in which there is significant conflict between the parents or between the parents and child around discipline and independence (White, 1984).

Because fecal retention is so common among these children, an initial treatment is usually some form of laxative. Mineral oil given one to two hours after a meal, will often help with regular bowel movements. It is also important that children be sent to the toilet and required to sit on the toilet several times a day for periods of about 5–10 minutes. These episodes should usually occur about one hour after each meal.

In cases of encopresis in which there is a manipulative component, it is often necessary to include attention to family dynamics. Structural intervention such as having parents agree on consistent discipline as well as helping parents respond in an emotionally neutral, nonpunitive manner to episodes of encopresis will be helpful.

ATTENTION-DEFICIT HYPERACTIVITY DISORDER (AD/HD)

Attention-deficit hyperactivity disorder is characterized by difficulties with focusing attention and concentrating as well as hyperactive and impulsive behavior

(*DSM–IV*, 1994). Inattention may take the form of difficulty remembering parental or teacher requests, being easily distracted by extraneous environmental cues, and an inability to focus on necessary detail (Searight, Nahlik, & Campbell, 1995). Hyperactivity may include motor restlessness, frequent talking, and difficulty remaining in one's seat in the classroom.

> Joey is a 7-year-old male referred by his school. Joey's first grade teacher sends a note to the provider that describes him as a "sweet child but always on the go ... he can't sit still, he bothers the other children, and he can't focus on his schoolwork for more than five minutes."
>
> Joey was born two months premature and had respiratory complications. He was in the hospital for about two weeks. Joey's mother says that in contrast to his older brother, Joey was always a "difficult child." He wouldn't sleep or eat regularly. Joey frequently wakes up during the night and it has always been difficult getting him into bed. ("We chase him back to bed for about two hours every night.") Mother reports he has always been "on the go" and is very distractible. ("He never stays seated for a meal; he's always reacting to everything in the room. The only time he ever focuses is when he plays video games or watches cartoons.")
>
> In the clinician's office, Joey is initially attentive and calm. After about 15 minutes, he begins to fidget in his chair. After 25 minutes, he is crawling on the floor and begins pulling books off the shelf. On screening tasks, he seems to have age-appropriate language skills and educational knowledge. However, Joey can only recall one of four words at a 15-minute interval and can only restate three numbers forward and two backward.

Symptoms of AD/HD must impair functioning in two arenas—social, academic, or occupational—and they must be present before the age of seven. This pattern must be consistently present for six months. This disorder appears to be diagnosed with increased frequency (Searight & McLaren, 1999).

The majority of these children are evaluated and treated by pediatricians and family physicians (Wolraich et al., 1990). There are two primary sub-types of AD/HD, hyperactive type and inattentive type. Each of these is defined by the primary form of symptomatology exhibited. The inattentive type is less frequent and appears to be more common among girls (Searight et al., 1995).

The overall prevalence of this disorder is about 3–5% in the general population. However, surveys of school-aged children, predominantly in the form of teachers' behavioral ratings, have found very high rates of core AD/HD symptoms reported—often in the 20–30% range (Searight & McLaren, 1999).

AD/HD's etiology is not well-established. However, there is evidence of central nervous system involvement with a possible imbalance in neurotransmitters as well as maturational deficits in the frontal cortex (Barkley, 1991, 1994). The disorder appears to continue into adolescence in about 70% of children affected with AD/HD. (Cantwell, 1996). The adolescent form of the disorder is somewhat more subtle with difficulties with attention and concentration predominating. Additionally, there are suggestions that the disorder continues into adulthood in about half of those patients who have childhood AD/HD (Cantwell, 1996). The symptom picture in adulthood often includes more subtle forms of impulsivity, labile mood, as well as difficulties with short-term memory, attention, and concentration (Wender, 1995).

Assessment of AD/HD in primary care should include several sources. Among children, parents and teachers should both be relied on as sources of the child's behavior at home and school, respectively. Use of structured rating forms such as the Connors Rating Scale are often helpful and efficient (Connors, 1989). Office-based tasks such as digit span, memory for a short passage, and computerized continuous performance tasks such as the Gordon diagnostic system are also compatible with a brief and focused assessment approach. It is noted, however, that a number of these children have comorbid learning disabilities. These children will likely require a referral for more detailed psycho-educational testing. The clinician should also seriously consider the possibility of oppositional defiant and conduct disturbance, either comorbid with AD/HD or as a differential diagnosis.

In most cases, treatment for attention-deficit hyperactivity disorder includes pharmacotherapy. Methylphenidate (Ritalin) is effective in about 70–80% of children with the disorder. The medication is typically administered at least twice a day, in the morning and at noon. Dosages range from 5 mg up to 20 mg. In older children who may have significant homework demands late in the afternoon, a third dose is sometimes given at around 3 p.m. An additional stimulant medication that is sometimes used is longer-acting Dextroamphetamine. The stimulants often may produce side-effects such as insomnia and irritability as well as decreased appetite. These should be closely monitored. A longer-acting stimulant medication that is occasionally employed is Pemoline. It has been suggested that about 20% of children who do not respond to an initial stimulant drug such as methylphenidate may demonstrate improvement when a different stimulant is employed (Searight et al., 1995). Among children placed on methylphenidate or dextroamphetamine, rapid improvement is generally the rule if the AD/HD diagnosis is correct. These children will demonstrate significantly improved attention and reduced impulsivity in the classroom environment usually within the first week. For children who do not respond to stimulant medications, several issues should be considered. First, the clinician should seriously consider whether the AD/HD diagnosis is correct. Additionally, the presence of comorbid psychopathology, in particular conduct disturbance or oppositional defiant disorder, should be considered. As noted above, learning disabilities occur in a significant proportion of AD/HD children. Childrens' inattention in a classroom, in these instances, may arise because they do not comprehend academic material. For children who cannot tolerate stimulants, the tricyclic antidepressants imipramine, desipramine and amitriptyline appear to be effective in reducing hyperactivity. However, they may not substantially improve cognitive functioning (Pliszka, 1987). Clonidine may also be helpful with AD/HD children who have comorbid problems with aggression (Schvehla, Mandoki, & Summer, 1994).

One common occurrence in managing the AD/HD child over time is that adults may indicate that stimulant medication that had previously been helpful has become less effective. Several issues should be considered when this problem arises. First, it is possible that the medication is not being given consistently. Children who are required to go to the nurse's or principal's office to get their medication at noon may become self-conscious about taking the medication and not be compliant. It is also possible that there is increased stress at home, which may reduce tolerance for the child's behavior. Parents sometimes will request medication reevaluation when children are exhibiting non-AD/HD behaviors such as fighting, arguing with siblings, or talking back to parents. Pliszka (1987) has described a behavioral "drift" phenomenon that may occur with AD/HD children being treated with medication. He notes that when treatment is initiated, improvement is usually fairly dramatic. However over time, the child's behavior, rather than being compared with their pre-medication state, is being compared with other non-AD/HD children. Clinically, AD/HD children on medication still exhibit some behavioral and cognitive deficits, although stimulants produce improvement.

CONDUCT DISORDER

Conduct disorder is probably best known as a predecessor to adult antisocial personality. The defining features of conduct disorder are a behavior pattern in which the rights of others are consistently violated and a failure to follow age-appropriate behavioral standards. Common behaviors include aggression to people or animals, theft or vandalism, lying, stealing, and serious violations of rules or laws (*DSM–IV*, 1994). Clues to conduct disturbance during the interview include reported encounters with the police, time spent in juvenile detention, suspensions from school, or frequent episodes of running away from home. In particular, early onset (prior to age 13 or 14) of sexual activity, smoking cigarettes, or drinking alcohol is often associated with conduct disturbance (Nahlik & Searight, 1996).

In the interview, these children are often very striking as they calmly describe their involvement in aggressive and destructive activities. They may describe in some detail and with little outward emotion how they set fire to a garage or vandalized a school. Older conduct-disordered adolescents will factually describe multiple trips to juvenile detention, drug use, drug sales, and gang involvement.

Twelve-year-old Jimmy is brought to the primary care provider by his mother after being suspended from school. Jimmy is on a two-week suspension for carrying a knife on school grounds. Jimmy's parents were divorced when he was very young; he has lived in his mother's or father's household for periods of 6–12 months since the divorce. Jimmy's mother says he came back to her home three months ago ("His dad threw him out after Jimmy stole $100 from his billfold and set the garage on fire.")

Further inquiry indicates that this is Jimmy's fifth school suspension in the past two years. Previous suspensions have been for swearing at teachers and physical fights with peers. Because one of these physical fights involved Jimmy breaking another child's nose, Jimmy was arrested and spent a week in juvenile detention.

In contrast to attention-deficit hyperactivity disorder, conduct disorder children do not exhibit pronounced distractibility or hyperactivity. The distinction between conduct disturbance and oppositional defiant disorder is that oppositional defiant children, while often argumentative, do not typically engage in overt illegal and physically aggressive and destructive behavior.

The *DSM–IV* (1994) makes a distinction between conduct disturbance that has its onset in childhood versus conduct disturbance that has its onset in adolescence. Early onset conduct disorder (before the age of 10) is associated with a worse prognosis. These children often engage in more disturbing behavior, such as fire-setting and killing or harming animals. Early onset conduct disorder is also associated with a more disturbed adolescent presentation including solitary aggression and property destruction. Acts such as fire-setting and vandalism often have a bizarre quality to them. Adolescent onset conduct disturbance is often associated with assimilation into a deviant subculture. In inner cities, a clinician will often see gang members who meet the criteria for conduct disturbance. These teenagers are usually not as psychologically disturbed as solitary, early-onset conduct-disordered children.

The prevalence of conduct disorder ranges from 6–16% of males under age 18 and for females is probably in the range of 2–9% (*DSM–IV*, 1994). Conduct-disordered males are more likely to be aggressive and engage in stealing and vandalism (Comer, 1995). Females are more likely to run away and be truant from school. It is likely that this disorder is increasing in frequency. As the author has experienced in inner city primary care settings, conduct-disordered children and teenagers are increasingly being brought in for treatment.

Although the etiology of conduct disturbance may include genetic as well as environmental factors, the families of conduct-disordered children are usually fairly disturbed (Miller & Prinz, 1990). Research indicates that one of the most salient predictors of conduct disorder in childhood is having one parent, usually the father, with a history of antisocial personality. Parents of conduct-disordered children are more likely to have problems with substance abuse and be physically or sexually abusive to or neglectful of their children. In addition, discipline is likely to be inconsistent, but when it occurs, it is frequently overly harsh (Comer, 1995).

Conduct disturbance has a guarded prognosis. The rule of thumb is that the earlier in life the intervention occurs, the more likely that more severe conduct disturbance in adolescence and antisocial personality in adulthood can be prevented. Children who have prior histories of fairly good functioning until early to mid adolescence and then develop conduct disturbance in the context of severe family distress, are likely to improve with aggressive treatment. For example, a 14-year-old girl with a history of good academic performance and no significant behavior problems who suddenly begins drinking, is truant from school, and runs away from home in the context of a conflictual parental divorce may improve if the family is stabilized and consistency is established fairly rapidly. Girls, in general, tend to have a later onset of conduct disturbance and usually have better outcomes. Factors associated with poorer outcomes include a significant legal history, particularly with serious offenses such as weapons charges, breaking and entering, and assault. Children whose only infractions are running away from home for brief periods of time or who have several school suspensions usually have better outcomes. As suggested above, long histories of disturbed behavior, particularly including property destruction and fire-setting, have a worse prognosis.

Clinically, it has been noted that many children with conduct disorder behavior may develop concurrent thought disturbance including hallucinations in adolescence. The combination of significant thought disorganization with conduct disturbance has a very poor prognosis. Children with long histories of residential placement such as group homes or foster homes generally have a poor outcome. Lastly, children who have lived for a number of years in an antisocial household or with parents who have spent time in jail or who have engaged in illegal activities such as selling drugs are likely to have worse outcomes.

The treatment of choice for conduct disturbance is consistent behavioral management. These children should be on a behavioral modification program with rewards and consequences that are regularly employed (Chamberlain & Rosicky, 1995). With teenagers, close parental monitoring of their whereabouts is extremely important. This monitoring can take place through face-to-face contact. However, in many households in which both parents work, this may not be feasible. Regular phoning in to check on the teenager may be fairly effective in monitoring the teenager's activities.

With children who are at significant risk of harming themselves or others as well as at risk for significant illegal behaviors and who are living with parents who cannot exert adequate control, residential placement should be considered as an option. As noted above, many parents of conduct disordered children exhibit significant psychopathology. As a result, they may not have the psychological resources to enact a consistent behavioral system and devote adequate energy to monitoring their child's activities as needed for effective treatment of this disorder.

OPPOSITIONAL DEFIANT DISORDER

Oppositional defiant disorder is characterized by chronic argumentativeness, resistance to adult demands, frequent temper tantrums, and overt expressions of hostile and negativistic mood (Barkley, 1991). Oppositional defiant disorder is distinct from the noncompliance of preschool children that may include temper outbursts and whining. In cases of oppositional defiant disorder, the pattern has to be consistent and in existence for six months. In addition, the degree of oppositional and defiant behavior is greater than would be expected for the child's developmental age.

These children may argue in response to all reasonable parental requests, have tantrums in which they slam doors or break things, and often do things to deliberately harass others. Their argumentativeness may include frequent swearing as well as blaming others for their own misbehavior. There are suggestions that oppositional defiant disorder initially begins at home and is usually more of a problem for mothers. However, as a child becomes older, fathers are more likely to be engaged and the behavior is likely to emerge in the school setting (Barkley, 1991). Parents may feel like they are "walking on eggshells." Parents of oppositional defiant children may verbalize complaints such as, "You know, he has the ability to do his work but he just refuses. He argues with his teacher all the time and he has already been sent to the principal's office five times this year for swearing at the teacher and refusing to do school work. I cannot get him to do anything at home without it being a major battle." This disorder appears to be somewhat more common in boys than girls. Prevalence rates are not clear, but probably include about 6–8% of school-aged children (*DSM–IV*, 1994). Although defiance and failure to follow rules are characteristics of both conduct disturbance and oppositional defiant disorder, oppositional defiant children tend not to have the degree of legal involvement or seriousness of rule infractions found in conduct disorder. In addition, while they are argumentative, oppositional defiant children rarely show serious physical aggression and are less likely to have significant contact with the police.

The treatments for oppositional defiant disorder and conduct disorder are somewhat similar. However, it is important to recognize that with the oppositional defiant child, any attention paid to them—positive or negative—is reinforcing. These children often will persist in antagonizing adults even though the response is an angry or rejecting one. These children are also fairly skilled at enlisting adults in arguments with them. For example, school-age children may be sent to their room for a half hour for refusing to do chores. After ten minutes in their room, the children may come out and insist to the parents that they are hungry and will become sick and dizzy if they do not eat. If the parents send them back to their room, the children will often escalate their complaints. It is important that parents and other caregivers of oppositional defiant children employ several basic principles. First, do not participate in arguments with the child. When the child does argue, it is important that the parent simply restate the consequence or expectations and indicate that there will be no discussion until the task is completed or the time-out is served. If the child persists and begins swearing or otherwise increases their argumentativeness, further consequence should be imposed (additional room time) with no argument or discussion of it. Once the room time or other consequence has been served, appropriate productive conversation with the child may be initiated. Structured anger management training modules for these children may be helpful. These often occur in specialized groups that focus on helping the child recognize anger in early stages and then develop self-control strategies as well as more appropriate means of expressing anger.

CHILDHOOD DEPRESSION

Both dysthymic disorder and depression occur in children and adolescents. Among children, mood disorders appear to be significantly less frequent than in adults. Estimated rates of major depression in children are about 2% (*DSM–IV*, 1994). However, by mid to late teens, mood disorders increase dramatically and begin to approach prevalence rates for adults. The symptoms of depression among children may differ somewhat from those in adults. Depressive symptoms are often difficult to evaluate in children because of their difficulty reporting psychological states as well as vegetative functioning over time. It is typically necessary to have a parent or other adult who knows the child well also serve as an informant. Young children (preschool and early elementary age children) may exhibit somewhat flat or sad facial expressions and apathy. They also may exhibit fearfulness and high levels of separation anxiety. Nightmares and sleep disturbances are not uncommon. Aggressive behavior is sometimes seen in young children, particularly boys. In middle childhood, poor self-esteem is often more apparent, as is social withdrawal. Academic performance tends to be an area of concern. Depressed latency age children also report vague somatic complaints including headache and stomachache. These children may meet criteria for both depression as well as somatization disorder. Among other vegetative symptoms, weight loss and a poor appetite may be somewhat more common among young children whereas weight gain may be a more prominent symptom in older children and young teenagers. It is important that the child be asked directly about the presence of sadness, crying episodes, and events associated with these. Structured questionnaires such as the Children's Depression Inventory may be helpful (Kovacs, 1983). The reading level of the Children's

Depression Inventory is around the mid-elementary school range. However, the clinician can read the items to the child. The CDI data alone, however, should not be used to diagnose depression, but as a source of information to direct further inquiry. Among teenagers, symptoms of depression may begin to become similar to those seen in adults. In terms of sleep disturbance, hypersomnia may be commonly seen in adolescents. Decline in concern for personal appearance as well as poor academic performance and social withdrawal are also seen. Irritability may be more prominent than sadness, particularly in early adolescents.

By gender, the prevalence of depression among boys and girls is about equal until adolescence. It is important that the clinician inquire about suicide. Suicide rates for both latency age children as well as adolescents have increased in frequency during the past 35 years (Comer, 1995). In diagnosing dysthymia, the clinician should be aware that symptoms need only be in place for one year for children and adolescents versus the two years required for adults.

In most children and adolescents, depressive symptoms are likely to have multiple causes. There does appear to be a hereditary predisposition for mood disorders. However, there is also likely to be significant family conflict as well as recent histories of loss (Pfeffer, 1986). This loss may take the form of parental death or divorce, or in teenagers, the breakup of a significant romantic relationship or loss of self-esteem through peer relationship problems or poor academic performance.

Treatment of mood disorders in childhood and adolescents almost always includes family or individual psychotherapy. There is not at present, strong evidence that antidepressant pharmacotherapy is consistently effective in children. While well-controlled studies are lacking, the overall effectiveness of medication does not appear to be as pronounced among children as with adults (Hodgman, Kaplan, Kazdin, & VanDalen, 1993).

PHYSICAL AND SEXUAL ABUSE

In primary care, abuse is likely to be somewhat less directly disclosed by the parent than in traditional mental health practice. Commonly, the abused child or adolescent will not report or exhibit clear-cut signs of physical or sexual trauma (Searight, 1997a). However, in some instances, children may present with evidence of genital trauma or of a sexually transmitted disease. Physical injuries inconsistent with parental reports (e.g., welts and bruises on the back as a sole injury sustained when tumbling down a flight of stairs) should similarly prompt concern about abuse.

With respect to sexual victimization, abuse may be "masked" by other behavioral symptoms. The child may present with somatization, increased fearfulness, aggression, or running away from home. There have been few consistent behavioral or psychological "markers" of underlying abuse (Searight, 1997a). As a general rule, it is not possible to differentiate children who have experienced abuse from children with other psychiatric disorders. Among children who have been sexually abused, the only significant behavioral indicator is sexual precociousness. Behavior such as excessive masturbation, sex play with peers, and sexualized interaction with adults is much more common among children who have been sexually abused when compared with those with other psychiatric disorders (Berliner & Conte, 1993).

While clinical interviews of possible abuse victims should ideally be staggered over multiple sessions, clinical and administrative realities often require that the evaluation be done in 30–60 minutes at the initial encounter. It is often useful to begin the evaluation with a game or expressive activities such as drawing or playing with clay (Searight, 1997a). The provider should refrain from asking "leading" inquiries and maintain a balance between open-ended questions to avoid suggestion as well as closed-ended questions when specific data are needed. Use of anatomical drawings and anatomically correct dolls is common among mental health professionals. If these tools are to be used in primary care or other health delivery settings, it is extremely important that professionals who include these procedures in their assessment have adequate training (American Psychological Association, 1991; Searight, 1997a).

Children should generally be interviewed alone. In addition, it is often helpful to separate adult care givers and interview them separately. Serious injuries that are reported to be self-induced should be regarded with considerable suspicion. Hayden and Gallagher (1992) have described physical injuries that should raise concern about abuse. Burns, skeletal injuries, abdominal trauma, head trauma, and cutaneous lesions are among the most common physical injuries associated with abuse. In the case of burns, immersion burns are fairly common forms of abuse. In these injuries, the history commonly reported involves the child falling into a hot bath or sitting in the tub when hot water was accidently turned on. One physical clue suggesting intentional burns is the presence of well-demarcated burns with an absence of splash marks. (Hayden & Gallagher, 1992). Contact burns occur when a child has a hot object held against them or the child is pressed against a hot object such as a radiator. Multiple cigarette burns should give rise to suspicion about abuse. Children may accidently back into a cigarette once, but are unlikely to do so repeatedly.

Fractures frequently involved in abuse include broken ribs as well as the humerus and femur. In particular, multiple fractures in various stages of healing without explanation are highly suggestive of physical abuse (Hayden & Gallagher, 1992). Abdominal injuries, while infrequent, are a common cause of death among abused children (Hayden & Gallagher, 1992). The most frequent cause of death through child abuse is head injury. Among small children, the most common is "shaken baby syndrome." These are generally infants who are shaken rapidly back and forth. There are often no external indications of injury, but the child sustains sub-dural hematomas (Hayden & Gallagher, 1992). Bruises and welts may be identified by hand marks or linear lesions that are associated with whipping such as with an extension cord. Bruising, particularly small half-moon-shaped bruises, often occur from pinching.

All states have mandatory reporting laws for both physical and sexual abuse. It is important for those working in medical settings to be cognizant of the fact that proof is not required for reporting abuse. The threshold is "reasonable suspicion." State laws usually include a penalty to providers for not reporting suspected abuse. Both physical and sexual abuse are required to be reported. However, a significant number of states do not include emotional, educational, or medical neglect in their statutes (Kalichman, 1993). Ambiguity is further confounded by the fact that most states legally permit some form of physical discipline. When nonspecific behavior possibly suggestive of abuse is present (aggression, somatization, enuresis, acting out) in the absence of other data, the majority of providers do not make a man-dated report (Kalichman, 1993). Only about half of official reports of abuse are substantiated by child welfare authorities. The general objective of these statutes is to detect as many cases as possible in as early a stage as possible. Sensitivity is emphasized over specificity (Kalichman, 1993). One strategy for these "gray areas" in which mandated reporting may not be clearly indicated is to contact the protective services hotline and provide the relevant details of the situation while initially keeping identities confidential. If the worker who receives the call indi-cates that this is indeed a situation requiring mandatory reporting, then the name of the patient can be disclosed.

CONCLUSION

Pediatric problems seen in primary care range from normal behavior that may be of concern to parents to more severe formal psychiatric disorders such as con-duct disturbance. It is very important that the primary care provider have a strong background in child and adolescent development so that he or she can distinguish normal from abnormal behavior. Additionally, with the erosion of extended fami-lies and the increased nuclearization of families in the United States, parents often have few "benchmarks" for determining whether their child's behavior is normal or problematic. Many behavioral and developmental concerns can be effectively addressed through brief, focused education as well as counseling around basic behavioral management strategies. A smaller percentage of patients will require pharmacological intervention such as in cases of attention-deficit hyperactivity disorder or longer term family or child therapy, such as with abuse or more severe behavioral disturbance.

Chapter 5

Family Dynamics and Primary Health Care

In contrast with tertiary care, family medicine and pediatrics have devoted considerable attention to the role of family factors in individual well being. Patients have families. Family dynamics play a significant role in coping with illness, help-seeking, and compliance. However, families often operate according to a set of unspoken rules that exist outside of awareness until they are broken. An analogy that demonstrates the potency of family rules is riding an elevator. We are never formally taught how to ride an elevator. There are no classes and no formal instruction. One simply gets in, pushes the button for the correct floor, and thinks little about it. Yet at the same time, there are implicit rules for elevator riders. These rules will become apparent when they are broken. If one of the passengers moves from standing side-by-side in the elevator and turns around with their back to the door and faces the others, discomfort arises. These unspoken norms are similar to how family rules operate (Searight, 1997c).

Most adults first become aware of the power of family rules when they begin to establish relationships outside of their family. This typically occurs in adolescence or young adulthood. At these developmental junctures, people become aware that families may differ widely in terms of expression of emotion, degree of individuality, tolerated boundaries between the family and the outside community, as well as gender roles. These differences are probably most dramatically apparent when someone develops an intimate relationship with someone of a different family background and the process of developing a new family begins.

CHANGES IN FAMILY STRUCTURE

Our definition of the family has changed dramatically in the last 40 years. The "Leave It to Beaver" family featuring a working father and the mother at home with one or more children is no longer the norm. Actually, fewer than 15% of American families fit this pattern. (McDaniel, Campbell, and Seaburn, 1990). During the 1970s and 1980s households with single parents and non-blood-related individuals became much more common. Single parent households now constitute close to 15% of households (McDaniel et al., 1990). There has also been a rise in nontraditional families, including heterosexual cohabiting couples with children as well as gay and lesbian couples (Searight et al., 1997).

Given these changes, it has been difficult to establish a consensually accepted definition of "family." In the past, a family was a group of people related by blood, adoption, or marriage that lived in the same household. This definition has its share of problems. For example, many college students who live away from home are considered part of the family on income tax forms. Most commonly, however, "family" has become equated with members of the same household. Increasingly, family includes whomever someone includes as a part of their kinship network.

The primary care specialties, particularly family medicine and pediatrics, have emphasized that patients should be viewed in a broader relationship context. Rather than a myocardial infarction or a case of otitis media, illness is seen as a social phenomenon that transcends disease (Kleinman, 1988). Although family health history is certainly useful in diagnosis, the impact of the family context on individual patient health is also seen as important. In family medicine, for example, patients' charts are often organized by family name, and the same provider frequently cares for all members of a particular family. This centralization of care provides a helpful longitudinal and developmental perspective on both the patient and family. Developing the ability to "see" how family members impact one another's physical and psychological distress is often challenging for the provider.

> The Buckmans are a family of four who became established in a family physician's practice about three years ago. The family includes Jack, 51, Margaret, 50, Jane, 17 and Theresa, 16. Jack initially presents because of lower back pain. After evaluation and treatment with medication, he exhibits some improvement. However, four months later, he reappears with complaints of fatigue and insomnia. A low dose of antidepressant medication is initiated. Several months later, he reappears with recurrent headaches as well as increased insomnia again. He has not been compliant with the antidepressant medication. Margaret is seen for the first time three months after Jack's first appearance in the office. She reports fatigue, dizziness and headaches. She is about 80 pounds overweight and has significant hypertension. The physician initiates antihypertensive medications and a referral to a nutritionist. For several months, she follows up with the physician but her blood pressure is not under control. She continues to gain weight—15 pounds in two months.
>
> Jack had been working two jobs because of financial distress. Margaret is an accountant but because of fatigue and headaches is working only part-time. Jack works about 70 hours a week. During the next year, there is increased conflict at home between Margaret and Jack as well as between Margaret and the children. Jane briefly moves in with a friend. Ten months after the family's initial presentation for

health care, both Jane and Theresa are suspended from high school for smoking in the restroom, arguments with teachers, and truancy.

Later that year, both young women are in the office for sore throats and coughs. Jack reports that things are a little better at home and the daughters are helping out and that he is sleeping somewhat better. Several months later, the provider receives an emergency call from Jack. Margaret and Jane have had a "blow out"—a major fight in which Jane left the house with the family car. The argument was precipitated by a conflict surrounding Jane's 30-year-old boyfriend and her continued truancy from school. A psychologist is consulted who engages in crisis intervention and establishes a behavioral contract for Jane and her parents around school attendance. Jane's school participation improves, she drops her older boyfriend, and the parents discontinue family therapy.

A similar pattern is repeated about 10 months later when Theresa is brought to the office by her parents. She reports that she is pregnant and is failing all her classes. She also describes a burning sensation with urination and a sexually transmitted disease is diagnosed. A similar school attendance contract is worked out with Theresa. She decides to terminate the pregnancy. Theresa responds well to the individual counseling and conjoint sessions with her father. Both Jack and Theresa report being angry with Margaret about her irritability with them and her unwillingness to follow through with health care, but seemed resigned to her noncompliance. Over the next year both Jane and Theresa return to the psychologist for individual counseling. Depression is diagnosed and both are placed on sertraline (Zoloft). Both young women improve. Margaret, however, continued to receive no treatment for her illness.

For several months, there is no contact with the family except for Jack, who is doing fairly well on his antidepressant. He says "nothing has really changed at home, I just try to live with it." Finally, a family conference is scheduled. Margaret appears at the family conference. Jack reports considerable frustration because she is home all the time and constantly irritable and fighting with Jane and Theresa over "trivia." Margaret is also angry with the girls about their past behavior. When her own health issues are raised, she sheepishly smiles and says "I know, I need to watch my diet and get some exercise." Some household tasks are redistributed and stress is reduced for a period of time.

This case illustrates how intricately family issues and dynamics are involved in health care. The mother's reduced involvement in her job and the subsequent increase in financial distress on the father and children are likely to be important factors. However, the mother's failure to address her health concerns is an ongoing issue underlying the acute presentation. Triangulation and detouring of conflict seem to occur when the daughters periodically act out. Jane and Theresa are being "helpful" to their mother by redirecting attention from her untreated health concerns to their own misbehavior. Family therapy directed toward getting appropriate health care for Margaret as well as increasing agreement between parents and structuring the household may be helpful in reducing distress in the family. Given the interplay of family issues, a simple "person-centered" educational intervention such as focusing on Margaret's hypertension would probably be ineffective in this family. Similarly, lecturing two daughters about "safe sex" and school attendance would be equally ineffective without attention to the broader family issues involving their parents.

FAMILY SYSTEMS CONCEPTS

As this case illustrates, families are interacting systems in which health and illness impact and are impacted by other family members. There are several useful concepts drawn from family therapy and general systems theory, which are helpful in understanding families and illness. The term family hierarchy refers to sources of power, influence, and authority in the family. As a general rule, parents have authority over important decisions surrounding their children such as school attendance, bed times, and health care. However, hierarchies may become unclear (Haley, 1976; McDaniel, Campbell, & Seaburn, 1990). A mother may inappropriately ask her 8-year-old daughter whether she should get a divorce from the child's father. This is a disturbed hierarchy and likely to be associated with significant family distress. Hierarchies may be reversed in other ways. One example the author commonly encounters is families in which teenagers have a baby. The baby's grandmother may actually be functioning as the parent. She is likely to be the family authority for seeking medical care and other outside services such as day care for the child. It is important in conducting developmental interviews to recognize this pattern because the grandmother will often be far more knowledgeable about the child's developmental milestones and medical history than the child's biological mother. Often, the biological mother behaves and is treated like an older sibling of the baby (Boyd-Franklin, 1989; Searight, 1997c).

Families also have coalitions. Coalitions commonly occur across generations, such as when a father frequently complains to his daughter about the mother's chronic low back pain (Haley, 1976; McDaniel et al., 1990). Coalitions also emerge among adult children such as when a mother frequently complains to an adult child about her husband's drinking or failure to stop smoking. Health care providers can also be brought into coalitions. A common example is when an elderly parent has a serious illness, such as cancer, and the adult child of the patient asks the provider not to disclose the diagnosis to the patient.

Family boundaries are another useful concept in the health care setting. These boundaries may be between individuals within the family or between the immediate family and the extended family. For example, when they enter adolescence, children may wish to have greater privacy and keep their door closed and even ask that a lock be installed. Boundaries between the immediate family and extended family often may also be a source of conflict:

> Mary, age 30, and Jay, age 39, were referred for a marital consultation by Mary's physician. Mary had been having tension headaches, insomnia, and abdominal pain for about 4 months. When she was asked about life stressors, Mary began crying and said she had "lost her husband to his mother."
>
> The maritial therapist learned that Jay and Mary had been married for 18 months after dating for 2 years. Mary's parents were divorced and lived in different cities about 500 miles away. Jay grew up about a mile from the couple's home. Jay was an only child and lived with his parents until he was 35. His mother and father had been supportive of his marriage to Mary and were subtly urging the couple to have children. The newly married couple saw Jay's parents at least once per week and Jay talked with his parents at least once a day. By contrast, Mary would see either her mother or father every 6 months and spoke with them by phone bimonthly at most. Although Mary sometimes felt "left out" by Jay's reliance on his parents for advice, she tried to be supportive of Jay's relationship with them.
>
> Nine months ago, Jay's father died suddenly after a heart attack. During the first months after his death, Jay saw his mother every day—often spending the evening at her home. Mary felt somewhat neglected, but tried to appreciate her mother-in-law's need for support. Although Mary anticipated that Jay would gradually refocus his energies on their marriage, as time went on, the reverse occurred. Jay began leaving home early in the morning to check on his mother before work and always stopped by her house for several hours on his way home. At night, Jay's mother would phone multiple times usually describing "strange noises" in the house and voicing fears that someone was climbing in her window.
>
> The marital therapist, after constructing a genogram, discussed the different relationships that Jay and Mary had with their families-of-origin. Mary readily saw her marriage as the primary focus, while Jay had always been trying to balance his commitment to Mary and his parents. Jay had been reasonably successful until his father died and his mother became dependent upon him. This "pull" left Mary feeling angry and abandoned. Mary felt somewhat guilty about her resentment towards Jay and his mother, which, in turn, led to somatization. As the therapist pointed out these dynamics, Mary was able to be more direct in her requests for Jay's presence. Jay had several individual sessions in which he developed strategies for balancing his concern for his mother with appropriate boundaries.

Alliances occur when there is a particularly close relationship between two family members. In general, parents should have a close alliance with one another. When parents do not have a close alliance or the alliance is between the parent and child, behavioral problems often emerge. One common example is a mother who tries to "reason" with her three-year-old when they have tantrums. Mother may say she does not want to squelch Susie's expressiveness, but Dad wants to use consistent discipline such as time outs. The inconsistency between the two parents associated with the alliance maintains and escalates the tantrums.

THE FAMILY IN HEALTH AND ILLNESS

Health promotion occurs through the family's support for illness risk factor reduction as well as through the ability to provide support while encouraging autonomy among family members who have acute or chronic physical disease.

Of the top ten causes of death in the United States, at least seven can be substantially reduced if persons at risk improved their diet, stopped smoking, reduced their alcohol intake, and took necessary antihypertensive medication on a regular basis (McDaniel et al., 1990).

In the case of smoking, smokers tend to be married to other smokers. With time, spouses synchronize their cigarette intake and smoking couples tend to quit smoking about the same time. Individual smokers have significantly better success in maintaining abstinence if other household members do not smoke. Spousal support has been demonstrated to be a consistent factor in smoking cessation (McDaniel et al., 1990; Venters et al., 1984).

Teenagers in households in which the same sex parent smokes are much more likely to take up the habit themselves. Among teens, in fact, parental smoking appears to be an independent risk factor apart from peer smoking (McDaniel et al., 1990). Whitehead and Doherty (1989) have suggested that smoking may serve a number of functions in a marriage. A husband may persist in smoking to exert independence from a wife he experiences as "controlling." This dynamic may be particularly prominent in newly married couples where loss of individual identity may be a source of anxiety. These passive–aggressive battles for control would still be present if smoking were not the issue. However, smoking provides content for these struggles.

Smoking may also serve as a distancing mechanism between partners. There may be an implicit understanding that conversation does not continue when one partner "lights up." The presence of stimulus cues such as ash trays, cigarettes, and lighters makes it far more difficult for patients to quit. As the following case example illustrates, smoking often has multiple functions within a relationship:

> Mr. Brandt is a 45-year-old White male with a history of multiple respiratory tract infections over the past two years. Mr. Brandt began smoking at age 15 and is currently smoking two and a half packs of cigarettes a day. He has been smoking at this level for the past 20 years.
>
> Mr. Brandt is referred to a psychotherapist for smoking cessation. The therapist asks Mr. Brandt to keep a "cigarette diary." In reviewing his smoking log, several issues become evident. First, Mr. Brandt smokes about two-thirds of his total cigarette

intake at home in the early morning and in the evening. Additionally, his overall intake has edged up to two and a half packs during the past two to three years. Mr. Brandt reports that he has "quit" smoking four times for periods of one to two days between ages 35 and 40, but has not initiated cessation since then.

Mr. Brandt has been married for 20 years. He and his wife have two children ages 16 and 14. Mrs. Brandt is also a smoker and began smoking shortly after the couple was married. The 14-year-old son has severe cerebral palsy and requires a high level of care from Mrs. Brandt. The 16-year-old daughter had been functioning fairly well until about two and a half years ago. At that time, she began having legal trouble for curfew violations and marijuana use. Mr. Brandt works full-time driving a delivery truck. Mrs. Brandt has been at home with the children since her son was born.

The clinician requested that Mrs. Brandt come to her husband's next office visit. In the session, she expresses concern about her husband's coughing and suggests that he may need "stronger medicine" for it. When the topic of smoking is raised, Mrs. Brandt becomes somewhat agitated and says that Mr. Brandt needs to "cut down a bit." When her own smoking is inquired about, Mrs. Brandt says: "When the kids are gone, maybe I can consider cutting back; I would be a mess if I quit. I tried four years ago and I was a nervous wreck; He doesn't have all the stress that I do." When the couple is asked about how they address their children's difficulties, Mrs. Brandt says, "*We* don't; That's *my* job. He makes the money. You know, he has already lost six days pay this year from being sick." The couple describes smoking together sitting side-by-side on the front porch or in the living room. When asked what they talk about during these times, Mr. and Mrs. Brandt say in unison: "We don't talk; When we light up, we go into our own thoughts. We both know not to talk to each other when we are smoking. The kids won't talk to us either."

Medication compliance is also affected by family climate. Involvement of a spouse or significant other appears to improve compliance with antihypertensive medication as well as overall blood pressure reduction (McDaniel et al., 1990; Morisky et al., 1983).

Just as issues such as medication compliance and risk behavior have been related to family functioning, family processes have also been related to immune disorders. Meyer and Haggerty (1962) examined families for a period of 12 months and kept records of distressing life events. It was noted that among children two years of age or older, a greater degree of family-related stress was found during a two-week period before the child developed a respiratory tract or streptococcal illness. A similar finding between stressful life situations and respiratory tract infections was reported by Boyce, Jensen, & Cassel (1977). Influenza Type B has also been associated with family dysfunction. Clover, Abell, Becker, Crawford, & Ramsey (1989) found that families that were more enmeshed, chaotic, or rigid were likely to have outbreaks of influenza B infection during an epidemic. Families that were more disengaged, however, demonstrated lower levels of infection than families that were more optimally balanced in terms of cohesiveness and adaptability. These studies are noteworthy in that they link family functioning to common diseases seen in primary care.

One of the most dramatic examples of the role of family factors in medical disorders is Minuchin's study of children who had recurrent diabetic ketoacidosis. In the study (Minuchin, Rosman, & Baker, 1978), investigators monitored free fatty acid levels of parents and children. (Free fatty acids are a precursor to diabetic ketoacidosis.) In a laboratory setting, parents were initially asked to discuss a recent disagreement between them. During this discussion, the free fatty acid levels of the parents rose. The diabetic child was then brought into the session. With the child's presence, the free fatty acid levels of the parents declined and those of the child rose. A concurrent behavioral change was that the focus of attention shifted from the parents' differences to concern about the child. This study provides a very elegant illustration of the parallel effects between physiological and behavioral processes. Minuchin and colleagues described these families as "enmeshed." They were overly close and did not permit differences to emerge between family members. The child's recurrent episodes of diabetic ketoacidosis served the distracting function of preventing the parents from addressing more significant marital problems. Recent research on the "diabetic family" has qualified Minuchin's findings. Families of children with diabetic control problems seem to be of several types: they maybe overly close as Minuchin described or they also maybe the opposite—disengaged. In this latter type of family, the parents are unavailable and don't monitor the child's illness closely enough (Coyne & Anderson, 1988).

THE FAMILY LIFE CYCLE

Mental health and medical providers are usually knowledgeable about individual developmental stages through the life span. However, families also go through developmental processes. The types of family interaction described earlier interact with developmental stages to increase family distress or enhance coping. To illustrate this interaction, consider two families consisting of a mother, father, and two children. One family has been rigidly organized around gender roles. The mother is in charge of the children and the father is solely responsible for earning income and managing finances. The second family has more flexible gender roles with both partners earning income and both being responsible for children and household maintenance. Mother and father manage the checkbook and pay the bills. In each family, their respective pattern has been operating for about fifteen years. Suddenly, the father has a myocardial infarction, and is hospitalized for several weeks and then comes home for several weeks of recovery. Which family is likely to cope better with this stressor? The family with more flexible rules is better equipped to manage an external challenge. Families with less flexibility are at greater risk for developing medical or behavioral problems within the next several months. The provider may see the mother in the office with tension headaches or one of the children may suddenly develop school behavior problems.

Clinically, it is helpful to consider the pre-existing organization of the family as a diathesis that will interact with external events to produce adaptive coping or illness depending on the type and level of external challenge as well as preexisting family resources.

The family life cycle is typically presented as a series of stages (Carter & McGoldrick, 1989; McDaniel et al., 1990). An early stage is the married couple without children. This type of arrangement may be established through a formal marriage ceremony. However, it may be less formal such as when a nonmarital couple establishes a household together. A frequent challenge here is to negotiate a new set of boundaries. A boundary should be established between the couple in relation to the outside world, particularly in relation to each partner's family of origin (Searight, 1997c). Each partner needs to maintain an individual identity apart from the relationship. There are also likely to be concrete issues including coordination of bill paying, shopping, cleaning, negotiating differences, and determining how each person's affectional and emotional needs will be met. Problems in this stage are often associated with each partner's original family. As in the earlier case example, one partner may be more removed from his or her parents and siblings whereas the other partner continues to be very involved with his or her original family (McGoldrick, 1989). In addition, the family of origin may intrude into the couple's efforts to establish their relationship by frequently being present in their household or becoming involved in decisions such as buying a home or appliances or even having children. In addition, the family of origin may exert a more symbolic intrusion into the new couples relationship. A newly married man attempting to fulfill his family of origin's mission for work success may have difficulty devoting adequate attention to his new partner.

Even in the "healthiest" of couples, the process of establishing a routine and appreciation of individual differences usually takes several years. Because of this time factor, it is often desirable for couples to wait several years before having children. Unlike developing a close relationship in which partners gradually get know each other better and then move in together and perhaps eventually get married, babies are sudden additions with little "transition time. The birth of the first child usually is associated with a decline in marital satisfaction. This decline may be reduced by factors including better communication between spouses, a father's involvement in child care, as well as maternal employment (Belsky, Perry-Jenkins, & Crouter, 1985). However, for all couples, a child brings about a decline in direct face-to-face communication as well as frequency of intimate interaction, including sex.

The couple's parents may have maintained a respectable distance during the early stage of the marriage. However, they may have difficulty maintaining that distance with a birth of a child. Particularly in overprotective parents, there is often an implicit message that the young couple is not adequately knowledgeable about child rearing and needs the benefit someone with more experience. Having young children at home, particularly two or more children who are close together in age, places nonemployed mothers at higher risk for depression (G. Brown & Harris, 1978).

When children are of school age, increased differences around philosophies of child rearing may emerge between parents. At this stage, the concept of boundaries is often helpful. Poor boundaries between a parent and one child may lead to an intergenerational coalition. Additionally, boundaries between the child and the larger community should be flexible. A parent may become anxious about loss of companionship when a child starts school. The result maybe over-involvement with the child—the child is not allowed to socialize with peers or participate in extracurricular activities. Although parental agreement around appropriate behavior for preschool children can usually occur, there tends to be much more disagreement about what to do when a child is receiving failing grades, at what age a child should stay overnight with a friend, or even basic routines like bedtime.

Adolescence only intensifies these issues. The family with teenagers often experiences conflicts around independence and personal privacy. Teenagers will usually want their own room and will usually want others to knock before they enter:

> James was a 17-year-old young man referred by his physician because of poor academic performance. He was in danger of being asked to leave the private school in which he was currently enrolled. Because of a history of poor grades, a developmental interview followed by psychometric and psychoeducational testing was conducted. During the intake interview, it was noted that the parents did not seem particularly concerned about James's poor grades. They seemed preoccupied, but it was difficult to determine exactly what was concerning them. Finally, with great distress and emotion, they indicated that they were disturbed because James spent time alone in his room with the door closed. There were several adolescent and young adult children at home and James was the youngest. None of them reportedly spent time alone. After the evaluation was completed and some recommendations were made to improve his academic performance, James's parents again wanted to know what the psychologist had "uncovered" around his "symptom" of needing privacy. The clinician suggested that privacy was normal for a young man of this age. This information was received with shock and viewed as a major threat to family cohesiveness.

For parents at this age, many decisions are particularly difficult: How old should a child be before they can go on a date? Should that date be a group date or a single date? This may also be a period in which there is increased tension between parents.

At this stage, parents are in mid life and frequently re-evaluating their career and/or marriage. Particularly if there are no other children in the family and the teenager is away from home a good deal of the time, longstanding differences between parents may emerge. These differences may lead parents to unconsciously keep the adolescent at home so that these past issues do not re-emerge. In extreme forms, this marital tension may develop into school refusal, somatic symptoms, eating disorders, or significant adolescent depression. These problems prevent the teenager from moving into age appropriate autonomy and keep them in an unhealthy dependence on parents (Haley, 1980).

The increased interest in sexual issues on the part of the teenager may raise issues around sexuality between the parents. If the marriage has been unsatisfying sexually for a number of years, one parent may sexualize the relationship with the opposite sexed adolescent. While this pattern may not take a form of overt sexual behavior, it may include subtle encouragement for the teenager to engage in irresponsible dating practices as well as pressure for them to discuss their sexual relationships with a parent.

When young adults do leave home, a major challenge is to be able to separate without breaking family ties. In highly enmeshed families, the only way that one can often break away is with a major explosion and a cut off from the family for a period of time (Searight, 1997c). It is important for the clinician to recognize that in multichild families, when the first child leaves home, the departure is a signal declaring that the family is moving into a new stage in which independence and separation is expected. This dynamic occurs even though there may be younger children in line who may not be leaving home until 10 to 15 years later. For families with children spread out over 10 to 15 years, the departure of the final child can have particular significance. In these families, routines have been child-focused, often for up to 20 to 30 years. Life styles, decisions, and marital interaction have all been devoted to children. When that focus is gone, spouses often have to renegotiate their relationships (McCullough & Rutenberg, 1989). Sometimes couples have the flexibility to taken on new roles and responsibilities, and sometimes they are unsuccessful.

> The Jacksons consist of Tom, Mary, and their five children. The only child remaining at home is 17-year-old Julie. Many years ago, Tom and Mary agreed that when their last child was gone they would be able to retire to Florida. This was a decision that the couple had made when the children were very young. Tom has been putting in substantial overtime for the last 10 years at his factory job. He has even taken on a second job for periods so that when the children are grown the couple could fulfill their dream. Over the years, however, Mary has decided that she does not really want to move. Her children live nearby and she has grandchildren as well. She has frequent contact with her children and grandchildren and strongly values these relationships.

With increased frequency Mary will make comments to Tom: "Isn't it nice that our children are nearby, not like the Johnson's next door whose children are scattered all over the country?" Julie is finding that she is having difficulty keeping focused on her school work. When she sits down to study, it always seems as if her mother or father are coming by and encouraging her to watch T.V. with one of them or help with some household project. The pressure to become involved in household tasks seems to have intensified in the past six months and her grades are suffering.

In these situations, the "contract" for the adolescent to fail is usually not conscious. In fact, it is unlikely that Mary, Tom, or Julie are aware of the underlying "agenda." However, the result of Julie's poor academic performance may be that she will not be able to graduate from high school on time or enter college. As such, she will be serving the function of preventing the smoldering marital conflict about Tom and Mary's future to emerge.

Our society provides relatively few good transitions for young adults when they leave their families of origin. Often adults in their late teens or early twenties enter large state universities or institutions such as the military. If parents are ambivalent about the young adult moving out and if their son or daughter exhibits distress, they may be encouraged to return home. It is not uncommon for freshmen living away from home at college to phone their patients during the first month or two complaining of how they are overwhelmed with school or feeling lonely. Parents may respond by encouraging them to return home and then try college again later. "Later" often never arrives (Openlander & Searight, 1983).

Successful transition from the family of origin involves balancing a connection with parents with establishing one's own independence. In healthy families, encouraging a balance between autonomy while providing adequate support helps this transition occur more smoothly.

In the later stages of the family life cycle, aging and mortality become key issues (Carter & McGoldrick, 1989). As parents become elderly, their physical health declines, and a role reversal may take place. The adult child becomes a parent to their own parent. If the relationship between parents and the adult child was conflictual, the adult child may feel considerable hostility, resentment, and/or a sense of being trapped when called upon to care for an aging parent. Issues between siblings—who is "mom's favorite"—may erupt. Adult children may also make a renewed attempt to get some validation or emotional support from parents that they saw as lacking during childhood. This striving to extract recognition or affirmation from a parent may lead to significant conflict and resentment when the desired response is not forthcoming.

At this time, many middle-aged adults still have children in college and may be paying for children's higher education while simultaneously having to help out with an aging parent (Walsh, 1989). Tasks may include helping a parent move into a nursing facility as well as assisting them with navigating the health care system.

Daughters and daughters-in-laws consistently carry the biggest burden for caring for elderly parents and parents-in-law. When an aging parent becomes acutely ill and is hospitalized, conflict may emerge between siblings around responsibility for mother or father. In families with multiple children, some of the adult children may live geographically closer to the parent. Those who live nearby often bear the greatest responsibility for checking on and providing assistance to the aging parent as well as helping them receive medical care. The siblings who live some distance often feel guilty about their lack of involvement. However, they often enact their guilt on the sibling who lives closer through criticism and second-guessing decisions. When the parent is hospitalized, the guilt often takes the form of anger by one sibling directed toward another sibling because he or she did not even notify the other about the parent's deteriorating health or take appropriate action.

Aging parents also often re-evaluate their own relationship with their children and spouse. This life review can be an emotionally painful process, particularly if they feel that they have been an unsatisfactory parent or spouse.

When parents die, adult children are often in middle-age and in the process of re-evaluating their own lives. Certainly the death of one's parent makes them aware of their own mortality. There is an increased awareness of life being limited, which may provoke re-evaluation of the quality of one's life. The death of a parent may also create a sense of relief. Many middle-aged adults experience an obligation to avoid specific life changes because of fear of upsetting their parents. For example, with Catholic clergy, one pattern that frequently emerged was that within a year after the death of a parent a middle-aged priest would leave the priesthood. These changes are accompanied by an implicit or explicit sense that the adult no longer has to fulfill parental expectations. Other life changes, such as obtaining a divorce, may be associated with a parent's death ("I never could do this when Mom was alive; it would have killed her.").

FAMILY CONFERENCES

When is a Family Conference Indicated?

In primary care settings, families are often seen for brief conferences consisting of one to two sessions rather than ongoing family intervention. There are a number of situations in which convening the family is likely to be helpful. In pregnancy, particularly when social support appears to be inadequate or psychosocial stress is high, supportive family involvement may reduce prenatal and perinatal complications. It is also helpful for the provider to pay attention to expectant fathers who may have a greater than average incidence of depression. This often presents as irritability or somatic distress (Schmidt, 1983).

Childhood disorders such as failure to thrive syndrome (FTTS) should also prompt a family conference. Family conflict has been found to discriminate with FTTS from controls (Mitchell, Gorrell, & Greenberg, 1980).

Family conferences should also be seriously considered whenever the presenting problem includes childhood behavioral difficulties. These may range from tantrums to noncompliance to disruptive behavior at school. There is a considerable body of research linking marital conflict to behavioral problems of childhood (as well as to maternal depression; E. M. Cummings & Davies, 1994). Major depressive episodes, particularly among women, should raise the possibility of convening a family conference. There is considerable evidence that marital conflict is associated with depression (E. M. Cummings & Davies, 1994).

Poor adherence to medical regimens including compliance with antihypertensive or diabetic medications may also be addressed in a family context. Lifestyle modifications such as smoking cessation or weight reduction as well as abstinence from alcohol are all more likely to be successful if significant others are involved and supportive (Campbell & Patterson, 1995). Patients who have heart disease and particularly those who are recovering from coronary artery bypass graft (CABG) surgery or patients who sustained a myocardial infarction seem to have better outcomes if they return to supportive family environments. In contrast, criticism on the part of spouse or significant other often will complicate recovery. It may also be useful to consider a family conference with patients who are high-frequency health care utilizers. These are patients who repeatedly come to their physician with relatively minor physical complaints. There is some data indicating that patients who have a poor social support network also have increased rates of medical utilization (Blake, Roberts, Mackey, & Hosokawa, 1980).

When terminal illness is present, a family conference is often very helpful. Discussing end of life decision-making issues as well as assuring family members that they are not responsible for the patient's medical condition results in a sense of family relief. This reduced guilt improves their ability to be emotionally supportive of the terminally ill patient.

The mental health specialist may be asked to facilitate a family conference with the physician or other medical personnel when there seems to be confusion about a patient's diagnosis or treatment recommendations. Although the technical aspects of the patient's medical status are generally outside of the realm of the mental health professional, they can be very helpful in clarifying communication as well as helping the physician to explain information in ways that patients and their families can understand.

There has been relatively little research conducted on family conferences. An older study (Comley, 1973) found that in the year following a conjoint family conference, there was an almost 50% decline in health care utilization as compared with a 10% increase in a control group. The majority of the patients who participated in family conferences received only one or two family sessions.

Available data also suggest that patients are usually receptive to family conferences. Patients were interested in having a family conference when there was serious medical illness and less interested in family conferences around psychiatric problems such as depression or anxiety (Kushner, Meyer, & Hansen, n.d.).

Conducting the Family Conference

During the preparation prior to the actual meeting, the provider has usually had contact with the patient or with the referral source. Before the session, it is helpful to have an understanding of the presenting concerns. If this is a consultation visit, it is helpful to know why the consultation is being requested. What goals does the referral source want met in this encounter? Who should attend the meeting?

Referral questions are often vaguely stated ("The patient's headaches seem to occur when he fights with his teenage son; therefore, it must be a family problem."). The physician may be seeking confirmation of a pattern relating symptoms to family issues. Medical providers may want mental health consultants to intervene or they may simply want a fuller picture of the case because they feel that they are missing something. This latter situation is often found with vague somatic complaints that are not clearly related to stressors, such as fatigue, stomachaches, headaches, etc. In terms of attendance, there are usually two options: Everyone in the household and sometimes beyond the immediate household (such as when grandparents are involved in the nuclear family's daily activities), or whoever in the family is most concerned about the problem. Additionally, the mental health professional should begin to form hypotheses about how or why this problem is emerging at this point in time. The family life cycle is a framework for generating hypotheses as well as providing clues about the external stressors that the family may be experiencing.

In the initial stage of the meeting, providers should introduce themselves and greet each member of the family. Individuals, one-to-one contact should be made with each family member—no matter how young. If an infant is present, the clinician can ask to hold the infant for a few minutes. Next, family members should be invited to be seated. Often, seating arrangements provide useful clinical information. A child may be seated between the mother and father, or one parent "pairs off" with the child.

The next phase focuses upon obtaining a picture of the family's basic composition. This would include basic demographic information from each family member including age, occupation, or grade in school and length of the marriage. When interviewing the family, it is often helpful to address the leader or the spokesperson first. This is typically the oldest person present, and in traditionally oriented families will usually be the oldest male. The clinician should make special efforts to engage the person who seems most distant. This is often the adult who did not initiate the medical or mental health contact. Also at this point, it is helpful to pay attention to nonverbal interaction. For example, if the teenage son rolls his eyes upward when the father launches into a monologue about his drug use, this behavior suggests that this narrative has been told many times before. With young elementary school age or preschool age children, it is often helpful to have activities such as drawing or coloring. The children can interact verbally for brief periods of time and then return to their activity.

The provider should then move on to identification of the problem. Before conveying specific information about a medical diagnosis, treatment, and prognosis, it is helpful to get an idea of how each family member understands the problem or what they understand about the patient's illness. Often, there are blatant misconceptions that can be readily be corrected. The question, "What do you perceive as being a problem or how do you understand John's illness"? should be asked of each individual family member. This inquiry should usually begin with the family member that seems most distant and conclude with the patient. In gathering this information, there are several follow-up questions that are often helpful, including "How does this problem impact you? When did you first notice it? What has been done with this problem in the past (with particular attention to previous treatment)? What sort of advice have you been given? What do you think of that advice?"

At this point, the provider should not offer information or directives, but should affirm each family member's contribution by restating or summarizing. If family members attempt to interrupt each other, the interruption should be blocked and each person reminded that they will have a turn to speak. The interviewer should not emphasize disagreements between family members.

When the presenting problem still does not seem to be clear or the provider is confused about some aspects of the problem (e.g., family members do not seem to be troubled by a child who has a terminal illness), alternative questioning styles may be useful. Family members may be asked to describe interaction of other members as they respond to the problem. This is a family therapy technique termed "circular questioning" (Boscolo, Cecchin, Hoffman, & Penn, 1987). For example, with an asthmatic adolescent, a circular question would be, "When your sister has an asthma attack, what does your mother do? Similarly, if the patient has panic disorder, the clinician may inquire: "When your mother gets panicky, what does your dad do?" Sometimes it is even helpful to have family members enact a problem: "Pretend you are having a migraine, what would your husband and son be doing?"

If a family member seems disengaged, the clinician may want to push engagement to assess the response. For example, if the children are acting out and disruptive during the session and the mother is trying to control them while the father is sitting back in his chair studying his fingernails, the provider may request that the father help find something for the children to play with.

During the closing and summarization phase of the family conference, the provider, often with the physician's assistance, may provide concrete information about the medical condition of the patient. In cases where an adult patient is seriously or terminally ill, it is helpful to use information previously obtained to know how much detail to provide regarding issues such as treatment course and prognosis. This information should then be summarized and the family encouraged to ask questions. After questions are answered, each family member should be encouraged to give a summary about what they understand. Again, in cases of medical illness, misconceptions can be clarified. The provider should ask family members as well as themselves about actions that every family member can take to improve their own coping and help the family cope.

If the presenting problem is psychiatric or psychosocial such as a child with behavioral problems or a depressed adult, every family member should be asked what they would like to see changed. Another helpful question is "What is the smallest change that might indicate that things are moving in a better direction" (Fisch, Weakland, & Segal, 1982). If the provider is still confused about the presenting problem or if family members seem anxious or resistant about disclosing information, they may be given a homework assignment to gather more information about the problem. In order to accentuate family strengths, the provider may ask family members what they do not want to change, or put differently, which aspects of their family they would like to remain the same (deShazer, 1983).

Follow-up recommendations from a family conference may vary and may range from formal therapy to no further contact. In situations where the goal of the family conference was primarily to convey medical information, it may be helpful to schedule a follow-up visit in several weeks to two months. With mental health–related problems or child behavior concerns, it may be necessary to schedule follow-up, diagnostic, or counseling visits in the more immediate future. With overt relationship conflict within the family, more extensive family counseling may be useful using behavioral (Stuart, 1980; Patterson, 1971), structural (Minuchin, 1974), or strategic (Haley, 1976) models.

CONCLUSION

The stage of the family life cycle is helpful to consider when meeting with families in medical settings. The life cycle will provide the clinician with hypotheses of the types of difficulties that are likely to be predominant. These life cycle issue will interact with illness as well as family boundaries, roles, and hierarchies. These interactions may exacerbate the developmental changes that take place at that stage so that the family becomes "stuck." For example, chronic illness situations such as an adolescent with insulin-dependent diabetes will often make it more difficult for parents to encourage separation while maintaining support and adequate control. The teenager may need some monitoring to be sure that they are maintaining their diet and insulin. At the same time, however, the diabetic teenager may experience this parental monitoring as particularly intrusive in a period when they are trying to establish their own independence. If boundaries between the teenager and parents have previously been diffuse, this age appropriate process will be more problematic. As a result, the teenager may overcompensate by refusing to take insulin as a way of demonstrating their independence. Incorporating this information into a family conference will hopefully help parents be appropriately supportive while encouraging age-appropriate autonomy.

Chapter 6

Cardiovascular Disease

Cardiovascular diseases are the most common cause of death in the United States. One out of three men and one in ten women will be affected by cardiovascular disease by age 60 (Gordon & Kannel, 1983; Levenson, 1993). Cardiovascular disease includes hypertension and coronary heart disease. Hypertension affects up to nearly one third of the general adult population (Levenson, 1993). Coronary heart disease is the primary cause of death in men beginning at about age 40 and in women beginning at about age 65 (Kannel & Thom, 1990).

HYPERTENSION

Hypertension (high blood pressure) is usually defined as a systolic blood pressure of 140 mm Hg or greater or a diastolic blood pressure of 90 mm Hg or greater (Rosen, Brondolo, & Kostis, 1993). Hypertension is about twice as common in Blacks as Whites. About 85% of people with hypertension are aware of their condition and 55% take medication regularly for blood pressure control (Rosen et al., 1993). Lifestyle issues such as obesity, lack of exercise, salt, and alcohol consumption all appear to play a significant role (Blair, Goodyear, Gibbons, & Cooper, 1994).

Most psychosocial interventions have focused on weight loss, dietary modification, and increasing exercise levels for mild levels of hypertension; these nondrug interventions alone may be recommended. In more advanced hypertension, these interventions are often combined with medication. Weight loss and salt restriction appear to be the most helpful nondrug therapies. Evidence for relaxation training alone as therapy for hypertension is not persuasive (Rosen et al., 1993). However, as Rosen and colleagues (1993) note, there have been few studies of combined drug and relaxation therapy.

CORONARY HEART DISEASE

Coronary Heart Disease (CHD) is primarily a function of atherosclerosis, the production of arterial plaques over multiple years (Scheidt, 1996). Atherosclerotic risk factors include older age, male gender, high blood pressure, high total blood cholesterol (LDL), low high-density lipoprotein (HDL or "good cholesterol"), diabetes, little physical exercise, and significant obesity (Scheidt, 1996).

Atherosclerosis emerges clinically as angina pectoris, acute myocardial function (MI or "heart attack") and sudden cardiac death. The "classical" presentation of angina is a middle-aged man with left chest tightening or pressure that often radiates into the left arm during physical activity. The pressure is usually relieved when the physical exertion stops or nitroglycerin is taken.

Common treatments of angina include angioplasty and coronary artery by-pass graft surgery (CABG). Angioplasty involves inserting a deflated balloon on the end of a catheter passed up the aorta to the blockage. The balloon is positioned next to the plaque and inflated to push aside the plaque. CABG surgery involves establishing new arteries to "re-route" the blood around an arterial segment blocked by the plaque. Both angioplasty and CABG surgery are safe treatments; angioplasty has an 0.5% and CABG surgery a 1–2% mortality rate (Scheidt, 1996).

Myocardial infarction (MI) or "heart attack" involves the death of heart muscle. Thrombosis (clotting) is associated with rupture of atherosclerotic plaque; plaque material comes into the bloodstream and triggers a chain of cardiovascular events. In order to prevent further damage, treatment to dissolve the obstructing clot should be initiated quickly (Scheidt, 1996).

Sudden cardiac death (SCD) accounts for one third to one half of all cardiac mortality. The standard definition of SCD is death within one hour of symptoms in someone not expected to die (Scheidt, 1996). SCD may include people who have had previous myocardial infarctions but who were not at imminent risk of death. Although deaths associated with other MIs have been reduced, SCD mortality has remained stable because many patients develop life-threatening arrhythmias in settings away from medical care. Among those patients without previously established coronary artery disease, traditional cardiac risk factors such as hypertension, smoking, and elevated cholesterol are predictive of SCD (Wyszynski & Wyszynski, 1996). There are suggestions that SCD may be associated with greater recent life stress and more immediate strong emotional reactions. In patients with preexisting arrhythmias, there is evidence that stress may decrease the threshold for ventricular fibrillation, in which electrical impulses through the myocardium become erratic (Scheidt, 1996).

Social Factors in Cardiac Disease

Mortality from coronary heart disease appears to be largely a 20th century pheno-menon. Myocardial infarctions were relatively rare until early in this century, and the MI deaths increase dramatically in the mid to latter part of this century (S. A. Taylor, 1991). The pace of modern life began to be examined as a possible risk fac-tor. Community and cross-national studies have demonstrated the role of changing social norms and "modernity" in coronary heart disease (S. A. Taylor, 1991).

Risk factor research in the 1950s and 1960s led to puzzling conclusions. For example, in Paris, people had cholesterol-rich diets and consumed more alcohol and cigarettes than those in comparably-sized cities in the United States. However, CHD incidence in Paris was significantly lower. In the midwestern United States, consumption of red meat was much greater than on the East Coast. However, CHD was less common in the Midwest (Davison & Neale, 1994). This pattern of seem-ingly inconsistent findings led investigators to examine behavioral and personality factors across different cultural and national groups.

In the 1960s, Roseto, Pennsylvania had much lower than average coronary death rates. Traditional health risk factors were not substantially lower in this ethnic Ital-ian community. Both men and women in Roseto tended to be overweight and their smoking and exercise levels were not significantly different from the norm. Neigh-borhoods were generally cohesive and personal problems were solved by consult-ing family members or the parish priest. By the mid 1970s, however, there was a dramatic increase in MIs in Roseto, particularly among men under age 55. By this time, there had been a number of changes in the community's quality of life. Social cohesiveness declined as young adults married outside the ethnic community and birth rates as well as church attendance declined (Bruhn, Chandler, & Miller, 1966).

One additional example of the cultural and ethnic factors in cardiovascular dis-ease is the comparative rates of CHD among Japanese and Japanese immigrants (Syme, Marmot, Kagan, Kato, & Rhoads, 1975). Among the three groups (Japanese immigrants in Hawaii and California and Japanese residing in Japan), Japanese residing in Japan had lower rates of CHD than Japanese immigrants in Hawaii or California, with the Hawaiian group having intermediate rates. In California, those Japanese immigrants who kept ethnic traditions had lower rates of cardiac illness than those who were more assimilated to mainstream American culture (Marmot et al., 1975).

Personality Factors and Heart Disease

An early opinion about the role of personality in cardiac patients was offered by William Osler (1910), who described the typical coronary patient as a "keen, ambitious man whose engines are set at full speed ahead." More contemporary work in this area was conducted by Friedman and Rosenman, who described a personality style, the Type A, that is seven times as likely to have an MI as their counterpart, the Type B.

Friedman and Rosenman (1959) described a behavior pattern characterized by time urgency and free-floating hostility that was more prevalent among persons with coronary heart disease. Longitudinal studies found that over an eight-year time period, healthy persons with this personality style (Type A behavior) were more likely to develop coronary heart disease than those without this pattern (called Type B).

Type A behavior is found among people who respond affirmatively to questions such as these:

1. Do you find it difficult to restrain yourself from hurrying others' speech (finishing their sentences for them)?
2. Do you often try to do more than one thing at a time (such as eat and read simultaneously)?
3. Do you find yourself racing through yellow lights when you drive?
4. Do you detest waiting in lines? (Friedman & Rosenman, 1974; Weiten, 1983)

The Type A behavior pattern has undergone considerable revision since it was initially described by Friedman and Rosenman (1959). The original Type A pattern was characterized by competitiveness, polyphasic behavior (doing more than one thing at a time), time urgency, free-floating hostility, and hypervigilance. Studies found that persons with this behavioral and personality style were more likely to have CHD symptoms than those without this behavior pattern (Type B). Subsequent investigations narrowed the predictors to time urgency and free-floating hostility (Friedman, Fleischman, & Price, 1996).

As a result of the behavioral focus of current Type A research, there has been a renewed emphasis on "time urgency" as the key component. In western society, time urgency has become increasingly normative and is often not consciously recognized. Hostility has been reconceptualized as the culmination of extensive time-urgent behavior.

Insecurity may be the core psychological issue from which time urgency and culminating hostility arise (Price, Friedman, & Ghandour, 1995). This insecurity includes poor self-confidence together with a view that this diminished self-esteem can be overcome by accomplishing more and more. These patients do not have an "internal monitor" of the number of projects to accomplish and the corresponding time allotment for these tasks: "I always do more and more until I've done too much. That's how I know I've done enough" (Price et al., 1995, p. 488). With the increasingly narrow focus on accomplishments, other activities (e.g., hobbies, exercise) become relegated to the background and overall life satisfaction actually declines. Accompanying this narrow task focus is increased irritability and hostility (Price et al., 1995). Insecurity is assessed by asking patients to answer questions such as "At your funeral or memorial service do you believe a large number of persons will attend?" and "Do you find it difficult to just sit and daydream and recall memories?" (Price et al., 1995, p. 489). Underlying insecurity may not be evidence until the patient begins to alter their Type A behavior by reducing hostility as well as urgent activity.

Assessment of Type A Behavior Pattern (TABP) was originally conducted with semistructured interviews or self-report questionnaires such as the Jenkins Activity Survey (Jenkins, Rosenman, & Zyzanski, 1974). The difficulty with these measures is that many TABP patients are unaware that they have the relevant behaviors and traits. (The patient who, drumming his fingers, yells "I'm never impatient" in response to a query.) More recently, Friedman and colleagues (1996) developed a videotaped clinical examination to assist in diagnosis of TABP. This videotaped evaluation includes attention to observed behaviors in addition to verbal responses to structured questions. These actions include rapid eyeball movements, inappropriate laughter, teeth grinding, and tic-like shoulder movements (Friedman Fleischman, & Price, 1996).

How hostility and time urgency become translated into CAD is not clear. It is possible that a mediating third variable such as smoking or alcohol consumption may play a major role in CAD. Increases in life stress may increase catecholamines that in turn, increase myocardial ischemia and reports of anginal pain. In laboratory studies, anger has exhibited a particularly strong relationship to CAD severity as demonstrated by angiogram (Dembrowski et al., 1995).

A physiological link between emotional reactivity and cardiac events has been suggested in case studies of ambulatory cardiac patients wearing heart monitors. Low-level stressors were associated with increased heart rate, premature ventricular contractions (PVCs), and ST depression (Gradman, Bell, & DeBusk, 1977; Lown, DeSilva, Reich, & Muraski, 1980; Powell, 1996). Under states of emotional arousal, catecholamine release, together with possible ischemia, may contribute to nonlethal PVCs degenerating to ventricular fibrillation (Powell, 1996).

The predictive power of Type A behavior for cardiac events appears to be greatest for middle-aged men. Type A characteristics do not appear to be as predictive of MIs among women or men over age 60 (Weiss, Anderson, & Weiss, 1991). This behavioral pattern has been reliably measured in children and adolescents. In younger people, Type A behavior may be associated with positive adjustment. While Type A children are more aggressive and more likely to experience negative life events than Type Bs, they are also more outgoing, talkative, and physically active (Matthews & Jennings, 1994; Matthews & Angulo, 1980; Visintainer & Matthews, 1987). Type A children do seem to have greater cardiovascular reactivity (Delameter, 1995).

Modifying Type A Behavior

Friedman, Thoresen and colleagues (1996) have developed a Type A behavior modification program that has successfully reduced the recurrence of coronary events in patients who have suffered a myocardial infarction. These programs have also been employed with persons at risk for cardiovascular disease because of time urgency, hostility, and insecurity. One difficulty in addressing these traits as part of a treatment package is that many individuals have come to associate Type A behaviors with success. For example, last minute "cramming" for exams or writing college term papers the night before they were due often "worked" for many students and has come to be almost superstitiously linked to success. Many people report that they do their best work under pressure, which forges an implicit link between time urgency and successful task performance.

Type A behavior patterns may be difficult for both physicians and mental health professionals to see in the patients because they may have many of these characteristics themselves. Certainly, advanced professional training is likely to reward the work-oriented provider who accomplishes more in less time.

One alternative to conceptualization has been suggested by Roskies (1987) who described an alternative pattern, the "Hardy Type A." This variation is characterized by a perception of tasks as challenges rather than as threats, being able to emotionally "let go" of external impediments to task accomplishments, and conscious efforts to reduce over-responding to frustration and provocation.

Intensive psychotherapy is probably not practical in most primary care contexts. However, educationally focused interventions—particularly those delivered in a group—can help patients target Type A behaviors and provide them with skills to begin modifying this pattern. Cognitively, core beliefs associated with insecurity can be isolated and subjected to critical examination and refutation (Bracke & Toheresen, 1996). Examples of these cognitive patterns include "My worth depends on the quantity, not the quality of my achievements; I must constantly prove my worth again and again because my past accomplishments don't count; I must do more than others to be worthy."

Other cognitive aspects include the likelihood of being "hooked" by the obstacles and provocations of daily life (Powell, 1996). The "hook" metaphor highlights that daily life events devoid of any direct, intended personal malice to the patient (e.g., being in a traffic jam) are associated with interpretations of being under personal attack or threat ("Why me?"; "They repaired this road on purpose during rush hour"; "It isn't fair.").

With time, "metacognitive" skills will hopefully develop such that frequently occurring stressors are noted as they arise in daily life and more adaptive alternative interpretations are substituted. For example, being stuck in traffic gives me the opportunity to think quietly about my vacation plans (Bracke & Toheresen,

1996). Patients initially benefit from keeping a daily log of events associated with emotional reactivity.

Behavioral strategies can also be taught efficiently. Patients can be instructed to monitor targeted Type A behaviors for a week at a time with a shift in focus from one observation time to the next. Examples include eating rapidly, finishing others' sentences, hypervigilance, not listening to family members or friends, or overscheduling. Patients are taught to alter one of these behaviors for a week and notice changes in others' reactions as well as their own emotionality. Altering behavior often, in turn, changes patients cognitive and affective reactions. Many coronary-prone individuals are cut-off from their thoughts and feelings. A behavioral emphasis on "doing" may be more readily incorporated by these persons.

Multifactorial intervention for Type A behavior may reduce the likelihood of coronary events. In particular, intervention directed toward this personality/behavioral pattern has been found to be more effective than "traditional" cardiac rehabilitation focusing on diet, exercise, and medication. Friedman and colleagues found that three years after an MI, patients receiving counseling addressing Type A issues in addition to cardiac rehabilitation were 44% less likely to have an MI during this period. This protective effect continued at 4.5 years (Friedman Thoresen et al., 1996).

In addition to sensitizing patients to recurring cognitive patterns and accompanying behaviors putting them at risk for cardiac disease, primary care patients can be efficiently instructed in relaxation training and encouraged to practice regularly. The importance of regular exercise and setting realistic work and recreational goals can also be included in primary care counseling. Involving the patient's spouse or other family members may also be helpful in obtaining additional information about Type A behavior as well as in encouraging the patient to practice newly acquired skills.

ACUTE MYOCARDIAL INFARCTION VERSUS PANIC DISORDER

On common dilemma in the Emergency Room is that many of the symptoms of panic disorder resemble those of a myocardial infarction ("heart attack"). As noted in an earlier chapter, MI symptoms such as chest pain, a sense of impending doom, dizziness, lightheadedness, and difficulty breathing all overlap with patients' reports of panic attack onset. Both MIs and panic attacks have a sudden onset and are often not directly related to an external stressor. As a rule, patients presenting with acute symptoms of this type should always be treated as if they are having a myocardial infarction. The diagnosis of panic disorder should be made by exclusion.

Some clinical and demographic features that may assist the clinician include female gender, younger age, and autonomic symptoms such as hyperventilation and bilateral diffuse chest pain, which are more suggestive of panic disorder. Loss of consciousness is more common with cardiac arrhythmias than with panic disorder. About 10% to 30% of patients who undergo cardiac catheterization have no clinically significant stenosis and essentially normal coronary arteries. Of this group, it is estimated that up to 50% have a psychiatric condition (Levenson, 1993) with anxiety disorders being the most common.

The picture may be further confounded by the diversity of individual responses to MI symptoms. Many patients have atypical symptoms and may attribute MI symptoms to other causes. Common sources of confusion including shoulder and arm pain attributed to arthritis or chest pain misinterpreted as indigestion (Scheidt, 1996). Confounding the picture further is that may patients may have "silent" MIs, in which the infarcts are discovered months or even years later. These occur without being noticed or the symptoms are not interpreted as a significant cardiac event. On the other hand, panic disorder patients are often preoccupied with a fear or belief that their symptoms reflect an, as yet, undetected organic condition.

Although a panic disorder diagnosis is suggested when there is a pre-existing personal or family history of anxiety disorder, the presence of panic disorder does not necessarily rule out the possibility of coronary artery disease—the two disorders may co-exist. Phobic anxiety may elevate the risk of sudden cardiac death. Pain episodes may precipitate ischemic pain, which in turn exacerbates anxiety and triggers panic: In the case which follows, the chronology of the patient's symptoms is particularly useful in that it portrays the recurrent use of emergency room services among these patients. In this particular case, the patient had a number of cardiac risk factors such that it was probably difficult for providers to determine the presence of panic disorder:

> Mr. Simpson is a 37-year-old African American male who becomes a new patient in the practice. In January 1994, his initial presenting problem is chest pain, which he describes as episodes of "sharp stabbing pain" lasting several seconds in duration with more frequent occurrences over the past few days.
>
> Mr. Simpson weighs an estimated 300 pounds and is about 5 feet 7 inches tall. He states he has always been overweight. He reports that he stopped smoking about 5 years ago and had previously smoked about a pack a day for 20 years. Mr. Simpson's family history is noteworthy for a father who died of a myocardial infarction at age 52 and two paternal brothers who died of myocardial infarctions in their mid-50's.
>
> By way of social history, Mr. Simpson is employed as a store clerk. He is married and has a preschool-aged child. Mr. Simpson graduated from high school and soon after began working in his current setting. He stated he does not use alcohol or marijuana. He says that in the past he was treated for about a year with Valium.

Mr. Simpson was referred to a cardiologist. A treadmill exercise test indicates normal exercise tolerance at 90% of age-predicted maximal exercise. The cardiologist also noted that Mr. Simpson had a low level of physical fitness.

In May 1994, Mr. Simpson returned to the clinic with similar complaints of chest tightening and stabbing pain. He was referred again to a cardiologist and had an electrocardiogram and an echocardiogram. Both were within normal limits. The cardiologist impression was "neuromuscular chest wall pain," with accompanying anxiety. Mr. Simpson is started on 0.75 mg alprazolam (Xanax)—4 times per day and 25 mg of nortriptyline (Pamelor) twice a day. He is referred to a mental health specialist. Mr. Simpson responds well to hypnosis and relaxation training. It is noted that he tends to take responsibility for a number of family issues and fails to tell his wife when he is becoming distressed. This pattern is pointed out to him and he becomes more direct with her. By August 1994, Mr. Simpson continues psychological treatment and has no anxiety episodes. His medication is continued as well. In October 1994, at the psychologist's direction and in conjunction with a primary care physician, Mr. Simpson begins to taper his Xanax in 0.25 mg per week increments. He has two full-blown "panic episodes" during the month and reported consistently high levels of anxiety. He was encouraged to use relaxation training.

In November 1994, he is admitted to the hospital because of chest pain. Cardiac studies again are negative. His Xanax is titrated back upwards to 2 mg a day. In April 1995, Mr. Simpson is reporting no cardiac attacks or significant chest pain. Again, psychological treatment, including biofeedback, is continued. Mr. Simpson is now taking 1.0 mg per day of Xanax (0.5 mg twice a day). He reports some episodes of break-through anxiety but is generally able to use deep breathing and relaxation training to prevent the panic from escalating. In June 1995, Mr. Simpson has an episode of acute chest pain and possible blacking out while at a family reunion. He is brought to the hospital by ambulance. Cardiac studies are negative. The diagnosis is "panic attack." The psychologist who has worked with him in the past is consulted. It is recommended that he be tried on a selective serotonin reuptake inhibitor and sertraline is initiated and titrated up to 250 mg/day.

During October 1996, Mr. Simpson has two panic episodes in one month. He reports that he discontinued sertraline (Zoloft) because it made him "jumpy." He reports continued episodes of chest tightening. Cardiac studies are again conducted and are negative. Xanax is reinitiated at 0.50 mg per day.

By March 1997, Mr. Simpson has had no panic episodes for 8 weeks. He is diagnosed with hypertension, however.

In June 1997, Mr. Simpson appears in the emergency room for chest pain, hyperventilation and headaches. A cardiac work-up is conducted again and is negative. He is initiated on buspirone (Buspar) with concurrent alprazolam treatment. Additional biofeedback instruction is provided through follow-up. By August 1997, the patient has no panic symptoms.

This case illustrates the interaction between physical symptoms and panic symptoms. Because of this patient's cardiac risk factors—his weight, history of smoking, and family history, it is important that his chest pain be treated as a possible myocardial infarction. However, the patient undergoes at least four cardiac work-ups during this time, all of which run at least $500.00–$3,000 and have no positive findings. Most panic disorder patients come under some control after a reasonable period of time. However, for many of them, the possibility of panic disorder is not considered for multiple years and particularly if they go to different physicians or emergency rooms, the cycle of emergency presentation and specialty referral persists.

Another cardiac abnormality which has been related to anxiety symptoms is mitral valve prolapse. Mitral valve prolapse (MVP) involves a decline in efficiency of the mitral valve, the valve between the left atrium and left ventricle. MVP is a congenital disorder in which the valve stretches over time. It is estimated that 6–10% of females and 4% of males are born with a defective valve (Scheidt, 1996). Of persons with this condition, 5–10% develop problems such as arrhythmias, chest pains, and elevated risk of subacute bacterial endocarditis, an infection of the heart valve (Scheidt, 1996). There may be an association between anxiety-related symptoms and MVP. Although it had been previously through that MVP had a strong association with panic disorder, more recent findings are equivocal. There are a number of panic disorder patients who do not have MVP (Scheidt, 1996).

PSYCHOLOGICAL SEQUELAE OF CARDIAC SURGERY

Coronary artery bypass graft surgery (CABG) is one of the most common surgical procedures employed in the United States (Gold, 1996). CABG surgery is performed to alleviate angina associated with atherosclerosis of coronary arteries and has been developed to the extent that mortality rates are only about 1% to 2% in low-risk cardiac patients (Gold, 1996).

There are several social and psychological issues associated with CABG surgery including functional role status, depression, and neuropsychological sequelae. Several studies have found high rates of retirement following CABG surgery: about 50% of patients retired within five years of surgery (Gold, 1996). Retirement occurs despite good exercise tolerance. Although some individuals may retire because of age-related work place policies, other patients (and their families) are likely to blame "job stress" for their cardiac difficulties. Employers may also present obstacles to returning to work, particularly if the job is physically demanding. Depression is also likely to be a factor contributing to functional limitations. Gold (1996) reports a 40% prevalence rate of significant depressive symptoms pre-operatively, which increased to 68% six months post-operatively. When these figures are examined in more detail, one-third of patients developed depression post-operatively with 40% remaining depressed prior to and after surgery. When demographic, marital, and medical (e.g., presence of comorbid illness) factors were examined, only social isolation was associated with increased post-surgical depression. Neuropsychological deficits including difficulties with attention, orientation, concentration, and short-term memory may arise from several causes including anesthesia as well as strokes associated with embolic events during surgery. Figures cited have varied considerably—between 1% and 10% (Gold, 1996).

More sensitive neuropsychological measures have indicated impaired cognitive functioning in up to one-third of patients undergoing coronary artery surgery (Pugsley, Klinger, Paschalis, Treasure, Harrison, & Newman, 1994). Primary neuropsychological deficits appear to center around verbal memory and related functions. There seems to be preserved cognitive functioning when surgery includes an arterial line filter or high intraoperative blood pressure is maintained (Gold, 1996). Both of these procedures reduce micro-emboli contributing to small strokes.

Delirium is fairly common in post-operative cardiac surgical patients. Kim, McCartney, Kaye, Boland, & Niaura (1996) found that 25% of patients undergoing open heart surgery exhibited post-operative delirium. Causes of post-operative delirium are not well-known. However, medications such as Cimetidine and Ranitidine, used to prevent GI bleeding after surgery, may contribute to acute mental status changes.

Post-cardiotomy delirium's etiology is not well-understood or established. A meta-analysis found that gender, previous psychiatric illness, and time on bypass were not significantly associated and that age was only slightly related to post-cardiotomy delirium (Smith & Dimsdale, 1989).

PSYCHOLOGICAL SEQUELAE OF MYOCARDIAL INFARCTION

Having a heart attack is, for many patients, a frightening experience of often traumatic proportions. Recovery after an MI appears to be strongly influenced by individual psychological issues such as the presence of depression and social issues including spousal support.

> Ms. Zarega is a 48-year-old Hispanic woman who is seen in the office 3 weeks after being discharged from the hospital following a myocardial infarction. Ms. Zarega experienced four to five episodes of angina during her hospital course, and a cardiologist expressed concern about a psychological condition as a contributing factor.

By way of social history, Ms. Zarega was separated from her husband about 3 years ago after a 20-year marriage. She has two children, ages 12 and 15. Ms. Zarega states that she left her husband because he reportedly drank and was seeing other women. Ms. Zarega and her children live with her sister. Ms. Zarega worked as a taxi driver until about 5 years ago when she reportedly sustained a back injury while in an accident. Since then, she has been developing her own business in property management. She reports working about 70 hours a week but has been having some difficulty financially. Ms. Zarega reports that about a year ago, she started a relationship with a man she met through her job. She states that she realizes that the relationship is "all wrong" because he disappears for several weeks at a time and she does not know his whereabouts. However, she seemed to have a hard time breaking off the relationship. Ms. Zarega reports no other social support. She has some contact with her mother but feels she is very critical of her. In addition, she and her sister have a conflictual relationship.

In the interview, Ms. Zarega presents as a well-dressed and groomed Hispanic female. Her thought processes are well-organized and coherent. However, she is very tearful, particularly when discussing family issues. Ms. Zarega reports muscle tension, fatigue, and GI distress of about 1-year duration. She also describes difficulty concentrating ("It is like my mind jumps all around.").

Ms. Zarega describes difficulty with sleep onset ("I just lie there for an hour and worry about all I have to do.") as well as terminal insomnia of about 3 months duration. She also reported bouts of passive suicidal ideation over the past 6 months but has no current or past suicidal plan or intent.

It is likely that Ms. Zarega's chest pain is partially exacerbated by depression and her emotional reactions to her life circumstances. To reduce the likelihood of a second MI, aggressive treatment of her depression and anxiety is necessary. Additionally, supportive and problem-solving psychotherapy should address her current relationship and work difficulties.

Post-MI patients should be encouraged to enter a cardiac rehabilitation program. These multidisciplinary programs have been effective in reducing the likelihood of a second myocardial infarction. The main difficulty with these programs is that they usually require fairly significant time commitment, particularly during the first two to three months. Patients typically come to the cardiac rehabilitation center for about two to three hours per day at least two to three days per week.

Cardiac rehabilitation usually includes a multiple-month program of diet, counseling, gradually increased exercise, relaxation training, and group support. Brief, individual psychotherapy is directed to patients with co-existing psychiatric illness (most commonly major depression or generalized anxiety). Meetings for patients and their spouses are typically included as well.

After an initial period of rehabilitation, patients are usually moved to a maintenance schedule in which they come to the center several times to once per month.

For patients who stay involved with the program and continue exercise and diet on their own, there is better recovery (Langosch, 1988).

Depression is very common among MI both before and after heart attack. Ten days after an MI, 20% to 25% of patients are likely to be experiencing an episode of major depression with an equivalent number reporting minor depressive symptoms.

During the six-month period following an MI, depressed patients have a mortality rate five to six times that of nondepressed patients. Frasure-Smith, Lesperance, & Talajic (1993) found death rates of 16% among depressed as compared with 3% in nondepressed patients at six months after an MI. Even subclinical depressive symptoms markedly increase the post-MI death rate (Frasure-Smith, Lesperance, & Talajic, 1995). The mechanisms mediating the relation between mortality and depression in these patients are not well-established.

Depressive symptoms among cardiac patients may differ somewhat from non-medically ill patients. Suicidal ideation is not as common among MI patients, whereas insomnia, social withdrawal, and lack of interest in usual activities are common experiences. The severity of cardiovascular disease does not appear to be directly predictive of level of depression. In addition to elevated general morbidity and mortality, cardiac patients with concurrent depression are less likely to return to work six months after MI and are more likely to have a second heart attack (Frasure-Smith et al., 1993; Ludwig, Rull, Breithardt, Buedde, & Borgreffe, 1994). Depression also adversely impacts medical compliance relative to cardiac risk. Among men in their 60s, daily aspirin regimens were less likely to be followed by those experiencing depression. While 70% of nondepressed men were compliant, fewer than 50% of depressed individuals maintained their aspirin regimen (Carney, Freedland, Eisen, Rich, & Jaffe, 1995).

Social support appears to be a buffer of stress and may reduce risk of coronary artery disease as well as of subsequent MIs after an initial episode. Among coronary prone men, the presence of a supportive context appears to exert its protective influence among Type A individuals. However, patients' social networks can also impede recovery following a cardiac event. Patients in cardiac rehabilitation programs whose family was overprotective, doubtful of recovery or discouraging, did not derive as much treatment benefit (Fleury, 1993).

Post-MI patients have been classified into several general "types" in terms of their coping style. Patients who are information-seeking, follow professional advice, and gradually increase their activity according to their physician's recommendations generally have the least complicated recovery patterns. These "optimal" patients make the necessary dietary changes, stop smoking, and reduce alcohol intake if necessary. Some patients develop "cardiac neurosis" and have internalized their Coronary Care Unit experience. These individuals felt a sense of security and safety on the CCU (Levenson, 1993). After hospital discharge, they may become preoccupied with "stressing" their heart and as a result become constricted emotionally as well as restricted physically. Each chest sensation is met with anxiety and alarm even if it occurs while walking up a flight of stairs. These patients may repeatedly bring themselves to the emergency department for another "rule-out MI" workup (Levenson, 1993). Another category of patients are those who deny the significance of their heart attack. They see it as a minor annoyance and push themselves to get back to their regular routine. In the short-term, patients who exhibit some denial may have better outcomes (Taylor, 1983). However, this denial may also prevent these patients from making necessary lifestyle changes including smoking cessation and participation in cardiac rehabilitation. When anginal pain does occur, these individuals may not bring themselves to the emergency room until it is too late. Anginal pain is often treated with nitroglycerine placed under the tongue. Tabrizi, Littman, Williams, & Schedit (1996) note that many patients are reluctant to use nitroglycerine when appropriate. This hesitation may stem from anxiety about alarming family or a view that stoically enduring anginal pain is a way of strengthening the constitution. Denial may also play a role in the reluctance to use nitroglycerine.

The marital relationship also appears to be important in recovery from an MI (Heinzelman & Bagley, 1970). Patients whose spouses are critical and pressuring ("If you keep smoking, you'll have another heart attack and die!" "I've told you, the doctor has told you; do you listen to us? No!") typically experience greater strain and little support. Similarly, intrusive spouses who foster dependence are likely to promote cardiac invalidism ("I don't want you doing anything to strain yourself." "I'll cut the grass, I'll pay the bills, you just rest." "Your poker-playing friends are no longer welcome in the house. Now, it's just because I love you.").

With respect to physical activity, cardiac invalidism has been altered by involving the nonpatient spouse in a supervised exercise program. C. Taylor, Bandura, Ewart, Miller, & DeBusk (1985) had wives of heart attack patients exercise on a treadmill at the same level of intensity as their husbands. Wives who actually walked on the treadmill rather than simply observing their husbands reported higher confidence in their husband's ability to engage in exercise. This in turn was associated with the patient's level of cardiovascular improvement at 11 and 26 weeks after the heart attack. Campbell and Patterson (1995) suggest that this intervention was helpful because it reduced the wives' overprotectiveness.

One often unspoken concern is resumption of sexual activity. Even when cleared by the cardiologist, may spouses of MI patients are reluctant to have sex because of fears of "provoking" another heart attack. Because of embarrassment, many patients will not raise these concerns. The health care provider should pro-actively raise the issue. ("Many couples are concerned about when they can begin having sexual relations again. This is a common worry.") The degree of exertion is approximately the same as a brisk walk up a flight of stairs.

PSYCHOPHARMACOTHERAPY WITH CARDIAC PATIENTS

Among MI patients, selective serotonin reuptake inhibitors (SSRIs) appear to be the antidepressant pharmacotherapy of choice. In particular, sertraline (Zoloft) is recommended over fluoxetine (Prozac) because of sertraline's shorter half-life (26 versus 72 hours). In addition, setraline does not have an active metabolite, which makes it safer for medically ill patients for whom the drug may need to be rapidly withdrawn.

The tricyclic antidepressants have been implicated in cardiac conduction problems (Wyszynski & Wyszynski, 1996). The SSRIs appear to be safe with cardiac patients. Fluoxetine (Prozac) may cause mild slowing of heart rate, but this appears to have no significant clinical implications. There is some concern about the SSRI's ability to inhibit hepatic (liver) enzymes (cytochrome P-450), which may alter drug metabolism (Tabrizi et al., 1996).

Psychostimulants such as methylphenidate appear to be fairly well tolerated by cardiac patients and are useful when a rapid response is needed. This is particularly true among the elderly and medically ill. Psychostimulants have been used with relative safety in patients with cardiovascular, pulmonary, neurological, endocrinological, urological, orthopedic, and gastrointestinal disorders (Masand, Pickett, & Murray, 1991). The only significant concern is the interaction of stimulants with other medications. For example, methylphenidate may increase levels of tricyclic antidepressants as well as of anticonvulsants (Wyszynski & Wyszynski, 1996).

Alprazolam (Xanax) appears to be useful in reducing catecholamine activity during physical activity. It appears to have no marked cardiotoxic effects. There are problems with withdrawal and anxiety surges between doses that are likely because of Alprazolam's relatively brief duration of action (Wyszynski & Wyszynski, 1996).

Interestingly, buspirone (Buspar) has been found to be helpful in reducing some Type A behavior in men without other psychiatric disturbance. There was some decline in hostility with more consistent reductions in time urgency, anxiety, and stress ratings (Littman, Fava, & McKool, 1993; Wyszynski & Wyszynski, 1996).

Several commonly used cardiac medications have psychological side effects. Beta-blockers are a category of medication used to treat hypertension, angina pectoris, and cardiac arrhythmias. These drugs are also helpful in reducing the likelihood of a second myocardial infarction. Patients taking beta-blockers often report nightmares, insomnia, decreased libido, fatigue, and difficulties maintaining concentration and alertness.

CONCLUSION

Behavioral factors play at least a moderate role in risk for cardiovascular disease. Patients with Type A behavior patterns will benefit from counseling about lifestyle modification including anger management. Mental health professionals are increasingly visible as members of cardiac rehabilitation teams. Identification and management of MI patients experiencing depression as well as family issues impairing recovery reduce the likelihood of further cardiac events. In the primary care setting, mental health professionals can be very helpful in assisting evaluation of the patient with atypical chest pain in which anxiety may be a component.

Chapter 7

Respiratory Disorders and Smoking Cessation

Historically, psychosomatic medicine has viewed underlying, unconscious dependency needs as associated with pulmonary diseases such as asthma, (Alexander, 1950). More recently, research has moved away from psychological factors as being etiological in pulmonary disease. There is evidence, however, that difficulty breathing (dyspnea), is influenced by emotional factors, with anxiety being predominant (Thompson & Thompson, 1993). Although not a causal factor, anxiety may play a significant role in exacerbation and maintenance of respiratory diseases such as COPD (chronic obstructive pulmonary disease) and asthma (Bender, 1996). One of the major causes of respiratory disorders is cigarette smoking. The latter section of this chapter touches on primary care strategies for smoking cessation.

ASTHMA

Asthma is characterized by hyper-reactivity of airways to allergens, nonspecific irritants (cold air), and infections. Physiological responses may include constrictions of the smooth muscle of the bronchial wall, swelling of the bronchial wall, and mucous secretion (Creer, Reynolds, & Kotses, 1991).

The result of hyper-reactivity is that the lung airways become inflamed, which in turn, results in shortness of breath and wheezing (Bender, 1996). Asthma affects approximately 12 million people in the United States, and includes 4 million children. There is evidence that the number of new onset of asthma cases in the United States may be growing.

Early research emphasized emotional aspects of asthma. In this perspective, asthmatic symptoms such as wheezing were seen as reflecting unresolved dependency needs (Alexander, 1950). Family issues were also seen as important causal agents in asthma.

Minuchin's classic description of "psychosomatic families," included those in which a child or adolescent had recurrent asthma (Minuchin, Rosman, & Baker, 1978). Minuchin argued that these children were likely to come from enmeshed families with poor boundaries between parents and children. The families were characterized by artificially low levels of conflict, excessive togetherness, and a pattern of treating adolescents as if they were developmentally much younger. Typically, there was a reduction in asthmatic episodes when appropriate boundaries between parents and children were established. More recent research, however, suggests that family interaction factors, although playing a moderating role, do not directly exacerbate asthma. Asthmatic families are probably more likely to be of two types. First, they may be enmeshed as Minuchin and colleagues suggested. However, they also may be highly disengaged. In disengaged families, there is little cohesiveness and members seem to lead "separate lives" (Searight, 1997c). Asthmatic children living in disengaged families may experience attacks because of inadequate parental monitoring to insure that medications are taken as required as well as adults' failure to recognize early states of respiratory episodes (Creer et al., 1991).

During the past 15 years, asthma has gradually been moved out of the "psychosomatic" category. Although interpersonal and emotional factors do not cause asthma, they may exacerbate respiratory symptoms and influence medication compliance. The role of psychological factors in exacerbating asthma has been demonstrated in the laboratory. When asthma patients are asked to inhale an inert substance labeled as a bronchoconstrictor, a number of them exhibit increased airflow resistance. (Creer et al., 1991). In addition, asthma patients have been found to demonstrate greater airflow resistance when they imagine experiencing fear and anger (Creer et al., 1991).

Among asthma patients, panic-like symptoms may be associated with the onset of respiratory distress among children and adults. Anxiety exacerbates the asthma symptoms and may interfere with the patient's ability to manage their attacks appropriately with medication. In addition, anxiety may contribute to confusion on the part of the patient and the health care provider about whether an asthma attack is actually occurring.

There are suggestions that anxiety disorders are more common among asthma patients with asthma (Creer et al., 1991). As dyspnea begins to occur, patients become increasingly frightened by their shortness of breath, which in turn increases their anxiety and makes it more difficult for them to breath. There is evidence that asthma patients with greater levels of panic–fear require higher dosages of medication and may have longer hospital stays (Baron et al., 1986).

> Ms. Barton is a 42-year-old White woman, who is seen about a week after she was brought to the emergency department by ambulance. Ms. Barton indicates that she has had an "attack" in which she could not breathe. She also reported diffuse tightness in her chest, lightheadedness, and "feeling like I was going pass out." Ms. Barton explained the episode came on very suddenly at work "... I felt like something

terrible was going to happen. My heart was beating both fast and slow." This is the second such episode of these symptoms in the past month. The first episode occurred at home and her husband called the paramedics.

Ms. Barton became a patient in the family practice clinic about 1 year ago. At that time, her medical history was noteworthy for asthma. She reported having had intermittent asthma attacks for about a 5-year period. She uses an inhaler as needed and her asthma is generally well-controlled.

Ms. Barton has been married about 12 years. The couple has one daughter—age eight. For the past 7 years, she has been employed as a union worker in an industrial plant. Her mother lives nearby. Ms. Barton's father died 1 year ago from myocardial infarction. Ms. Barton stated she has had asthma attacks in the past but can usually prevent these from escalating with use of the inhaler. Her first episode was about three months ago. She noted it occurred on Father's Day.

In the interview, Ms. Barton presents as a well-dressed and groomed White female. She appears somewhat tense and frightened, particularly when describing her symptoms. Ms. Barton describes generally unreactive mood and denies suicidal ideation or intent. Her thought processes are generally intact although she provides somewhat over-elaborated answers with excessive circumstantial detail. Ms. Barton reports sleeping about 4 hours per night. She attributes this pattern to her work schedule but reports requiring about an hour to fall asleep. She denies fatigue or changes in weight or appetite. She is started on alprazolam (Xanax) 0.25 milligrams, twice per day. About a week later, her husband calls the physician, says that Ms. Barton is very short of breath and cannot speak. He is told to call an ambulance. She is brought to the emergency room and, again, there is no evidence of any cardiac abnormality. She is seen again in the office by the physician who switches her medication to sertraline (Zoloft). She also sees a mental health professional who instructs her in progressive relaxation and includes some biofeedback training. She sees the mental health specialist for about four sessions based over a 2-month time period. During this time, she reports having periodic asthma attacks at work but these do not require emergency attention.

About 1 year later, both providers are contacted again. The patient's mother has reportedly died about a month ago. Ms. Barton appears in the emergency room, again brought by ambulance with similar symptoms as her initial presentation. She had stopped the Zoloft and indicates that she had not been practicing relaxation training because she felt like she was "all better." Again, she is seen by the mental health professional for several months and reinitiated on Zoloft. While she has several asthma episodes at work, these are not severe.

In contrast to those with higher levels of panic–fear, patients with very low levels of panic–fear may underestimate the severity of asthma symptoms. As a result, they may be less likely to use medications and be discharged from hospitals prematurely with subsequent rehospitalization (Thompson & Thompson, 1993).

Similar to many chronically ill patients requiring regular medication regimens, asthmatics often have problems with treatment compliance. Studies in which microchip counters were placed in inhalers indicate that patients often do not take their medication as directed (Milgrom, Bender, Sarlin, & Leung, 1994). There is evidence that patients under-report their inhaler use to health care personnel. There are also suggestions that as doses increase, patients may actually become less compliant (Bender, 1996).

In addition to addressing medication compliance, psychological treatments such as biofeedback, autogenic training, and progressive relaxation have been beneficial in decreasing airflow resistance (Creer et al., 1991). Asthmatic children have been found to have lower levels of social confidence and self-esteem (Bender, 1996). Increased peer activities and possibly social skill–oriented group treatment may be helpful with these children.

CHRONIC OBSTRUCTIVE PULMONARY DISEASE (COPD)

COPD patients do not appear to have increased levels of anxiety or depression as compared with other chronically medically ill patients (Sandhu, 1986; Thompson & Thompson, 1993). However, panic-like symptoms do occur among COPD patients, particularly those in later stages of illness. Significant anxiety may make it difficult for the late stage COPD patient to determine their degree of dyspnea and may exacerbate respiratory problems. Other evidence suggesting a role for psychological factors in COPD is that although there is a relatively modest relationship between lung function and degree of disability, a much stronger relationship exists between dyspnea and disability (Williams, 1989; Williams & Bury, 1989). At a practical level, it is important for the clinician to be aware that a very high percentage of COPD patients acquired their condition through smoking. Smokers, in turn, are much more likely to drink alcohol. Thus, the clinician should be aware that alcohol abuse may be higher among patients with COPD.

COPD patients may have multiple episodes of severe hypoxia (Thompson & Thompson, 1993). Hypoxia may produce mental status changes. In extreme situations, the patient may appear delirious. Paranoid ideation, along with psychosis has also been reported (Thompson & Thompson, 1993). These cognitive symptoms are usually reversible with oxygen.

> Ms. Page is an 82-year-old African American woman who is brought to the emergency room in restraints by the emergency medical technicians and the police. She is agitated, combative and is talking about the CIA and secret radio transmissions to the Pentagon. Initially, she is incoherent and disoriented. The medical personnel cannot obtain a history from her.
>
> Ms. Page's son is contacted. He says his mother was fine until several days ago. She has lived on her own since her husband died 25 years ago. Ms. Page was diagnosed with chronic obstructive pulmonary disease some years ago and is currently

receiving home oxygen. The son recalls a phone call from his mother's visiting nurse about a week ago. The nurse described "weird behavior." "Mom thought her oxygen canister was a radio transmitter and would not let the nurse near it. She told the nurse if she touched it, she would expose the secret code and start World War III."

On mental status testing, Ms. Page is inconsistent. When she is asked to name or draw an item or picture, she performs well. When asked orientation questions, she verbalized incoherent answers about "spies and nuclear war"; however, she could repeat six digits forward and five digits backwards. Her performance on short-term memory and other cognitive tasks was very poor; she did not seem to understand what she was being asked to do. However, at the end of the interview, she said, "Doctor, how did I do? ... I can't think quite straight." Radiographic studies of the brain are normal.

While this case example describe the effects of oxygen deprivation on cognitive functions, delirium occurs in patients with other conditions. Acute delirium occurs in up to half of patients undergoing surgery for a hip fracture (Francis & Kapoor, 1990; Gustafson et al., 1988). Predisposing factors for delirium following hip fracture include older age and the presence of pre-existing illness involving disruptions in respiration, kidney, or cerebral–vascular function. Medications with anticholinergic effects are a common precipitant. A number of hip fracture patients are on these medications prior to injury. The hypotensive side effects of these drugs are a contributing factor to the fall in which the patient sustained the fracture.

CIGARETTE SMOKING

Demographics

One of the primary risk factors for respiratory disease is cigarette smoking. Although the prevalence of new smokers has plateaued during the past decade, about one in five Americans are smokers. There has been a 10% decline in the number of smokers in the United States since 1976 (Brown, Goldstein, Niaura, Emmons, & Abrams, 1993, U.S. Department of Health and Human Services, 1988). Demographically, African Americans are more likely to smoke than Whites. Approximately equal numbers of men and women are smokers. However, it is estimated that by the year 2000 more women will be smoking than men. The number of women who smoked increased during the late 1960s. There is generally an inverse relationship between educational level and smoking. Those who have less than a high school education are less likely to have stopped smoking. However, those with college education are more likely to successfully complete smoking cessation efforts (Escobedo, Anda, Smith, Remington, & Mast, 1990).

Developmentally, cigarette smoking begins at about age 11 and with a second surge in smokers at around age 13. However, the most common age for initiating smoking is between 17 to 19 (Escobedo, Anda, Smith, Remington, & Mast, 1990).

With respect to developmental patterns, teenagers are more likely to smoke if they have parents who smoke or peers who smoke (Krosnick & Judd, 1982). In addition, teens who are experiencing depressive symptoms are more likely to initiate smoking (Kandel & Davies, 1986).

Nicotine Dependence

Nicotine, the psychoactive component of cigarettes, has its maximum brain concentration within one minute of ingestion. In laboratory studies nicotine has been shown to improve attention and memory (R. A. Brown et al., 1993). There are suggestions that its effects are particularly pronounced in situations involving lower levels of environmental stimulation such as repetitive tasks. Nicotine also appears to decrease adverse affective states (Hughes, 1988). Nicotine-dependence syndrome has a similar pattern as addiction to other psychoactive drugs (Milhorn, 1989). Individuals often require increased amounts of nicotine to achieve the same effect and gradually increase the number of cigarettes consumed. Cessation of nicotine after extended use is associated with a withdrawal syndrome. Common characteristics of nicotine withdrawal include irritability, preoccupation with smoking, craving for cigarettes, anxiety, difficulty concentrating, dysphoric mood, decreased heart rate, and increased appetite or weight (*DSM–IV*, 1994; American Psychiatric R. A. Brown et al., 1993). The initial symptoms of nicotine withdrawal often occur within two hours after the last cigarette and usually become most pronounced 24 to 48 hours after the most recent smoking episode. Withdrawal symptoms may last for several days to a week (R. A. Brown et al., 1993). Nicotine replacement therapy such as nicotine gum or transdermal patches are based on the idea that nicotine is an addictive drug. The replacement therapies operate through the gradual downward titration of nicotine.

Stages of Habit Change and Smoking Cessation

Prochaska and DiClemente (1983) developed a broad model for habit change that is useful for assessing smokers. Health care professionals should evaluate the patient's relative motivation for habit change. Prochaska and DiClemente (1983) note that considerable frustration occurs when clinicians attempt to engage patients in a program of smoking cessation without assessing the patient's motivation and readiness to begin such a program.

In the initial stage of smoking cessation, precontemplation, patients generally do not view their smoking as a problem. At this stage, the benefits of smoking are viewed as significantly outweighing any liabilities. Contemplation, the second stage, usually involves ambivalence about smoking. Patients are aware of both the benefits as well as adverse effects of smoking. However, they do not verbalize any particular commitment to beginning a systematic process of smoking cessation. The third phase, preparation, is often characterized by a vaguely formulated plan to stop smoking at some unspecified time in the future. Individuals in this phase are often beginning to be much more conscious of the number of cigarettes they smoke as well as some of the environmental cues for smoking. Patients may begin to reduce the number of cigarettes they smoke. In addition, they may make attempts to delay the period of time between which they experience an internal prompting for a cigarette to the time they actually begin smoking. In the action phase, individuals move to a serious planful attempt to stop smoking. Lastly, maintenance, is characterized by lapse prevention. The exsmoker will often experience periodic urges to reinitiate smoking. Particularly in stressful circumstances, former smokers will find themselves craving a cigarette. In addition, many former smokers find that they do indeed relapse and re-initiate smoking for periods of time. Patients who are, in the long run, successful in their smoking cessation efforts are able to keep these lapse periods relatively isolated in time. As maintenance continues, the number of lapses become fewer with greater time intervals in between these episodes (Prochaska & DiClemente, 1983).

Smoking Cessation: Assessment and Counseling in Primary Care

The majority of people who stop smoking successfully quit on their own without any professional assistance. In evaluating a patient's readiness to stop smoking, it is important for health care providers to remember this principle as well as to consider the patient's motivation is light of Prochaska and DiClemente's (1983) stages. For patients who are in the precontemplative phase, it is important that the provider send low-key yet consistent messages about smoking. These are often as simple as asking the patient at each visit, "Are you still smoking?" or "Have you cut down on your smoking any?" (Husten & Manley, 1990). Some medical clinics have stickers on patients' charts to remind the provider that the patient is a smoker. Interestingly, surveys of patients suggest that the majority of smokers state that their doctor has never recommended that they stop smoking (Anda, Remington, Sinenko, & Davis, 1987). For the patient who is not seriously considering quitting; it is important that the provider avoid cajoling or lecturing them. If patients are made to feel anxious, uncomfortable, or in some way that they have disappointed the provider, it unlikely that they will return for further care.

When a patient responds to the provider with interest in reducing smoking, the provider should spend some time determining why the patient wants to stop smoking and their reasons for wanting to stop at this particular time. Patients often will spontaneously respond with "Yeah, I'd like to stop, but I just can't seem to do it." or "This cough, it keeps coming back and it's really got my wife worried. I'd like to quit but I've tried several times and I just can't stay away from the cigarettes for more than a day." When interviewing the patient at this stage, it is helpful to determine if their motivation is internal or external. It is also important to determine whether the patient is genuinely worried about their own health or are responding to family members' concerns.

Although the extent of smoking is often assessed in terms of packs of cigarettes per day, it is also valuable to ask the patient about the duration between the time they wake up in the morning until they have their first cigarette (Husten & Manley, 1990). Someone who begins smoking less than 30 minutes after awakening usually has a strong addiction to nicotine. In this exploration process, it is also important to ask the patient if they have tried to quit before. Patients should be asked what types of strategies they previously used to stop smoking. The relative success of prior efforts as well as lengths of abstinence are also important. The greater the period of abstinence, the better the prognosis for subsequent smoking cessation efforts. If a patient was able to be abstinent for a period of time, the provider should ask about the circumstances around which they began smoking again. Most patients who have been abstinent for more than six months usually report that a particularly stressful life event triggered their return to smoking. ("My mom just had a heart attack; I was a mess." "I got a new boss at work; he was a real slave driver.") These individuals will typically be able to go through a period of initial cessation, but are likely to have more difficulty during the maintenance period.

Successful smoking cessation will be far more challenging when there are a number of environmental cues for smoking. One of the most common cues is the presence of other smokers in the household. If a spouse or significant other smokes, it is recommended that the provider invite this other person for conjoint office visit to discuss smoking cessation. The spouse's interest in stopping smoking should be assessed. The spouse's motivation may be for their own health or a desire to support their husband or wife. In situations in which the husband or wife refuses to participate, the provider should be aware that successful smoking cessation is going to be more difficult. However, this information is essential in developing a smoking cessation plan for the patient. The presence of stimulus cues such as cigarettes, ashtrays, lighters, and matches will make it much harder to achieve successful smoking cessation.

As noted in an earlier chapter, smoking often becomes part of a power struggle between couples (Whitehead and Doherty, 1989). These couples are often middle-aged adults who have been smoking for 10–20 years. A wife may be antagonized by her husband's smoking (although she won't say so directly) and is fearful about the impact on his health. As a result, she frequently points out to him that he is killing himself and in an angry tone, repeatedly urges him not to smoke. Smoking may also become the content of a passive–aggressive dynamic. In situations in which both spouses are smoking, the spouse that is attempting to quit may be a threat to the one who continues to smoke.

It is important that the clinician not become discouraged when treating patients who have tried to stop smoking and have failed before. It is estimated that fewer than 20% of smokers succeed on their first attempt (Miller, Golish, & Cox, 1992). With these patients, the clinician should inquire about how the individual attempted to stop in the past and the circumstances surrounding the lack of success. The next step involves establishing a quit date. The quit date should be about one to two weeks in the future. During the ensuing time interval, the patient should monitor their smoking patterns. A simple way to obtain data about smoking patterns is to have the patient attach an index card to their cigarette pack and make a mark each time they smoke. In addition, it may be useful to have the patient note the settings in which they are smoking and possibly any thoughts or feelings that they have at these times. It is important to recognize that simply as a function of monitoring their smoking patterns, the patient is likely to smoke less. However, the clinician will still be able to obtain a useful profile of their patient's smoking habits with respect to time of day and situation. Common situational cues for smoking include having coffee in the morning, remaining at the dinner table after a meal, driving in heavy traffic, or talking on the telephone. After these high risk situations have been targeted, the clinician can work with the patient around developing alternative behaviors. For example, the patient who consistently has a cigarette with their morning coffee and newspaper can be encouraged to have their morning coffee and newspaper at their office where smoking is prohibited.

At this stage, when the provider begins to encourage a critical process of examining and changing lifestyle patterns, some patients become resistant. Patients who respond to suggestions such as those mentioned above with, "Oh, I could never do that" should prompt a re-evaluation along the lines of the model by Prochaska and DiClmente (1983). These patients may need additional education that nicotine is an addiction that cannot be broken without major life style change (Richards, 1992). For example, one patient was consistently in the habit of going to the local tavern after work. Bars, in addition to being settings for a number of people to smoke, also feature alcohol, which is likely to reduce inhibition around smoking. The patient was gently encouraged to find another setting such as a no-smoking section of a restaurant, to "wind down" after work.

Nicotine Replacement Therapy

Nicotine replacement therapy is based on the concept of providing patients with safer forms of nicotine to reduce withdrawal symptoms and help the patient in gradual cessation of nicotine use (R. A. Brown et al., 1993). Replacement therapies take two forms: gum or transdermal patches. Nicotine resin complex (gum) has been found to be more efficacious than a placebo when used in conjunction with a behaviorally oriented smoking cessation program (Miller et al., 1992). Overall, research suggests that nicotine gum is helpful in reducing smoking over short periods of time, but is not as successful with long-term abstinence. Outcome almost always improves by at least 10%–15% when gum is used in conjunction with a behaviorally oriented program (Health & Public Policy Committee, American College of Physicians, 1986). Although the gum is a short-term treatment in therapy to curb the withdrawal symptoms, among those who abstain from smoking, up to 50% are still using the gum at six months and 25% use it at one year (R. A. Brown et al., 1993).

The nicotine transdermal patch delivers nicotine through the skin. The patches appear to be effective in reducing nicotine withdrawal, but may not be as consistent in reducing nicotine craving. (Daughton, Heatley, & Pendergast, 1991) Both the patch and gum are generally associated with relatively good short-term success rates averaging about 50% to 60% at six weeks (Westman, Levin, & Rose, 1993). However, at one year, success rates typically fall below twenty percent (Lam, Sze, Sacks, & Chalmers, 1987; Westman et al., 1993). For both gum and the patch, quit rates at three and six months are about 10% to 15% better than for placebo.

The initial two weeks of a smoking cessation program with nicotine replacement therapy is generally a good predictor of longer term outcome. One study found that three quarters of patients who were back to smoking at six months re-initiated smoking by week two of their cessation program (Kenford, Fiore, Jorenby, Smith, Wetter, & Baker, 1994). Of those patients who are abstinent by the second week, almost half are abstinent at six months. Research suggests that there are several interventions that may improve outcome. Among heavier smokers who lapse by week two, it may be helpful to consider an additional extra 5- to 10-mg patch or switching to a higher dose (21-mg patch). Those started on lower doses with sustained provider contact during the initial smoking cessation period had some improvement in success rates. Patients who had phone contact from a nurse or participated in a psychoeducational support group for a sustained period (at least 10–12 weeks into the smoking cessation program) were about 5–10% more likely to be successful (Transdermal Nicotine Study Group, 1991; Sachs, Sawe, & Leischow, 1993). One of the current areas for research is to define subgroups of smokers who are and are not responsive to standard nicotine replacement and behavioral interventions and generate specific approaches for these more difficult to reach patients.

One primary obstacle to smoking cessation is weight gain. This problem appears to be of particular concern among women. Although early smoking cessation studies generally suggested that the amount of weight gain was relatively low (four to eight pounds), a more recent study indicated a 13-pound weight gain at one year after follow up among patients who were successfully abstinent from smoking (Klesges et al., 1997). Of interest, patients who continued to smoke only gained about two and a half pounds during this time period. Patients who had some relapse during the one-year period but were abstinent at follow up gained about six and a half pounds.

Initial Cessation and Relapse Preparation

Patients should be seen in the office close to their stopping date. In addition to providing social reinforcement for their decision, it is important to review the patient's smoking diary with them and ask them what they are going to do differently in periods when their cigarette consumption has been high.

In the first two weeks of smoking cessation, the major triggers will be nicotine withdrawal. It is important to prepare patients for this experience by explaining to them that nicotine is an addictive drug and that they will be irritable, depressed, and have trouble sleeping. However, the worst will be over in about 10–14 days. Patients often do not recognize the time-limited nature of this discomfort and believe that they will always experience significant distress.

Subjectively, many patients report that the craving period seems interminable. When these individuals are asked more objectively about the length of time involved, the period lasts only about 10 minutes at the upper extreme. This is a useful perspective to emphasize with patients to highlight that these craving episodes are time limited. This point can be emphasized by encouraging patients to reflect on their experiences during periods of reduced smoking. During the baseline period prior to the quit date, many patients actually do try to stop or reduce their cigarette intake. Rather than being an extended period of misery, patients tend to report that they can tolerate not smoking and even extended time intervals when the patient doesn't think about smoking.

It is also helpful for patients to establish some sort of reward system. Many patients rely exclusively on long-term regards and say something like, "If I don't smoke for a year, I will have nearly a thousand dollars so I will use that to take a trip to Hawaii." While this does provide some incentive, it is generally too far in the future to modify behavior on a daily or hourly basis. It is important that the patient has some built in rewards for much shorter time periods. It may also be useful to enlist family members or friends in this regard. For example, the patient may say, "If I don't smoke today, I won't have to do the dishes after dinner" or "If I don't smoke this week, my teenaged daughter will cut the grass."

As indicated by the number of times that smokers initiate cessation before being successful, patients will undoubtedly lapse. There will likely be high risk periods that the provider or patient had not yet considered. In clinical practice, patients seem to "slip" around interpersonal stress (Marlatt & Gordon, 1985). In situations in which the patient lapses, it is helpful to have them develop some skills to manage the lapse. One strategy is simply for the patient to say to themselves,

"I'll wait five more minutes before I light up." Second, it is helpful for them to review the reasons for quitting at these high risk times. Third, they should consider how disappointed family members and friends will be if they lapse. Lastly, they should think about how bad they will feel about themselves tomorrow if they lapse.

Even when these guidelines and strategies are followed, patients will still often lapse. The provider should use this lapse as a learning experience. The patient encountered a new situation that had not been predicted. It is also important that the provider and patient try to isolate the lapse in time. For example, saying to the patient "Even though you did give in for two days, you haven't smoked for the last ten days." The urge to smoke did not spread like "wildfire." Another strategy is to encourage the patient to "give in less" (Marlatt & Gordon, 1985) each time they light up a cigarette. Thus, the patient may be encouraged to wait a period of time before beginning to smoke, confine themselves to one cigarette every thirty minutes, or inhale less. These activities all help the patient to experience some control and direct them more quickly back to abstinence. Research on smoking cessation underscores this point. Only about 20% of smokers succeed at their first attempt at smoking cessation. Fewer than 50% of smokers succeed at their seventh attempt (Milhorn, 1989).

PSYCHIATRIC DISORDERS AND SMOKING CESSATION

There is considerable evidence that psychiatric patients are much more likely to be smokers (R. A. Brown et al., 1993). Patients with schizophrenia, anxiety disorders, as well as unipolar and bipolar affective illness are more likely to smoke than the general population (Kick & Cooley, 1997). Primary care practitioners will commonly encounter depressed patients who are smokers. In particular, patients with depression who undergo smoking cessation are less likely to succeed (Glassman et al., 1990). Depressed patients are also less likely to initiate smoking cessation. The reverse pattern also appears to be true. In large samples of clinically depressed inpatients, up to half may be smokers. As the severity of depression increases, the likelihood of smoking also appears to increase (R. A. Brown et al., 1993).

It has been suggested that the "normal" dysphoria and irritability that smokers experience during nicotine withdrawal are probably more pronounced among depressed patients (Glassman et al., 1990). Thus, when patients with dysphoria try to stop, they are much more likely to return to smoking after a brief period of time. For providers addressing smoking cessation, the possibility of depression should be seriously considered with patients who have made multiple attempts at quitting smoking without success. In addition, patients who report a sharp decline in mood when they do try to stop smoking are probably at higher risk for relapse. It may be useful to evaluate and treat these patients for depression prior to or concurrent with smoking cessation effort.

SPECIALIZED PSYCHOLOGICAL INTERVENTIONS FOR SMOKING CESSATION

Controlled Smoking

Controlled smoking involves a major reduction in the number of cigarettes consumed without complete cessation. Clinically, it is not uncommon for patients to report that they have recently reduced their daily cigarette intake to 10 cigarettes after a 15-year period of smoking 30 cigarettes per day. As a broad-based treatment strategy, controlled smoking does not appear to be maintained. Patients tend to return to their earlier pattern of heavy use. It is likely that there is a subgroup of previously heavy smokers who can be successful at controlled smoking. However, the characteristics of this subset are not established.

Aversive Conditioning

Counterconditioning with aversive techniques often have been used by psychologists. The general process is to link cigarettes to a number of unpleasant sensations thereby decreasing frequency (Miller et al., 1992). Electric shock has been used in individual therapy. In this situation, the person imagines themselves smoking or actually smokes and receives an electric shock. An aversive procedure with limited established effectiveness is rapid smoking. This technique has the patient smoke two or three cigarettes in rapid succession with no pauses. For example, they will take a puff every six to eight seconds until tolerance is reached and often until the individual feels nauseous. This protocol is followed daily for about a week. The median quit rate for rapid smoking appears to be about 30% (Schwartz, 1987).

There are several problems with aversive conditioning procedure such as electric shock or rapid smoking. Their effectiveness is often short-term. If there are several maintenance sessions, aversive procedures will often be initially helpful for patients who may need some motivational assistance at the beginning of their smoking cessation efforts. However, as these procedures are repeated, their effectiveness tends to diminish. In addition, these procedures are not very attractive to the patient, who will often not continue with them. Lastly, rapid smoking may produce unpleasant side effects as well as possible medical problems such as cardiovascular complications (Lichenstein & Brown, 1982).

Hypnosis

Hypnosis is very popular among patients. The author practices hypnosis for smoking cessation and often receives a number of requests for this treatment. By itself, hypnosis produces rather modest results (Schwartz, 1987). However in conjunction with behavioral interventions, hypnosis can be helpful during initial phases of smoking cessation. Generally speaking, abstinence rates for hypnotic therapy are around 60% at one to two months, but decline to 20% to 30% at one year (Health & Public Policy Committee, American College of Physicians, 1986). Patients who are highly motivated, have the capacity for hypnotic imagery, and are suggestible will often have a positive initial response to hypnosis. In the author's practice, hypnosis is never used alone, but in conjunction with contingency contracting and stimulus control. Hypnosis can also be conducted with aversive conditioning. The patient is put into a state of relaxation and then very unpleasant images associated with smoking are described. For example, the patient may crave a cigarette; the craving is very strong. They walk along the street and find a charred cigarette butt in a pool of vomit. They reach into the vomit, and smoke the cigarette all covered with vomit, and smell and taste the vomit while they get a few empty drags off the cigarette butt (Kroger & Fezler, 1976).

Progressive relaxation is also useful in smoking cessation. Relaxation provides the patient with a useful coping strategy particularly for patients who smoke in response to anxiety and tension.

CONCLUSION

While asthma is no longer viewed as a "psychosomatic" condition, anxiety may exacerbate asthma symptoms and psychological issues may prevent medication compliance. Chronic obstructive pulmonary disease may present as cognitive changes prompting psychological assessment. Cigarette smoking is a main contributor to respiratory problems. Providers should recognize that smoking cessation is a relatively long-term process. Although pharmacotherapy in the form of transdermal patches or nicotine gum may be helpful in weaning from the addiction to nicotine, long-term therapy involves behavioral modification and life style change. A new strategy for smoking cessation involves regular dosages of buproprion (wellbutrin), an antidepressant. To date, it has not been thoroughly evaluated over an extended time period.

Chapter 8

Diabetes, Weight Loss, and Eating Disorders

Although three distinct topic areas—diabetes, obesity, and eating disorders—are discussed in this chapter, these problems often co-exist. Maintenance of proper weight, diet, and activity levels are important interventions for patients with these disorders.

DIABETES

About five and a half million people in the United States are currently believed to have diabetes mellitus. There are two primary types of the disease. In both forms, chronic hyperglycemia (abnormally high levels of blood glucose) are the central feature. Type I diabetes or insulin-dependent diabetes mellitus, has its onset in childhood or adolescence with the destruction of pancreatic beta cells that secrete insulin. The reductions in insulin prevent glucose from being absorbed into the tissues. This, in turn, leads to hyperglycemia and a metabolic breakdown of fats. In its extreme form, this process may lead to ketoacidosis, coma, and in some instances, death. The second type of diabetes, Type II or non-insulin-dependent diabetes mellitus usually occurs after age 40. In these patients, chronic hyperglycemia stems from insulin resistance along with abnormal beta cell activity (Polonsky, 1993). The majority of Type II diabetics are obese. Type II diabetes is estimated to be 7–10 times more prevalent than Type I diabetes (Polonsky, 1993).

Uncontrolled diabetes is associated with a number of other health complications including renal failure, blindness, and cardiovascular disease. A high percentage of diabetic patients do develop serious complications. At the metabolic level, the primary treatment objective is to prevent hyperglycemia by keeping blood glucose levels within the normal range (80–120 mg/dl) (Polonsky, 1993).

Type I diabetics usually take at least one injection of insulin per day, with a number of Type I patients requiring multiple injections per day. For non-insulin-dependent (Type II) patients, weight loss and diet are often used for control along with oral hypoglycemic medications.

Neuropathy is a further complication of diabetes. Typically, this takes the form of loss of sensation as well as paresthesia equally affecting both limbs. In addition, there is often accompanying pain, particularly in the legs (Kornstein & Gardner, 1993).

Diabetic Control

Injectable insulin is the primary treatment for Type I diabetic patients. Oral medication is more common among Type II diabetics. Type I diabetics often require multiple daily injections of insulin. One problem with insulin therapy is that overly high levels of insulin can result in hypoglycemia. These occur when the blood sugar levels become too low. A number of related symptoms occur including increased heart rate, trembling, and lightheadedness. Anecdotally, patients with hypoglycemia have been accused of being drunk because of their confusion, slurred speech, and difficulties with gross motor coordination.

There are two customary methods of monitoring glucose levels. These include daily urine tests that may indicate the presence of ketones associated with significant hyperglycemia. Blood samples obtained through finger pricks are also commonly employed.

Cox and colleagues (1991) note that by about the age of ten, children should be responsible for at least part of their own diabetic self-treatment. At this age, tasks could include performing self-tests of blood or urine and being able to give their own insulin injections. By ages 12–14, teenagers should be able to engage in complete self-care of their illness. One problem with diabetic children and adolescents is that a pattern of overdependence on parental care of the illness often becomes established at younger ages and then continues unabated through adolescence.

Diabetic Compliance

Compliance with medication, exercise, and diet is often problematic among diabetic patients. Kurtz (1990) reports that 80% of patients did not take their insulin in the appropriate manner. Between 35% and 75% of diabetic patients did not adhere to their diet, and over 40% failed to perform urine glucose tests in a regular manner (Kurtz, 1990). Over three-quarters of patients in another study reported that they were noncompliant with their dietary regimen on at least a weekly basis (Christensen, Terry, Wyatt, Pichert, & Lorenz, 1983). Longer term studies suggest that patients have more difficulty maintaining appropriate diet and exercise regimens than adhering to medication and regular testing. However, studies have found that between 10% and 40% of women with insulin-dependent diabetes purposefully miss insulin on a regular basis (Polonsky, 1993). Other data indicate that physicians should view self-reported blood glucose monitoring with some suspicion. When patients used glucometers with built-in memory, it was found that patients often reported taking 30–40% more readings than objective counts indicated (Polonsky, 1993).

Personality and behavioral research indicates that there is not a strong relationship among compliance with various aspects of diabetic regimens. Thus, patients who exercise regularly may not follow dietary recommendations and patients who follow their diet may not administer urine tests regularly. Additionally, glycemic control does not appear to be directly related to patient's knowledge of their illness (Jacobson, Adler, Wolsdorf, Anderson, & Derby, 1990).

Individual Coping Styles among Diabetics

The coping styles of diabetic patients have been classified into three types: adaptive copers, low support–low involvement, and spousal overinvolvement (Nouwen, Gingras, Talbot, & Bouchard, 1997). The adaptive copers tend to regard their diabetes as less disruptive and do not see it as significantly disturbing their daily life. The low support–low involvement patients viewed significant others including spouses as well as health professionals as nonsupportive. These patients also did not see themselves as able to carry out many basic self-care behaviors surrounding diabetes. The spousal overinvolvement group received both appropriately reinforcing actions from others, but also higher levels of "misguided support behaviors" (Nouwen et al., 1997, p. 265). This taxonomy was initially developed on a mixed group of Type I and Type II diabetics and then cross validated with patients with greater than five years of Type II diabetes. Over 85% of the cross-validation sample fit into one of the three categories. Although the implications of these typologies for primary care interventions have not been empirically examined, it is likely that the focus of compliance efforts would vary across the three groups. For example, the spousal overinvolvement group would probably benefit from both nutritional as well as brief marital counseling directed toward increasing supportiveness in a nonintrusive manner.

Social Factors in Diabetic Self-Care and Compliance

The interaction of social support with diabetic compliance is a complex relationship. With children and adolescents, family support and cohesiveness has been related to improved glycemic control and overall compliance. However, among adults, relationships are less direct. Interestingly, reported satisfaction with one's social support network is associated with better glycemic control for non-insulin diabetic women, but not for men. Men who reported greater satisfaction with their social network exhibited poor levels of glycemic control (Kaplan & Hartwell, 1987; Polonsky, 1993).

There have been few systematic studies of the relationship of the health care provider and the diabetic patient. Clinically, there are several communication patterns that are likely to improve diabetic compliance. First, the provider should be very specific about terms such as diet and exercise. For example, telling a patient simply, "You need to exercise" may be translated into a 10-minute walk once per week. Similarly, a recommendation to "decrease your sugar intake" may result in the patient continuing to consume large amounts of sugar-containing beverages while eliminating deserts. Additionally, there are suggestions that physicians should, at each office visit, systematically review and encourage the patient to discuss their blood glucose test results. Patients should be socially reinforced for continuing their testing and bringing this data into the physician. Given the data about poor diabetic compliance described earlier, it is likely that patients engaged in some "impression management" with their physician to prevent disappointing them. Thus, patients may report better adherence to both diet and exercise as well as even falsifying glucose testing data so that the physician will not be disappointed in them. With diabetics and other patients who are on a regular medication regimen, one useful routine question is, "How many times have you missed your medicine in the past week/month?" By asking the question in this way, the episodes of nonadherence are in some respects "normalized" and validity of self-report is enhanced. All health care providers need to recognize that with Type I and with many Type II diabetics, their illness is a long-term chronic condition that can be controlled, but not cured. Health care providers often have difficulties maintaining regular contact and providing ongoing care to patients with chronic conditions because of the absence of "cure." The idea of managing chronic illness is in many respects antithetical to a world view that with science, all disease may be reversed. The health care provider needs to re-orient themselves to the value of small achievable goals and control of symptoms rather than eradication.

Stress, Depression, and Diabetes

Although psychosocial stressors certainly appear to be related to poor glycemic control, the exact relationship between stress and diabetes is not well understood. Laboratory studies have not consistently related autonomic stress to blood glucose (Polonsky, 1993). At the same time, when directly asked, many diabetic patients report significant worries about the future and concern about long-term health consequences, guilt and anxiety regarding managing of their diabetic regimen (Polonsky, 1993), as well as anger about diet and insulin injection. Among adolescents who have been diagnosed with diabetes prior to puberty, there is often anger about being different than peers. This anger may take the form of self-destructive behavior such as refusing to take insulin. A common presentation in the emergency room is the teenager in acute ketoacidosis who has refused insulin. This anger about being different is often intermingled with rebelliousness toward parents and may contribute to diabetic noncompliance. Lastly, beginning heterosexual and dating relationships produces great anxiety around whether the teenager should disclose his or her diabetic status to a boyfriend or girlfriend. Children's diabetic noncompliance may also serve seemingly "benevolent" functions in enmeshed families (Madanes, 1981):

> Renaldo is a 16-year-old Hispanic male, who was diagnosed with Type I diabetes at age 15. His blood sugars are fairly well-controlled. He, however, is not compliant with his diet and frequently consumes large quantities of sweets. Renaldo is referred because of noncompliance with insulin. In addition, he has not attended school for the past 10 days.
>
> Renaldo resides with his mother, a 10-year-old brother and a 6-year-old sister. His parents separated about 3 years ago. His father maintains intermittent contact with the children but does not pay child support. Of note, Renaldo's mother has a history of insulin-dependent diabetes and is currently on insulin. She also has had episodes of significant anxiety. When she becomes anxious, she does not take her insulin and has had to be admitted to the hospital several times. Renaldo reports being a B average student and has been involved in sports and other social activities through school. However, he states that he now feels he needs to stay home to "watch out for mother." He explains that his father's girlfriend keeps calling the house and threatening his mother. Renaldo indicates that he needs to intercept these calls so his mother does not become more anxious and stop taking her insulin again. Jonathan also has been taking more responsibility for his younger siblings. His school attendance has actually been rather sporadic for the past 6 months.
>
> When asked about specific psychiatric symptoms, Renaldo reports being somewhat "tense" but denies any dysphoria. His sleeping and appetite generally appear normal. He denies use of alcohol, nicotine, or other drugs. He states that he has not been taking his insulin for the past week, because "nothing is wrong with me. I feel fine without it. Besides, my mother needs it more than I do."

Clinical depression appears to be fairly common among persons with diabetes. It is estimated that about 20–30% of patients with either Type I or Type II diabetes meet criteria for a major depressive episode (Rouchell, Pounds & Tierney, 1996). Evaluation of depression in diabetic patients is often confounded by symptoms associated with glycemic control. Sexual dysfunction, fatigue, and low energy level may stem from hypoglycemia. Eating disorders also appear to co-exist with diabetes, particularly among adolescents and young adults. Suggestions that an eating disorder may be confounding the clinical picture include rapid weight change, poor or erratic glycemic control, unusually elevated glycosylated hemoglobin values, and distorted body image (Marcus & Wing, 1990).

Antidepressant therapy also appears to be helpful in reducing pain associated with neuropathy. Most available studies have involved tricyclic antidepressants (Kornstein & Gardner, 1993). It is also important to recognize the complicated array of psychological and social factors that are associated with diabetic noncompliance. When patients have exhibited a chronic pattern of noncompliance with medication and diet, the provider should consider the patient's life circumstances. Usually, in these cases, direct education is an inadequate response:

> Mr. Osgood is a 55-year-old White male. He was diagnosed with Type II diabetes about 12 years ago. He was also diagnosed with hypertension about 4 years ago. Mr. Osgood's record indicates a long history of noncompliance with medication since becoming a patient in the clinic about 5 years ago. His blood sugars over the past year have frequently been out of control. He has had multiple hospitalizations over the past 2 years for diabetic noncompliance as well as additional medical problems that include hypertension, angina, and diabetic retinopathy.
>
> By way of social history, Mr. Osgood was divorced in 1990. The couple has a 13-year-old son. He reports his ex-wife continues to harass him for child support. Mr. Osgood worked as a plumber for about 20 years until his vision became worse. He has been on Supplemental Social Security Income since 1991 for complications associated with diabetes. He does report that he has his own computer repair business and works at it sporadically. About 4 years ago, he remarried. His wife has a 10-year-old daughter. Mr. Osgood recently obtained custody of his 13-year-old son by his first marriage. She says that the two children fight with each other "like cats and dogs." He also reports frequent conflict between himself and his new wife. These conflicts center around the children and his ex-wife.
>
> With respect to his medication, Mr. Osgood states he does not "like taking medication" and he frequently stops abruptly. One year ago, he stopped all his medicines for 2 weeks. During the past month, he reports missing about 7 days of his insulin. He says the medicine makes him weak. Review of his record indicates that he provides no consistent reasons for his noncompliance. Reasons are typically vague and include "forgetting," "running out of medicine," or being "too tired." Physicians have repeatedly pointed out to Mr. Osgood that he may eventually require dialysis.
>
> In the psychological interview, Mr. Osgood is very pleasant, respectful, and talkative. He does report dysphoric mood of about 4 months duration. He reports being held overnight in jail after threatening his ex-wife. Mr. Osgood reports intermittent insomnia, frequently staying awake for at least an hour several times a night. This appears to be unrelated to his medical problems. He also reports a sense of helplessness about his medical problems and his domestic situation. He says that "none of my problems are going to change, I am just going to get worse." He also describes a poor appetite and says that he tends to go a day or two with eating very little and then will eat a great deal on the 2nd or 3rd day. He also denies alcohol use. There is no evidence of psychotic behavior.

Mr. Osgood is referred back to his physician for antidepressant medication. He is placed on Zoloft and his sleeping and mood improve. Through psychotherapy, he is able to disengage himself from his family when conflict arises. While this does not eliminate the conflict entirely, Mr. Osgood becomes less reactive to it. In addition, he forms a good relationship with the mental health provider who "holds him accountable" regarding his medication compliance.

Sexual Dysfunction and Diabetes

Sexual dysfunction, particularly erectile dysfunction in men, is a common problem among diabetics. Prevalence rates for diabetic men have been reported to be as high as 50–60% (Cox et al., 1991; Ellenberg, 1983). In nondiabetic men, most instances of erectile dysfunction are attributable to psychological or relationship issues. Organic or neurologic causes are at least partially implicated in erectile dysfunction among Type I diabetics. In reality, the dichotomous distinction between psychological and organic causes of erectile dysfunction is a false dichotomy. Although autonomic neuropathy plays a major role in difficulties obtaining and maintaining an erection, psychological factors that may be secondary to other aspects of diabetes may be involved as well. Usually, erectile difficulties associated with autonomic neuropathy follow a gradual course and develop over a period of months or years. Erections become less frequent and less firm while libido usually remains (Cox et al., 1991). However, there may be an interaction between this array of factors. For example, failing eye sight, depression, and other medical problems associated with diabetes may make the patient feel less interested in sex or less attractive. As the patient begins to notice difficulties with maintaining an erection, performance anxiety may increase, which only makes attaining an erection more difficult.

Among women, sexual dysfunction in diabetes has not been as well studies. There have been suggestions that contrary to expectations, that women with Type II diabetes are more likely to have sexual dysfunction. Thus, it has been suggested that with early onset of Type I diabetes, women may be able to incorporate the disease into their sexual development as well as relationships. The onset of Type II diabetes at a later point in life may create difficulties with self-concept and perceptions of oneself as attractive (Cox et al., 1991).

Diabetes and Eating Disorders

Recently, there has been concern about the relationship between eating disorders among diabetics, particularly in adolescent and young adult women. Research suggests that among diabetic women, there is a significantly greater prevalence of abnormal eating attitudes as assessed by survey instruments (Marcus & Wing, 1990). Even when symptoms that would be influenced directly by diabetes are controlled, there appears to be a much greater concern about the food, body weight, body image, and deliberate efforts to eliminate calories. In the case of diabetics, there appears to be a pattern of reducing insulin doses to achieve this end rather than relying upon vomiting or purging. Diabetic women who appear to have greater eating-disordered behaviors were those that were likely to have gained significant amounts of weight rapidly following their initial diagnosis. One pattern that often occurs is that with the start of treatment, diabetics often re-gain lost weight very quickly because of the effects of insulin and rehydration. For many young women this rapid weight gain is particularly frightening (Steel, Young, Lloyd, & MacIntyre, 1989). This dynamic may be a contributor to the higher level of abnormal eating attitudes among young diabetic women (Marcus & Wing, 1990). In addition, similar to nondiabetics with eating disorders, there is emphasis on food and strong guilt feelings if diets are not followed. It was noted that women with diabetes who had disordered eating were also much more aware of internal states, experience themselves as ineffective, and were less trusting of others. These patterns are also very common among non-diabetic women who have eating disorders (Steel, Young, Lloyd, & MacIntyre, 1989).

There does appear to be a pattern in which patients with eating disorders have a higher incidence of diabetic complications. In particular, elevated glycosylated hemoglobin levels and retinopathy are significantly more common among women with eating disorders. Again, this may reflect self-induced glycosuria, the goal-directed efforts at weight control through reductions in insulin, which is a purging method unique to diabetics. (Franz, 1990). It has been suggested that patients who repeatedly present with elevated hemoglobin A1C levels be evaluated for the possibility of an underlying eating disorder.

OBESITY AND WEIGHT LOSS

In the United States, obesity is becoming a major public health problem. Among persons age 20 and older, 35% of women and 31% of men are overweight. About 25% of children and adolescents are obese (Institute of Medicine, 1995). Although commercial and self-directed weight loss programs abound, the majority of persons who successfully complete them gain two thirds of their weight back in one year, with all of the lost weight usually regained in five years (Institute of Medicine, 1995).

Weight loss is similar to other forms of habit control such as smoking cessation. First, as noted above, weight loss is a difficult goal to achieve, with long-term success being particularly elusive. Second, the majority of people who successfully loose weight do so on their own without a formal program. Third, success requires behavior modification on an individual level and particular reliance on stimulus control strategies. Fourth, the average person who attempts to lose weight through a self-directed program actually initiates a program on the average of 5–10 times before being "successful" (Brownell & Wadden, 1992; Institute of Medicine, 1995; Argas, 1987).

Primary Care Approach to Weight Loss

In primary care settings, the number of contacts with patients who are seeking to lose weight are likely to be limited and each particular contact is likely to be relatively brief. Given these parameters, it will be particularly important that the patient have basic skills that they can employ on a regular basis to reduce high caloric food consumption and increase their exercise or activity level. The provider's communication style around weight loss is particularly important. The optimal message is one that arouses adequate concern on the part of the patient, but does not overwhelm them with anxiety. In addition, concern about weight should be linked to some concrete physical symptoms such as blood pressure, diabetic control, or joint pain. For example saying to the patient, "Your blood pressure, I've noticed, has been high for the last three office visits. There are probably several things that are contributing to your high blood pressure. One of them is your weight. I am wondering if you are concerned about your weight?" One observation that health care providers have made with significantly obese patients (350–400 pounds) is that they frequently verbalize a high degree of denial about the impact of the weight on their health. Patients who are 150–200 pounds overweight will often come to the physician saying, "Doctor, my knees are killing me. You've got to do something about it." Or, "I don't know why, doc, but I get winded so easily just walking up two flights of stairs. It leaves me gasping for air. Why is this happening to me?" When providers hear statements like this from patients who are seriously overweight, it is important that the issue of weight loss be gradually introduced over time. These patients are likely to be extremely well defended. A question that might be helpful in these circumstances is, "I wonder if other doctors or family members have raised the issue of weight loss with you? (pause) What was your reaction?" A direct educative approach is unlikely to be helpful with these patients. A more useful initial approach with these more extreme or intractable cases of obesity is one in which the provider exhibits a curious inquiry.

The most effective weight loss programs are those in which patients meet on a group basis. Workplace-based programs appear to be particularly effective (Institute of Medicine, 1995). However, if the patient is not interested or able in

participating in an organized weight loss program, an individually focused program can be conducted successfully. The first step is having the patient maintain
a food diary. The patient should list what they eat, when they eat it, as well as
quantities consumed (Agras, 1987). It is also helpful to ask patients to briefly
note any mood states or particular stressors that may be associated with overeating. Once the patient has gathered this information for about one to two weeks,
it is important to look for patterns. For example, it may be that a patient con-
sumes 70% of their calories between 5:00 p.m. and 9:00 p.m. This gives the
provider a time frame around which to target reduction in food consumption. The
clinician should also be aware that self-monitoring is inherently reactive. Thus,
the patient who is keeping a food diary may actually reduce their food intake
simply as a result of the process of paying closer attention to their food consumption.

It is important that patients' weight loss programs be tailored to their overall
life style. This is particularly true with exercise, which will usually be necessary
to maintain any weight loss. For example, patients who have always been late
sleepers are, even with the best of intentions, unlikely to start getting up in the
morning at 5:30 to run five miles. For these patients, it is important that they
attempt to embed their exercise routine into their overall life style. For example,
if they like to watch television for several hours in the evening, encourage the
patient to obtain an exercise bicycle that they can ride while watching TV. The less
disruptive exercise, dietary, and other life style alterations to the patient's overall
life pattern, the more likely that these changes will become maintained. Third,
it is important that patients have a short-term self reinforcement plan. Often in
cases of weight loss, the goal is to lose 30 or 40 pounds for the summer swim
season or for a particular event such as a family wedding. These long-term goals,
although useful, are usually inadequate to sustain day-to-day efforts. It is helpful
to encourage the patient to have weekly goals. For example, if they stick to their
diet 80% of the time, they will be able to rent two movies that they like on Friday
night.

The concept of stimulus control is also very important in any habit change
program (Agras, 1987). All habits have environmental cues. Cues for eating are
nearly everywhere. It is important that patients learn about the cues in their particular environment that trigger excessive eating. It is often very difficult for people
on weight reduction programs to linger around the dinner table without continuing to eat. In addition, restaurants featuring "all you can eat buffets" should be
avoided. Patients should be advised to leave the table immediately after eating.
Socialization should be conducted away from food. For many patients, watching
TV is often an environmental cue for eating. In cases of TV viewing, patients are
often unaware of how much they actually are consuming because their attention

is focused on the television. In this case, it would be useful to recommend that the patient engage in another activity during TV time, such as crocheting. It is also helpful to enlist as much social support as possible. Patients should be encouraged to tell family members and friends of their weight reduction and diet program. It is helpful if significant others do not "nag" the patient if they see them not following through with diet or exercise. Simply having told others often times makes the patient acutely self-conscious should they feel like overeating in front of them. This alone is often a significant deterrent. A helpful response from a friend or family member to someone who is embarking on a weight loss program is simply, "How can I help you?" Patients should be encouraged to think about this issue and be able to describe to significant others exactly what types of behavior they would find supportive.

It is extremely important that patients be aware that they are very likely to lapse. Marlatt and Gordon (1985) have emphasized that in nearly all significant life style alterations, including smoking cessation, cessation of alcohol consumption, time management, and regular exercise, change is not an all or nothing process. Habit control occurs gradually with frequent lapses being the rule rather than the exception. It is important that these lapses, however, be contained and not lead to a significant relapse where the individual totally abandons their diet. The following scenario is one that the author presents to family medicine residents who may be trying to lose weight:

> You have been doing a great job with your diet since Sunday. You have stuck to your calorie count. You are feeling very good about your success. Today, though, you had a terrible day. You were on call last night and had to admit seven patients to the hospital. You only got about one hour of sleep. In the office this afternoon, they double-booked you by mistake. You had to see twice as many patients. You finally arrive home to find a certified letter from the student loan company. Apparently, you neglected to inform them about your whereabouts for the past year and they are telling you that you are going to have to pay $50,000 on the spot. Before you know it, you are standing in front of an open refrigerator spraying whipped cream out of an aerosol can directly into your mouth. You wash it down with a can of chocolate syrup. You say to yourself, "Oh, what the hell. I was born to eat. There is no way I can lose weight. Now, where is the number for that pizza delivery company."

Patients need to be prepared for similar experiences. What typically happens is that patients will have one or two episodes like the above and decide that they can't lose weight. In addition, they will not follow up with their physician or other provider because they are too embarrassed. They are afraid of being criticized for failing at their diet.

By alerting patients at the outset to the likelihood that they will lapse, the provider will normalize these experiences when they occur. In addition, when the patient comes into the office after having lapsed, a thorough description of the situation should be obtained (Marlatt & Gordon, 1985). This account will be very helpful in highlighting situations that trigger overeating. It is likely that they will include issues such as fatigue, work stress, or family-related conflicts. Then, the clinician and the patient can together generate a strategy for managing these stressors when the next occur. In addition, patients should be supported for their ability to stop the lapse at any point and prevent relapse from occurring. In the above example, if the call to the pizza delivery company was not made, the patient should be applauded for their ability stop the lapse from escalating further. Even if they had followed through and eaten the pizza, if they were able to get back on their diet the next day, the patient should be reinforced for their ability to gain control. It is important that the provider point this out to patients because in most instances, patients are able to regain control after some period of time. However, when they lapse, patients often make the misattribution that these episodes are "proof" that overeating is outside of their control and that they are "doomed" to obesity.

Commercial Weight Loss Programs

There are relatively few well controlled studies of popular widely advertised weight loss programs. Optifast, Nutri Systems, Overeaters Anonymous, Weight Watchers, and other commercial programs have often been closed to outside investigators. Studies conducted in the early 1980s found that the average person in a commercial weight loss program remained for about 34 weeks with an average weight loss of 19 pounds. However, 50–70% of participants had dropped out by 26 weeks. For those who remain in the program at one year, they were able to keep about half to two thirds of the lost weight off (Institute of Medicine, 1995).

Among formal weight loss programs that are effective, there are several key components that seem to enhance efficacy. In addition to workplace settings, programs that include an active exercise component as well as long-term contact appear to have better outcomes. It is imperative for weight loss programs to have an extended maintenance period after an initial active intervention period. During the maintenance period, participants may come to the program site once a week for a period of about a year. They are weighed and often participate in group discussions (Institute of Medicine, 1995).

Pharmacological Approaches to Weight Loss

People who become obese tend to self-select a diet that exceeds their calorie expenditure (Elks, 1996). There has been considerable research that suggests that most individuals have a "set point" for their weight. One currently popular approach to weight control that is largely based on set point theory is the use of appetite suppressants. It has been suggested that these medications result in re-establishing the set point at a lower level (Elks, 1996). Medications that have been recently employed for weight control include fenfluramine hydrochloride (Pondimin) and phentermine (Ionamin, Fastin). Short-term weight loss rates associated with these medications have exceeded those for placebos. There did appear to be a stabilization of weight loss at 20 to 24 weeks (Elks, 1996). It appears, however, that only about half of the patients who use these medications will be successful. In addition, there have been concerns about the safety of these medications. Several of them have recently been disapproved for weight loss. A high proportion of patients using them dropped out because of the side effects, personal problems with the treatment, or absence of weight loss (Elks, 1996). It is important to recognize that in the absence of life style change including diet and regular exercise, gains associated with appetite suppressant pharmacotherapy do not appear to be maintained (Carek, Sherer, & Carson, 1997). However, because of the significant cardiac risks as well as prevalence of diabetes among patients who are obese, weight loss often is medically necessary, and these medications help achieve an initial significant weight decline. There have been additional concerns about use of appetite-suppressing medications for persons of average weight who wish to become thinner. In particular, women who want to emulate models have been reported anecdotally to be misusing these medications (Elks, 1996).

Developmental Aspects of Disordered Eating

Dieting may be a factor in the development of eating disorders. Among U.S. adolescent girls who diet, about 20% developed an eating disorder within one year of beginning dieting. Girls as young as five or six years of age report being concerned about their eating and weight. Many of 11- to 13-year-olds have attempted to "diet." However, "diet" in this sense is usually rather informal. The goal is to lose about 5–10 pounds. A young teenager or a pre-teen girl would initiate a "diet" in phone conversation with a girl friend. The weight loss plan may be carried over into skipping breakfast in the morning or having a "diet soda" breakfast. This "meal" may be followed by a lunch consisting of splitting a salad with a friend. By late afternoon, however, the teen begins to consume Cokes and candy bars while saying, "I know I should not be eating this, but tomorrow I'm going to go on a diet." Reasons behind this struggle are fueled by social pressure and paradoxical treatment of diet in the media. Teenage magazines often include stories about girls' obsessions with eating and diet that are frequently sandwiched between pictures of anorexic models. Among older adolescent girls (16 and above) dieting is extremely common. Studies have found very high prevalence rates of eating-disordered behavior among high school girls, including bingeing and vomiting at some point.

EATING DISORDERS

Anorexia Nervosa

Anorexia nervosa is characterized by a pattern of refusing to maintain appropriate body weight for one's height and frame. Anorectic patients also exhibit preoccupation and fearfulness regarding weight gain and are similarly preoccupied with the shape or size of their body. Frequently, these patients have distorted perceptions of their body build. The majority of these patients are female. Anorexia nervosa generally has its onset in early adolescence. Overall prevalence according to the *DSM–IV* (1994) is 0.5% to 1.0% in the general adult population. In addition to early onset at around age 14, there appears to be a later period of onset at about age 18. The disorder appears to be primarily found in industrialized societies particular in Western cultures such as the United States and Europe. Anorexia nervosa has a number of medical complications including anemia, cardiac problems, and disturbances in electrolytes (*DSM–IV*, 1994).

Anorexia nervosa probably has a multifactorial etiology. Many clinical commentators have emphasized the cultural value placed on thinness among young women. Family theorists have emphasized the role of interaction patterns. In clinical settings, Minuchin et al. (1978) described families of anorectic young women as highly enmeshed. Disagreements were seen as unacceptable and even low levels of conflict were avoided. It has also been suggested that these families have exhibited a high degree of perfectionism. One of the striking aspects of Minuchin's characterization is that the families tended to have little recognition of the role of family issues in their daughter's extreme weight loss because they viewed themselves as a "all-American family" that was free of any discord.

With respect to personality dynamics, anorectic patients are often compulsive and perfectionistic with strong needs for control. Additionally, there is often a history of being mildly overweight (Hall, 1996).

Bulimia

Like anorexia, bulimia is a disorder found predominantly among young women concerned about their weight. Criteria include binge eating and "inappropriate compensatory behavior" twice a week for a period of three months (*DSM–IV*, 1994). Binge eating on the part of bulimics tends to include high-calorie food that is consumed rapidly and in secret. The patient will often consume food until they are nauseous and then will induce vomiting (*DSM–IV*, 1994). In addition to vomiting, which is the most common method of purging, patients will also use laxatives and diuretics. Lastly, these patients may engage in exercise for of up to four to five hours a day.

The majority of young women with bulimia nervosa are of average weight. There are suggestions that in the past, some of them have been overweight. However, there also seems to be a pattern in which anorexia nervosa may develop into bulimia in later adolescence and young adulthood.

Bulimia's prevalence ranges from 1% to close to 19% of young adult women. It appears to be significantly higher among college women. Prevalence rates approaching 20% have often been found among female college students. (Drewnowski, Hopkins, & Kessler, 1988; Freund, Graham, Lesky, & Moskowitz, 1993).

Bulimic behavior may not be obvious. Unlike anorexia, women who have bulimia are very secretive about their abnormal eating and purging patterns. Two questions, "Do you ever eat in secret?" and "Are you satisfied with your eating patterns?" were found to have very good sensitivity and specificity in a hospital-based primary care practice (Freund et al., 1993). Given the fairly high prevalence among college-age women, it is recommended that these questions be included in standard clinical interviews within this demographic group. Additional clues to the possibility of bulimic behavior should be abdominal pain, gastrointestinal bleeding associated with tears in the esophagus, electrolyte imbalances, and pancreatitis (Freund et al., 1993).

The current understanding of bulimia suggests that these patients—who are predominantly young woman—have issues regarding security and nurturance. Often families are disengaged and nonsupportive. The bingeing behavior is seen as a way of obtaining basic nurturance that is under the patient's control. Independence/dependence is core conflict among these young women. This tension makes it difficult for them to engage in treatment because they, at some level, have to be dependent on the provider:

> Ms. Shannon is a 25-year-old White woman referred by the emergency room physician. She presented in the emergency with light-headedness and a recent episode of passing out. It was noted that she had been dehydrated secondary to self-induced vomiting. Additional symptoms that she reports include stomach pains, rapid heart rate, chest pain, bleeding throat, weakness, and constipation. Ms. Shannon says she has headaches almost constantly as well as low blood pressure. She stated that this is the fifth time in the past two months that she has passed out. This most recent episode happened at work and she was brought to the emergency room by coworkers.
>
> Ms. Shannon is 5'3" tall and weighs 120 pounds, although, she reports her weight as 110. Ms. Shannon reports that she views herself as overweight and says for the past five years she has engaged in self-induced vomiting. She currently vomits about twice per day. Ms. Shannon states she has used laxatives in the past and is currently using over-the-counter diet pills and various diuretics. She reports that she will go up to two days without a meal and will also exercise up to three hours per day.
>
> Ms. Shannon indicates that she is currently working as a secretary. She left school during the eleventh grade to take a modeling position. However, she turned it down

because she did not want to leave her community. Ms. Shannon's parents continue to live together, although their relationship is described as very conflictual. Ms. Shannon states that she alternates in terms of closeness, "sometimes I am tight with my dad and other times I am close with my mom. I am never close to both of them at the same time though." Ms. Shannon has lived with several boyfriends over the past seven years. At present she is living with her parents after recently breaking up with a boyfriend.

Ms. Shannon indicates that she is sleeping only about four hours per night and that this has been her pattern for about two years. She describes frequent mood swings including angry and irritable outbursts. She reports periodic suicidal ideation. Two years ago she indicated that she took an overdose of Tylenol. She has self-inflicted burns on the inside of her arms. She denies any drug or alcohol use. She states she has been on antidepressant medication in the past but stopped it because "I don't like medicine having control over me."

As indicated by the above case, patients with eating disorders often have serious medical as well as psychiatric concerns (Herzog & Copeland, 1985). In this case, the patient appears to have a number of indicators of borderline personality disorder. This is likely to make successful treatment particularly difficult. In addition, she places a high reliance on self-control and has had a history of poor relationships with others. These are all likely to make developing a successful therapeutic alliance with Ms. Shannon particularly challenging.

There is also evidence of a relationship between bulimia and other addictive behavior including drug and alcohol abuse. Up to one third of bulimics in a recent survey met criteria for alcohol problems based on the CAGE screening. (Freund et al., 1993).

Treatment of Anorexia and Bulimia

Among anorexics, immediate treatment focuses on weight gain. As outpatients, anorexics should gain about one half to two pounds per week until a weight goal has been met. If weight gain occurs more quickly, there is a possibility of cardiac failure (Rome, 1996). A nutritional consultation should also be included. The patients themselves should take the responsibility for the meal plan in order to reduce parental conflicts. Some patients also become anxious around eating solid foods and may have difficulty swallowing. Liquid supplements would be useful in these cases (Rome, 1996). Behavioral intervention with short-term rewards for weight gain should be part of the treatment plan.

With mild cases of bulimia and anorexia, the primary care mental health specialist should conduct a thorough assessment with particular attention to the degree of control that the patient experiences over their disordered eating and weight as well as the presence of family support. In addition, the clinician should carefully attend to the probable presence of other psychiatric disorders including substance abuse and depression, which if present, are likely to place serious limits on treatment efficacy. If the complicating factors are treated and under control or are absent, the mental health professional may begin the treatment combining cognitive behavioral as well as structurally oriented family therapy. However, this treatment should occur in conjunction with a primary care physician as well as nutritionist. If improvement is not made fairly rapidly, a referral to a specialized eating-disorder program should be seriously considered.

Specialized treatment may be necessary for anorexia because the disorder tends to have life-threatening complications fairly quickly. Anorectic patients may require treatment in an inpatient facility until adequate weight is gained and cardiac status is stable.

Long-term outcome studies of anorexic patients indicate that this disorder is frequently chronic. As follow-up times increase, the numbers of patients who are both cured and eventually die increase as well. Mortality rates are 1% after 6 years and 18% after 33 years. Highest rates of recovery tend to occur between the second and sixth year of follow up. Overall recovery rates do not appear to exceed 20% per year (Herzog, Schellberg, & Deter, 1997). There are suggestions that bulimia is more difficult to treat than anorexia. Patients are generally older and have longer periods of bulimic behavior before coming to treatment. Both bulimics and anorexics tend to exhibit significant cognitive distortion. As noted, bulimics are generally older and are probably more likely to be responsive to a cognitive therapy approach. There does tend to a be a "superstitious" quality to these patients' thought processes around food ("If I eat two pieces of bread I won't be able to stop and I will just continue to get bigger and bigger." or "Since I have already eaten this bag of french fries, I am off my diet. I have no control and I might as well eat three hamburgers.") (Muscari, 1996). For bulimics who engage in bingeing, the patient should have their eating restricted to one room of the house so that hiding food around the house is less likely to occur. Additionally, patients should be taught the affective states associated with bulimic behavior and taught to substitute other behaviors. These should be selfnurturing acts such as watching a movie, taking a walk, or a hot bath. It should also be pointed out to the patient that the urge to binge is time-limited, although it does recur. The patient should be taught strategies to get through this very difficult period with the recognition that the intensity of the desire to binge will decline. Patients who have more intractable bulimia will require specialized treatment. However, Fairburn and colleagues (Fairburn & Peveler, 1990; Fairburn et al., 1995) have developed primary care treatment approaches for bulimia. Their model focuses on modified cognitive behavioral therapy that can be conducted by a nurse specialist or primary care physician. Sessions are about 20 minutes in length, and patients are seen for a total of eight weekly sessions. Patients are educated about the role of maladaptive cognitions as they contribute to binge eating. In a small study, 6 of 11 patients who were treated through this model were found to have substantially improved eating. Fairburn has also developed a self-help model that is based on cognitive behavioral therapy. Patients move through a self-help text over three to four months. The patients keep rigorous food consumption records. The patient's progress is reviewed in six to eight sessions occurring over the three to four month period. Each contact involves reviewing records as well as identifying problems that arose and helping the patient to identify potential solutions as well as providing general support to continue the self-help modules. Although these studies involving relatively brief and limited contact with providers are somewhat promising, most data with eating disorders has been less optimistic (Campbell & Patterson, 1995).

Treatment of bulimia and anorexia nervosa is usually a long-term process conducted by specialists. A study conducted by Dare and colleagues (Dare, Eisler, Russell, & Szmukler, 1990) followed patients for up to a year and employed both family and individual therapy. It was found that the younger anorectic patients with briefer duration of symptoms did better with family than individual treatment. Anorectic patients with a longer duration of illness as well as bulimic patients did not demonstrate as much improvement as the younger anorectic group. In particular, the older bulimic patients had the poorest outcome, and there did not seem to be any particular advantage for individual or family therapy. The provider should keep in mind that many bulimic patients have had active symptomatology for many years prior to seeking assistance.

CONCLUSION

Behavioral and psychological factors have a significant impact on exacerbation and treatment of illnesses involving metabolic control. Obesity and early stages of disordered eating are risk factors for Type II diabetes as well as indirect contributors to gastrointestinal problems, electrolyte imbalance, and hypertension. The mental health professional's role varies considerably in the illnesses discussed in this chapter. For diabetics, detection and treatment of depression and adjustment problems can be readily conducted in the primary care setting. Behavioral intervention for diet and obesity is also generally problem-focused and time-limited. Although early stages of anorexia nervosa and bulimia may be treated by the generalist mental health practitioner, more significant symptoms of longer duration will require referral to a specialized eating disorders program.

Chapter 9

Psychosocial Aspects of Infectious Disease

There are a number of illnesses arising from viral, bacterial, fungal, or parasitic organisms. The transmission of these organisms is often associated with behavioral factors. Life style changes, such as use of condoms among those at risk for sexually transmitted diseases or compliance with medication regimens, play a major role in prevention and treatment of infectious diseases. In addition, those diagnosed with infectious diseases such as AIDS may develop psychiatric illnesses that influence their successful coping with the illness. Lastly, some infectious diseases affect the central nervous system. In some cases, behavioral or cognitive changes are the initial symptom of an infectious process that brings the patient to a physician. (Summergrad, Rauch, & Neal 1993).

HUMAN IMMUNODEFICIENCY VIRUS (HIV/AIDS)

Epidemiology

It is estimated that up to 1.5 million people in the United States are currently infected with HIV (Rubin, 1988; Osmond, 1994). Each year, about 5% to 10% of these individuals develop frank AIDS (Mann, Tarantola, & Netter, 1992). AIDS is currently the second leading cause of death for young adult men and the sixth leading cause of death for young adult women in the United States (MacQueen, 1994).

In the early days of the epidemic, gay males and intravenous drug users were the primary HIV risk groups. However, recently, the incidence of new cases among gay males has leveled off, and the greatest rates of increase are among women and drug users. Sexual transmission of HIV occurs much more readily from males to females than vice versa (Pizzi, 1992). About one third of HIV-positive women become infected through sexual contact with infected males (MacQueen, 1994). Intravenous drug users constitute about 25% of reported AIDS cases, with 5% to

10% of these individuals being male intravenous drug users who have sex with other men (MacQueen, 1994).

HIV Counseling and Testing

Most mental health professionals have seen patients who have expressed concern about their risk for HIV (Berger, Handal, Searight, & Katz, 1998). In the United States, about one third of adults have been tested for HIV. However, it is important to recognize that nearly half of U.S. adults who have established HIV risk factors have not undergone serological testing (O'Connel, 1993; Searight & McLaren, 1997).

Patients who describe HIV risk behavior such as multiple sexual partners, casual sexual contacts, or drug use are at elevated risk for HIV infection. It is also important for the practitioner to recognize that several of these factors interact and amplify risk. For example, patients who have nonmonogamous sex under the influence of drugs are likely to elevate their risk through decreased use of condoms and increased high-risk sexual practices such as receptive anal sex.

In evaluating HIV risk, it is important that the interviewer adopt a nonjudgmental, neutral stance toward the interview content. As a general rule, it is most helpful to proceed from less sensitive to more sensitive issues. Thus, asking the patient about their current relationships and social support should precede discussion of specific sexual or drug use practices. It is also important that the interviewer avoid "trait-like" labels in conducting the interview. Thus, rather than asking the patient if they are "gay or straight," patients should be asked: "Do you have sex with men, women, or both?" There are a significant proportion of self-identified heterosexuals who have same-sex sexual contact and would not be identified if terms like "gay" or "straight" were employed (Searight & McLaren, 1997). Similarly, rather than asking "Are you promiscuous or do you have sex with a large number of people?" the interviewer should ask for more specific data such as: "How many sexual partners have you had in the past five years?" Lastly, rather than using the label "prostitution," it is more helpful to ask: "Have you ever had sex in exchange for money or drugs?" (Kassler & Wu, 1992; O'Connel, 1993).

Some patients will be specifically requesting HIV testing. It is always helpful to use this request as an opportunity for further education. These patients should be asked specifically about their reasons for requesting HIV testing. Forstein (1990) suggests that HIV testing be conducted with a similar informed consent procedure as any medical test. He notes that HIV testing has benefits but also is accompanied by psychological risks.

Mental health professionals will readily recognize that a patient's response to a positive test result is likely to be influenced by their premorbid psychological adjustment. Thus, if possible, patients should undergo a psychosocial interview with particular attention to their previous psychiatric status. Patients with pre-existing mental health histories or current evidence of psychiatric illness are much more likely to have difficulty coping with a positive test result.

In addition to gathering this information, it has been strongly recommended that patients be asked directly prior to testing about their reaction to the result: "What will be your reaction if the test is positive?" or "What behaviors will you change if the test is negative?" (Searight & McLaren, 1997).

There does appear to be a high rate of premorbid psychiatric disorder among persons seeking HIV testing. These include mood disorders as well as personality disorders (Wyszynski & Wyszynski, 1996). Of particular interest are studies that indicate that despite preconceptions, suicidal ideation does not increase after notification of a positive HIV test result. Although suicidal ideation predictably decreased in the week following notification among sero-negative patients, it did not significantly increase among those who were sero-positive (Perry, Jacobsberg, & Fishman, 1990). Of particular note was that two months later, suicidal ideation had declined in a sero-positive sample. Thus, it appears to be that it is not knowing about one's HIV status that is associated with elevated psychological distress. However, at the same time, about 15% of both sero-positive and sero-negative patients continued to manifest significant suicidal ideation (Perry et al., 1990; Perry et al., 1993). It also appears that patients who suspect themselves to be HIV positive who have their suspicion confirmed through testing are more likely to reduce high-risk behavior, whereas those who test negative do not make significant changes (Forstein, 1990).

Psychiatric Disorders among HIV-Positive Patients

Within the last 5–10 years, there has been a developing literature on mental health problems of patients who are HIV-positive or who have developed frank AIDS. There are suggestions that HIV-positive individuals may have a greater prevalence of premorbid psychiatric disturbance (Searight & McLaren, 1997). Disorders commonly found among these patients include major depression, bipolar illness with particularly pronounced prevalence of manic episodes, substance abuse, and personality disorders.

As studies continue to accrue, there is evidence that when gay men are compared with matched groups in the general population, there may not be a greater prevalence of depressive illness among these with HIV (Johnson, Williams, Rabkin, Goetz, & Remien, 1995). However, there are several difficulties in accurate diagnosis of depression among HIV-positive patients. There is evidence that AIDS patients exhibit subtle cognitive symptoms. It may be that these symptoms are misinterpreted as indicative of depression. Certainly, in cases of AIDS dementia, which will be discussed below, the symptoms of apathy, social withdrawal, and decreased cognitive efficiency can be readily confused with symptoms of depression. It is, however, a mistake to view depression as a "normal" reaction to an HIV-positive test result or the development of frank AIDS. As noted earlier, depression is not a "natural" reaction to a diagnosis of a life-threatening chronic illness. Failure to adequately evaluate and treat depression adversely impacts the ill patient's quality of life.

There have been several studies examining the relationship of depression and immune status. There were concerns that the presence of depression or significant life events could result in alterations in CD4 and CD8 cell counts in those patients with already compromised immune systems. Overall, there does not appear to be a consistent relationship between immune status and the presence of depression. However, this association may be mediated by factors such as the clinical course of the illness and practical difficulties linking mood disorder symptoms and stressful life events to immunological functioning (Wyszynski & Wyszynski, 1996).

Although early reports of suicidal ideation among patients with HIV spectrum disease reported extremely high rates (Marzuk et al., 1988), recent studies have reported a much lower rate. However, the base rate for suicide among HIV-positive men does appear to be about seven times that of noninfected males (Searight & McLaren, 1997).

One finding that is emerging with consistency is that rates of mania appear to be significantly higher among patients who have AIDS. Prevalence rates for AIDS patients have ranged from 2.5% up to 30% (Searight & McLaren, 1997) compared with a 1% prevalence rate in the general population. Possible explanations have included the impact of the disease on the central nervous system as well as possible side effects of medications that are used to treat AIDS-related illnesses.

Personality disorders appear to be common among patients who are being tested for HIV as well as among HIV-positive persons. In one study, about one third of HIV-positive gay males exhibited evidence of personality disorder compared with 15% of HIV-negative gay men (Perkins, Davidson, Lesserman, Liao, & Evans, 1993). Borderline personality was a common diagnosis among these patients. The sexual practices of patients with borderline personality include a number of behaviors elevating risk for HIV infection (Zubenko, George, Soloff & Schulz, 1987). In addition, personality disorder patients are more likely to use maladaptive coping styles such as denial and helplessness (Wyszynski & Wyszynski, 1996). Lastly, the presence of a personality disorder, often together with an Axis I syndrome such as major depression or substance abuse, increases the likelihood of high-risk behavior among those who are HIV-positive. These patients present particularly difficult ethical dilemmas in the mental health sector. (Searight & Pound, 1994).

Substance abuse is a primary risk factor for HIV. Although considerable attention has been focused on needle sharing among intravenous users, it should be recognized that non-IV drugs such as cocaine or alcohol increase the potential for high risk sexual behavior. Non-IV users are much more likely to engage in trading sex for drugs, have more sexual partners, and use drugs such as amphetamines or cocaine to amplify sexual arousal (Searight & McLaren, 1997).

Reports of acute psychosis among HIV-positive patients have also emerged. It is likely that this is attributable to encephalopathy and is less likely to be a "functional" psychotic illness (Searight & McLaren, 1997). It is important to recognize that the chronically mentally ill such as those with schizophrenia engage in a number of high risk behaviors for HIV transmission. One study of chronically mentally ill patients found that a very high percentage engaged in trading sex for money, drugs, or a place to stay. Additionally, 20% of the subjects had met their sexual partners in public settings such as in the street or in parks. About one third had been treated for sexually transmitted diseases other than HIV infection (Kelly, Murphy, & Bahr, 1992). These patients' high risk behavior raises particularly troublesome legal and ethical issues in hospital or group living settings:

> A 35-year-old male is admitted to an impatient psychiatric facility with suicidal ideation. The patient had just learned that his wife was diagnosed with AIDS. The patient and his wife report a history of IV drug use. In addition they indicate that they are "swingers" and engage in heterosexual and homosexual sex with other couples. On the psychiatric ward, the patient is observed to be developing romantic relationships with several of the female patients.

Sexual contact between hospitalized psychiatric patients, although often discouraged, is not uncommon. Macklin (1991) notes that staff often consider these relationships to be inappropriate. A major issue is that the patient may be having unprotected sex with other patients without notifying them of his HIV risk and subsequent positive status. The issue for hospital staff is centered around whether they should notify other patients and if so, which patients? Should all patients be notified or only those that the infected patient has been seen with? A further concern was whether this forced disclosure would only intensify the patient's depression and suicidal thoughts. Other staff members suggested "quarantining" the patient in a locked room on the unit. The patient's capacity for responsible sexual behavior was questionable. However, it is unclear specifically who should be warned.

AIDS Dementia

As AIDS became more common, it became apparent that a number of patients presented with cognitive symptoms. Patients who were often nonsymptomatic in other respects, described difficulties with decision-making, a general "slowing" of cognitive processes, difficulty with maintaining a focus of concentration, and short-term memory difficulties. In addition, patients or those around them would report apathy and personality changes. Some of these patients exhibited acquired fine motor coordination problems and tremors (Wyszynski & Wyszynski, 1996). After the patients were tested and it was established that they had an HIV-positive test result, it was often thought that many of these symptoms were associated with emotional reactions to the illness. However, over time, it has become well-established that AIDS affects the central nervous system. AIDS dementia complex (ADC) appears to occur in about 7% of patients with the illness. However, about 20% of patients with AIDS appear to exhibit at least minor cognitive impairment (Wyszynski & Wyszynski, 1996).

AIDS dementia is a subcortical dementia and, as such, presents differently than the "classical" dementias of Alzheimer's type. In contrast to cortical dementias such as Alzheimer's, the symptoms of AIDS dementia are more subtle. Gross mental status evaluations such as the minimental state examination often do not detect existing impairment among patients with AIDS dementia complex. Instead, tasks assessing speeded information processing and cognitive flexibility, such as the Trailmaking Test, are probably more sensitive to the impairment associated with ADC. A useful screening test assessing cognitive flexibility among AIDS patients has been described by Jones, Teng, Folstein, & Harrison (1993). This is a timed test in which the patient is asked to count from 1 to 20, then recite the alphabet, and finally say letters and numbers in an alternating pattern (i.e., 1-A, 2-B, 3-C, etc.). The total score is based on the number of correct pairs verbalized in 30 seconds. A cut-off score of 15 has fairly good sensitivity and reasonable specificity.

One current ongoing controversy centers around whether asymptomatic HIV-positive patients exhibit subtle cognitive impairment. Presently, findings are inconsistent. However, when these deficits do occur, cognitive changes appear to be fairly subtle and appear to have little impact on patient's social functioning (Wyszynski & Wyszynski, 1996).

Treatment Issues

Research suggests that the mental health of HIV-positive men is enhanced through available social support, including emotional sensitivity as well as concrete assistance such as money and transportation. A patient's sense of connectedness—feeling that they belong and are not isolated—appears to enhance well-being (Montauk & Gebhardt, 1997).

Among women with HIV, family issues and diminished energy level appear to be primary concerns (Montauk & Gebhardt, 1997) Case management and attention to practical issues such as the children's future guardianship as well as disclosure of diagnosis to partners, extended family members, and children are areas that should be addressed with these women.

Psychotherapy that includes attention to the patient's premorbid psychological functioning should address both pragmatic and "psychodynamic" concerns. Pragmatic issues include safe sex guidelines, disclosure of the illness to significant others and family, future educational/career planning, and advanced health care directives. In particular, enhancing patients' use of their current support network or helping them develop a support network is helpful. Group psychotherapy has been found to be a useful treatment modality for these patients (Fawzy, Namir, & Wolcott, 1989). Clinically ill patients who undergo group therapy have been found to exhibit decreased emotional stress, better health status, and even longer survival time. A particularly helpful emphasis with severe illness such as AIDS includes a supportive–expressive treatment focus. In this model, emotional expression of thoughts and feelings, improved group support, and development of coping strategies are salient therapeutic processes. In addition, patients are encouraged to focus on current and future events rather than rehearsing the past (Spira & Spiegel, 1993). Behaviorally oriented coping skills such as relaxation training, stress reduction, and pain management may be a useful addition.

Psychotropic medications for AIDS patients have been discussed in some detail (Searight & McLaren, 1997). For depression, selective serotonin reuptake inhibitors are probably the psychopharmacology of choice. They have fewer side effects, and because of concern about suicide, these medications are less likely to be toxic in overdose. Stimulant medications such as methylphenidate (Ritalin) have been recommended for patients who exhibit significant cognitive impairment or are highly apathetic. Anxiety in HIV-infected patients often is effectively managed with Lorazepam (Ativan) or Alprazolam (Xanax).

Ethical and Legal Issues

Those working with HIV-positive patients are likely to confront a number of ethical and legal issues. At present, there is no known cure for AIDS. Thus, at some point, patients will have to address end-of-life issues. Research suggests that patients with AIDS want to review life-sustaining treatment options and code status. However, at the same time, these patients report that their physicians often do not raise these issues with them (Fogel & Mor, 1993). Although the specific medical treatments available late in life should be addressed with the patient by their physician, the mental health professional can help the patient review options in the context of their particular values. It is important that these discussions should be carried out prior to the onset of serious illness. Later in the illness course, the presence of AIDS dementia and its impact on attention and concentration as well as memory are likely to impair the patient's ability to formulate plans. There is also some evidence that depression may interact with patient decision-making around these issues.

Depression does play a moderate role in patients' desire for aggressive medical treatment. For example, Fogel and Mor (1993) found that among AIDS patients, fewer than 10% were accepting of a respirator and less than 20% accepted a nursing home. The presence of depression increased their rates of nonacceptance somewhat and the alleviation of depression reduced rejection of options. However, among patients with other chronic illnesses, patients with more severe levels of depression do appear to change their wishes in the direction of more aggressive treatment after mood disorder symptoms have been alleviated (Ganzini, Lee, Heintz, Bloom, & Fenn 1994).

Most mental health professionals are well aware of their duty to inform potential victims when a patient makes a specific threat. This warning, the Tarasoff Standard, is usually implemented in cases when a patient threatens physical harm to another and will be discussed in a later chapter. Some states have legislated a duty to warn when an HIV-positive patient is engaging in high-risk behavior toward a known party (Searight & Pound, 1994). Although most jurisdictions require patients who test positive to be reported to the local health department, notification may not be adequate as a warning:

> Mr. Bullock is a hospitalized 26-year-old African-American gay man who sustained a broken leg, concussion, and lacerations in a car accident. He reports that he was found to be HIV-positive about 18 months ago but is currently asymptomatic. Laboratory tests confirm the patient's HIV status. Immediately before the accident, the patient and his lover of 3 months had been drinking and having an argument. Mr. Bullock stormed out of the house and began driving while intoxicated. The patient reported that he and his lover would typically consume 3–5 mixed drinks per night. However, Mr. Bullock did not consider his drinking to be problematic and refused an evaluation from the substance abuse treatment program. He indicated that the auto accident occurred when he angrily left the house after learning that his lover had had a one-night affair with another man.
>
> Mr. Bullock stated that he had informed his partner of his HIV status. When asked about their sexual practices, the patient indicated that they used condoms "most of the time" and usually had sex after drinking "quite a bit." The patient said that periodically his partner would want to have sex without condoms and that he would agree. In talking with Mr. Bullock's lover, all of the information was confirmed. A conjoint interview indicated a high degree of conflict in the relationship.

The legal and ethical obligation to inform the patient's partner had already been fulfilled by the patient himself. The partner's current HIV-status was reportedly negative. However, he was putting himself and others at risk through unprotected sex with the patient. In addition, the extensive use of alcohol by the couple is likely to impair judgment and consistent use of "safe sex" practices. However, other than recommending substance abuse or psychiatric treatment, other preventive courses of action are unclear.

As noted earlier, patients with personality disorders, schizophrenia, and disinhibition associated with more advanced AIDS dementia may not self-regulate their behavior. In these circumstances and when the patient poses a risk to an identifiable person, it may be necessary to break confidentiality. The American Medical Association has suggested that providers engage in a specific protocol in this situation. Initially, the provider should attempt to persuade the patient to stop high-risk activities. If the patient appears to be responsible and rational and agree to cease behavior placing others at risk, the obligation has probably been fulfilled but should be documented in the record. If a patient cannot be persuaded to stop high-risk actions, the health department should be notified, if this notification has not already occurred. (As stated earlier, in many states, HIV-positive test results must be reported to the state or county health departments.) If the health department does not take appropriate action, confidentiality can be further abrogated and an identifiable person at risk can be notified. Ideally, this should be done collaboratively with the patient (Council on Ethical and Judicial Affairs, 1987).

CHRONIC FATIGUE SYNDROME

Fatigue is a common presenting problem in primary care. Many patients report tiredness, weariness, lethargy, and a lack of motivation (Ruffin & Cohen, 1994). Chronic fatigue syndrome is a controversial disorder. The disease has been described as resulting from infectious, psychiatric, and environmental causes. To achieve a diagnosis of chronic fatigue syndrome (CFS), fatigue should be persistently present for at least six months. Additionally, in CFS, bed rest does not improve functioning, and average daily activity level is reduced by at least 50% (Holmes, Kaplan, & Gantz, 1988). Chronic fatigue patients exhibit fever/chills, sore throat, muscle weakness, lymph node pain, headache, arthralgia, and neuropsychiatric symptoms including forgetfulness, irritability, difficulty concentrating, and depression. Sleep disturbance, either involving excessive or decreased sleeping, is also common. The onset of chronic fatigue syndrome is usually associated with a significant viral illness or episode of some type. In primary care settings, studies have found that up to 24% of patients present with fatigue as being one of the primary reasons for their office visit (Kroenke, Wood, & Mangelsdorff, 1988).

Etiological explanations for CFS include the following models: infectious disease, immune disorder, sleep disorder, muscle disorder, psychiatric disorder, and sociocultural phenomenon (Anfinson, 1995). Infection has been one of the most commonly described causes. Several viral etiologies have been suggested in this regard. Other explanations include environmental or food allergies as well as abnormalities of the immune system (Anfinson, 1995). Studies conducted by mental health professionals have highlighted a high degree of depression and somatization disorder among chronic fatigue patients. However, it has also been noted that there do seem to be some differences with respect to symptom presentation as well as possible immune functioning among chronic fatigue syndrome patients and those with major depression. The high incidence of depression among chronic fatigue patients may be attributable to the overlap between chronic fatigue symptoms and those of depression as well as the likelihood that chronic fatigue syndrome may result in depression.

In patients with chronic fatigue syndrome, there are some features that tend to make it distinct from common presentations of major depression: the degree of dysphoria or sadness is often less; there is an absence of suicidal ideation or intent; the patient tends not to be guilt-ridden; the degree of helplessness and pessimism is usually not as pronounced; poor premorbid social and occupational functioning is less common; and cognitive difficulties with memory and concentration are somewhat more commonly reported. Chronic fatigue patients are also much more likely to describe their syndrome as occurring relatively abruptly after a viral illness (Anfinson, 1995; Ruffin & Cohen, 1994).

Chronic fatigue highlights the observation that across cultures, symptoms may have very different meanings. Depressed patients from Asian cultures as well as some patients from Arab cultures may present with fatigue rather than clear-cut (DSM–IV) depressive symptoms. These patients may not experience dysphoric mood or anhedonia, but instead experience chronic tiredness. In mainland China for example, Chairman Mao's dictum is still often heeded: mental illness is not an illness—only wrong political thinking (Kleinman, 1988). In cultures such as mainland China, mental illness historically has carried a strong stigma. Kleinman (1988) has noted that neurasthenia, a disorder similar to chronic fatigue syndrome, is a medical diagnosis that is very common in mainland China. Kleinman points out that it has similar consequences as mental illness in western culture. Patients with neurasthenia may receive disability benefits or an easier job assignment, and may even be permitted to move to the countryside where it is "less stressful." He notes that a neurasthenia diagnosis gives a sense of control in a society in which many people do not individually determine their destiny. It is also interesting to note that in mainland China, fatigue patients are viewed by both traditional and nontraditional practitioners similarly to how many chronic pain patients are viewed in the United States. Kleinman (1988) points out that even herbalists and acupuncturists tend to have poor outcomes with them.

Regardless of the etiological model adopted, the importance of obtaining a thorough psychosocial history with these patients cannot be understated. These patients are likely to have many arenas of their life disrupted by their symptoms. The growing recognition of the synergy between psychosocial and biomedical factors among these patients makes it particularly difficult to classify the disorder as a physiological versus psychological (Ruffin & Cohen, 1994).

In intervening with these patients, it is important for the practitioner to approach these patients similarly to other patients with chronic illnesses. In this regard, improved functioning, rather than cure, is a good outcome. Similar to chronic pain patients, it is helpful to set modest goals of improved activity level rather than return to premorbid functioning. Patients should be encouraged to increase their activity level on a gradual basis. For example, they may initially be instructed to walk for five minutes per day every day with a one-minute increase in walking time each week. Additionally, patients' cognitive distortions should be challenged. Many chronic fatigue patients will say "I am tired; I have been doing too much." The clinician should gently challenge this assumption by pointing out that they may be tired because they have become less active (Anfinson, 1995). The cycle of deconditioning in which patients exercise less and then feel more fatigued should be pointed out to them. In addition, patients should be encouraged to maintain their daily regimen of exercise regardless of how they feel. When patients say, "I can't do this because I don't feel like it," the practitioner should respond with, "I understand you don't feel like it, but it is important to do it anyway."

It is also important to have care centralized for these patients. The mental health provider should be working closely with the primary care physician. All patient referrals to specialists as well as requests for medical testing should be directed to the primary care physician. Centralizing care will reduce the tendency of these patients to continue to search for an elusive diagnosis. Antidepressant medication should also be seriously considered. It is important when introducing the idea of antidepressant medication to these patients that pharmacotherapy be described as an adjunctive treatment. Thus, the practitioner may emphasize to the patient that the antidepressant medication will help some with sleeping, appetite, and perhaps with some improvement in energy. It will also be less threatening to the patient if the depression is "connected" to chronic fatigue in a similar manner as chronic pain or somatoform symptoms are linked to psychiatric illness. ("Certainly, with the long-time fatigue that you have been experiencing, it is likely that your mood, motivation, and relations with others have all been affected.")

It is important for the clinician to recognize that CFS patients are very likely to adhere to a biomedical explanation for their symptoms. Similar to patients with somatization disorder, chronic fatigue patients are often not open to psychological perspectives on their illness.

CONCLUSION

Although infectious diseases have traditionally been seen as unrelated to psychological and behavioral dimensions, the AIDS epidemic has made this distinction obsolete. Acquisition and transmission of HIV or other sexually transmitted diseases, and even tuberculosis, are strongly affected by cultural norms, cognitive appraisal of risk, and comorbid psychiatric illness. These discussions raise ethical and legal questions that many mental health professionals have addressed in other contexts, such as violence and abuse. Chronic fatigue syndrome is a relatively new, continually evolving, entity in which the mental health professional may play an important part in the assessment of psychiatric illness as well as cognitive and behavioral treatment.

Chapter 10

Psychosocial Aspects of Neurological Disorders

Cognitive, behavioral, and social changes are often early indicators of many neurological disorders. The mental health professional should possess a working knowledge of these syndromes to prevent misdiagnosis. Because symptoms of many neurological disorders such as dementia and delirium may be similar to those of psychiatric illnesses such as depression or psychosis, there is a serious danger of failing to recognize a neurological disorder. The converse is also true—older patients with declines in memory and concentration may be misdiagnosed with a neurological condition (dementia) rather than a readily treatable psychiatric condition such as depression.

This chapter focuses primarily on differential diagnosis of dementia and delirium. Distinguishing delirium from dementia as well as dementia from depression are common diagnostic dilemmas in both hospital and ambulatory settings. Seizure disorders are a common neurological condition in the general population. Although patients with ongoing seizures will usually be managed by neurologists, these individuals appear to have a higher incidence of psychiatric disorders. The mental health professional may be asked to address these concerns as well as patients' psychosocial adjustment to a long-term seizure disorder.

DEMENTIA: AN OVERVIEW

Dementia is a cognitive–behavioral syndrome with at least 70 different etiologies (Cummings, 1987). Some causes of dementia can be determined through imaging procedures such as a CT scan or magnetic resonance imaging (MRI). Examples of these types of dementia include normal pressure hydrocephalus, subdural hematomas, or tumors. However, the most common form of dementia, senile dementia of Alzheimer's type, is often only diagnosable in its early stages through cognitive and behavioral changes. The other difficulty with diagnosing many dementias is that, in early stages, they also appear similar to common psychiatric disorders—major depression, in particular. One final confounding factor is that these are primarily diseases of the elderly. Adults undergo a normal decline in some cognitive functions such as short-term recall and reaction time as part of the aging process, and in and of itself, this is not pathological (Gray & Cummings, 1996). From a neuroanatomical perspective, enlargement of the brain ventricles also occurs during normal aging. Diagnostically, the most common question centers around whether a progressive dementia is present or if the patient has a treatable cause for mental status changes.

ALZHEIMER'S DISEASE

About 50–70% of dementia patients have Alzheimer's disease. Although the overall population prevalence is about 1% for men and 3% for women, the disorder affects a large proportion of patients who live into their 80s. It is estimated that up to about 50% of patients over age 85 have the disorder (Roth, 1993). Patients who have symptom onset before the age of 70 are likely to have a family history of the condition. A hereditary predisposition for Alzheimer's is suggested by data that indicates that among those with a sibling with early onset of Alzheimer's disease (prior to age 70), close to 50% had developed the syndrome by the age of 85 (Hayman et al., 1983; O'Brien, 1994).

Patients with Alzheimer's disease are often placed into mild, moderate, or severe levels of impairment. In the early stages of Alzheimer's disease, the changes are relatively subtle. These symptoms may include difficulties with learning new information or retaining recently required information. Knowledge of spatial relationships may also be impaired, and the patient may have difficulty traveling independently in the community. Patients often will exhibit difficulties in mental status testing on delayed recall tests (retaining four words at a 5- or 10-minute delay). However, historical information such as where the patient went to school and other childhood memories remain intact. In the middle stage, there is more severe disorientation. The patient may not be aware of the season of the year or the month. Higher cognitive functions such as the ability to perform numerical calculations as well as read and spell also become progressively more impaired. In later stages, patients become increasingly disoriented and their verbal output becomes reduced. They eventually become mute and unable to walk independently (O'Brien, 1994).

Patients who progress beyond relatively early stages of dementia usually require supervision in their living situation. Wandering out of their home and becoming lost in previously familiar places becomes a concern. Their memory difficulties are such that fire-setting (failing to remember that the stove is on) or forgetting to take their medication can become issues. The overall course of Alzheimer's disease may range from 6 to 15 years (O'Brien, 1994).

Causes of Alzheimer's disease are not well-established. The pathology involves atrophy of large neurons and synapses. This process appears to be more pronounced in the hippocampal region, which is known to be involved with short-term memory. Reduction in acetylcholine transferase activity in the cortex and hippocampus also seems to be involved (O'Brien, 1994).

As noted above, in the early stages of Alzheimer's disease, deficits are often fairly pronounced before changes appear on a CT scan. It is not uncommon to see patients clinically who have a fairly pronounced dementia process but whose CT scan shows very minimal changes or is normal.

Multi-Infarct Dementia

Multi-infarct dementia is the second most common type of dementia. Multi-infarct dementia accounts for about 25% of dementia patients. There are some noteworthy differences between multi-infarct and Alzheimer's dementia. Multi-infarct dementia typically occurs in patients with vascular risk factors and is more common among patients with hypertension or diabetes (O'Brien, 1994). In multi-infarct dementia, the patient has a series of infarcts that are the result of small strokes. This disorder is more common in men, particularly men ages 45–65 (O'Brien, 1994).

Whereas the course of Alzheimer's disease is gradual and progressive, the course of multi-infarct dementia is intermittent and fluctuating. The patient's cognitive changes occur much more suddenly and abruptly, and the changes follow a stair-step pattern. If the patient is seen only once in the office, it may be difficult to distinguish multi-infarct from Alzheimer's dementia based on cognitive testing or a mental status examination alone (Erker, Searight, & Peterson, 1995). In multi-infarct patients, there is likely to be somewhat greater variability in the types of cognitive deficits exhibited. This variability reflects the different regions of the brain involved. There is usually evidence of vascular disease on a CT scan.

While multi-infarct and Alzheimer's disease are commonly presented as competing diagnoses, a significant percentage of older patients actually have both processes. The presence of both multi-infarct and Alzheimer's dementia appears to be associated with substantially greater functional impairment.

Additional Dementia Syndromes

Other dementia processes, including long-term alcohol use, can result in a specific dementia. As noted in an earlier chapter, short-term memory deficits are usually the most predominant symptom among alcohol-involved patients, but abstract thinking may also be impaired. Furthermore, alcohol-involved patients commonly exhibit ataxia. Normal pressure hydrocephalus is occasionally encountered in the primary care setting. These patients have dilations of the lateral ventricles. Normal pressure hydrocephalus patients have a distinct symptom pattern: dementia symptoms (most pronounced on concentration and short-term recall tasks), gait disturbance, and urinary incontinence. This condition often is treatable through use of shunts to reduce intracerebral pressure (O'Brien, 1994).

Many demented patients also exhibit marked personality changes. These may take the form of a decline in personal hygiene or wearing inappropriate clothes. Additionally, patients who exhibited unusual personality traits prior to dementia will exhibit amplifications of these characteristics. For example, someone who was suspicious prior to the onset of the dementia process, may exhibit extreme paranoia when dementia ensues. Patients who were a little eccentric with schizoid or schizotypical features may become bizarre.

FOCUSED ASSESSMENT OF DEMENTIA SYMPTOMS

A useful approach for evaluating and documenting most dementias, particularly in the early stages, is through a careful mental status examination or standardized neuropsychological/cognitive testing. One commonly used tool in primary care is Folstein's Mini-Mental Status Examination (Folstein, Folstein, & McHugh, 1975). The Mini-Mental Status Exam consists of 30 items and includes short-term memory, concentration, language, and visual/spatial tasks. A cut-off score of 23 is commonly used. However, recent research suggests that average scores in the general population are affected both by age as well as level of education. It is strongly recommended that clinicians using the Mini-Mental Status Exam include attention to these factors by using the conversion table developed by Crum, Anthony, Bassett, & Folstein (1993).

It is also useful to include more demanding tests of memory than those found in the Mini-Mental Status Exam. In particular, reading the patient a passage of several sentences and asking them to repeat it back is a relatively sensitive tool for assessing immediate recall. By including a delay period of several minutes, with some interference tasks in between, the patient's short-term memory can be assessed (Strub & Black, 1993). Visual spatial skills can be assessed by asking the patient to copy geometric figures.

DISTINGUISHING DEMENTIA FROM DEPRESSION

Clinical Issues

Distinguishing dementia from depression is a common challenge in primary care. In these situations, a patient age 60 or older typically will report a decline in cognitive functioning. In particular, they will describe memory loss, (particularly in short-term memory), a subjective sense that their thought processes are "slowing," as well as difficulties with attention and concentration. Many elderly patients who are depressed will present with predominantly cognitive rather than affective or vegetative symptoms (Caine, Lyness, Caine, & Connor, 1994). In outpatient settings, roughly 10–20% of all geriatric patients have significant depressive symptoms (Barrett, Barrett, Oxman, & Gerber 1988). The provider may note the patient's presenting cognitive symptoms in the context of the patient's age and erroneously conclude that they are experiencing early signs of a degenerative dementia process. There is evidence that this misdiagnosis frequently occurs. It is estimated that 10–30% of patients initially diagnosed with degenerative dementia of Alzheimer's type because of cognitive symptoms are actually depressed (Katzman, Lasker, & Bernstein, 1988). Whereas depression is a readily treatable condition, degenerative dementias cannot be reversed, and have a poorer prognosis. Thus, the practical and humanitarian costs of misdiagnosis are considerable. The clinical picture is frequently ambiguous.

> Mr. Koop is a 69-year-old African-American male who presents with increasing forgetfulness. He states that he has been more aware of this problem during the past 6 months. Examples include forgetting directions to familiar places and entering a room or going to a store and then forgetting why he was there. Mr. Koop states that he has never been truly "lost." Mr. Koop is a retired accountant. His wife of 45 years died suddenly 18 months ago after being bedridden for several years following a stroke. The patient has three grown children who he sees regularly. Mr. Koop's medical history includes mild hypertension. One year ago, Mr. Koop had pancreatitis.
>
> In an interview, Mr. Koop says his mood is more irritable than previously. He reports several angry outbursts. He denies any crying spells or suicidal ideation. Mr. Koop reports some decline in his appetite as well as periodic episodes of intermittent insomnia. He describes a 25-year history of daily drinking which ended about a year ago. He typically drank about a six pack of beer per day and occasional hard liquor but stopped after his illness. He is not on any medication. When asked about his response to his wife's death, Mr. Koop indicates that he feels some sadness but feels his wife is "better off now" because she is "not in pain." He says that he and his wife used to sit on the porch and drink in the evening and that he misses her most at this time.

Assessment

Differentiating early stage dementia from depression is difficult for several reasons. Both dementia and depression are usually initially diagnosed clinically without the benefit of laboratory tests. As noted earlier, radiographic studies may not demonstrate abnormalities in early degenerative dementias. The history as well as the clinical examination and mental status examination are usually the most helpful in differentiating the two diagnoses.

In contrast to degenerative dementia, the onset of depression is usually relatively sudden. Depression is often related to specific life events such as the death of a spouse or a geographic move. A very common life event occurring with elderly people is the development of multiple medical problems that reduce their independence. In cases of depression, the mood disturbance and social withdrawal clearly precede the cognitive changes. In cases of dementia, the cognitive changes are usually more gradual and they are usually not associated with a event (McAllister, 1985). However, life changes such as the death of a spouse who had provided a lot of direct care for the patient, or a move to a new setting such as a retirement community, may make cognitive deterioration much more apparent. This pattern also occurs when patients are hospitalized. An elderly patient may fracture their hip or develop congestive heart failure requiring hospitalization. The patient had been experiencing a slow deterioration in cognitive functioning prior to their hospital admissions. However, the abrupt change in their daily routine made these deficits much more apparent. Over time, family members and significant others have often unreflectively adapted to the patient's gradual cognitive deterioration, and it may not be as apparent to them until the patient is moved to an unfamiliar setting such as a hospital. Elderly patients who are depressed are much more likely to have a previous history of psychiatric illness. A positive psychiatric history should direct the clinician to a greater likelihood of depression.

On the mental status examination and the clinical interview, there are some specific patterns that often assist with a differential diagnosis. Orientation is much more likely to be problematic with demented patients. In particular, orientation to time is more likely to be impaired in dementia (Kazniak & Christenson, 1994). With respect to attention and concentration, preserved ability to perform tasks such as digit span or serial 7s is usually suggestive of depression. However, depressed patients may occasionally do poorly on these tasks. A noteworthy distinction is that depressed patients show much more subjective distress about their poor performance than demented patients. Tasks that are usually more sensitive to dementia are recent/delayed memory tasks. Four-word recall with a time delay and asking the patient to remember items hidden in different parts of the room will be more difficult for demented patients than patients who are depressed. It is also useful to have the patient perform some simple constructional tasks such as having them reproduce geometric figures. Depressed patients usually have no difficulty with this. They may be slow and self-critical of their performance, but will usually be able to reproduce the gestalt fairly accurately.

There are several qualitative dimensions of the interview that are helpful. Depressed patients are much more likely to say, "I don't know" or give up without really trying when they are asked to perform tasks (Kazniak & Christenson, 1994; McAllister, 1985). They also more likely to be self-deprecating. Dementia patients will show more "near miss" or tangential responses and they usually put forth more effort in trying to answer the questions. In contrast to those with dementia, depressed patients will show more variability in their performance on cognitive tasks. For example, when presented with serial 7s (count backwards from 100 by 7s), depressed patients will often insist that they cannot perform the task. However, with encouragement, they will make no errors until they reach the number 58, and then be off by ten or more afterwards. Patients with degenerative dementia tend to show more consistent and global patterns of impairment (Kazniak & Christenson, 1994; McAllister, 1985).

Changes in social behavior also take a somewhat different form in patients with depression versus degenerative dementia. In cases of depression, the social withdrawal tends to occur prior to or simultaneously with the decline in cognitive functioning. In cases of dementia, social withdrawal tends to occur relatively later in the illness course.

Specific verbal tasks that have been useful in differentiating depression from early dementia include word fluency and memory tasks. In word fluency, a patient may be asked to say all the words that they can remember beginning with the letter "T" in a 60-second period. A cut off of 30–32 words has been suggested with less than this range being suggestive of dementia (Butters, Salmon, & Butters, 1994). Additionally, recognition memory often holds up much better in depression than in cases of dementia. An example of testing recognition memory would be to ask patients to remember a list of paired associated words. After the patient is tested in an open-ended manner (e.g., "What word went with 'black'?" "That's right, it was white"), the patient is then asked to select the associated word from a list. This same format can be used with an open recall task in which the patient is asked to remember four to six words. If the patient cannot remember the words, they can be presented with a list in which the target words are embedded with words that were not presented earlier.

Treatment Implications

As noted earlier, there is no independent "gold standard" for diagnosing depression or early-stage degenerative dementia of the Alzheimer's type. In Alzheimer's patients, imaging procedures tend to have nonspecific results and typically are characterized by "mild ventricular enlargement" or "mild cerebral atrophy consistent with normal aging." In addition, particularly in early stages of dementia, there is no consistent relationship between the degree of atrophy or ventricular dilation and cognitive or functional impairment (Ford & Winter, 1981; McAllister, 1985). It has often been suggested that when in doubt, the patient should be treated as if they were depressed. The reason behind this guideline is that degenerative dementia has no known effective treatment. Depression is a treatable condition and even in cases where depression and dementia co-exist, treatment of depression is likely to result in some cognitive improvement as well as some enhancement the patient's quality of life. As the newer antidepressants have minimal adverse effects, there are relatively few medical contraindications for initiating a trial of a selective serotonin reuptake inhibitor.

CARE AND TREATMENT OF DEMENTIA

Although some of the risk factors for vascular dementias—such as hypertension—may be modifiable, dementia is generally regarded as a progressive disorder that is unable to be "cured." There are several exceptions to this poor prognosis. Secondary dementias such as normal pressure hydrocephalus or cognitive changes associated with vitamin deficiencies and medication interaction may be reversible (O'Brien, 1994). Additionally, patients with small areas of brain involvement following a stroke may return to premorbid functioning.

Several medications have recently been developed that may slow the cognitive decline seen in Alzheimer's patients. The best studied of these, tacrine, has been found to stabilize the cognitive functioning in about 30–40% of Alzheimer's patients. Although tacrine appears to be associated with maintenance of cognitive functioning on formal mental status testing (Davis, Thal, Gamzu et al., 1992), it has not been particularly effective in improving functional daily living skills.

A number of behavioral interventions for dementia have been developed. These have included frequent orientation to person, place, and time. Patients should also be kept on a consistent schedule for mealtimes, recreation, and sleeping. Responding to the patient in a gentle and calm manner when they are becoming confused or disoriented will be reassuring. In addition, when patients become demanding or highly agitated, they should be redirected to another activity.

Many family members are concerned about the progression of the disease. Practical decisions such as the necessity for greater degrees of supervision in the home environment and nursing home care are common concerns of those caring for a family member with Alzheimer's disease.

> Ms. Bunn is a 78-year-old divorced woman who comes to the office with her only daughter, Ms. James. Ms. Bunn's daughter has come to visit her mother for several weeks and insists that her mother see a physician. Ms. Bunn states that she is "just fine" and says she has "no idea" why she is seeing a physician. Ms. Bunn's daughter, however, appears anxious and tense. The physician has Ms. Bunn undergo physical examination that is essentially normal. Her weight and blood pressure are also unremarkable. She obtains a score of 20 on the Mini-Mental Status Exam (slightly below the cut-off). During the interview, Ms. Bunn is pleasant but somewhat guarded. When she is asked about her memory and concentration, she says "I am 78. I don't remember as well as I used to. What do you expect? ... My daughter just wants my money." Ms. James asks to speak with the doctor alone and her mother agrees.

Ms. James states that she has not seen her mother for about three months although she spoke with her by phone about twice a month. "My mom's house is a like a cesspool ... There are dirty dishes everywhere, stacks of magazines and newspapers, and food ground into the rug. My mom has never been too clean, but she has never been this bad. What really worries me is her spending. She is a sucker for anyone who calls her ... Mom has magazine subscriptions to *Teen Beat, Hot Rod World, Snowboarding Monthly, Biker World,* and *Heavy Metal Review.* What is more, she is playing the lottery through these 900 phone numbers. She has racked up $12,000 in debt! She is running through her savings like it is water. When I talked to her about it, she says "I'm old. Let me spend my money before I die. You are just looking for a big inheritance." A CT scan is normal. Report states Ms. Bunn has "mild ventricular enlargement, not inconsistent with normal aging."

Although specific case-by-case prediction of outcome among demented patients is not currently possible, there is evidence that certain factors are predictive of the need for nursing home or equivalent care. These include presence of extrapyramidal signs, psychotic symptoms, younger age at onset, poor cognitive functioning, and longer illness duration. Stern and colleagues (1997) found that of those patients who had a score of 1.0 on their health-related facility care index (a composite of the variables just described), 25% of those over the age of 73 were likely to require the equivalent of nursing home care in about nine months. By contrast, of those under the age of 73 who had a composite score of 3.0, 25% were likely to require nursing home placement in 31 months.

DELIRIUM

Delirium and dementia are often confused, particularly in acutely ill patients encountered in the hospital or emergency room. The delirious patient exhibits a "clouding" of consciousness. Patients are often unaware of their surroundings, are not oriented to time or even to person. In some instances, this impaired consciousness will alternate with periods of intact and clear consciousness. Hallucinations—most commonly visual—may also be present (Francis & Kapoor, 1990). The symptom pattern fluctuates throughout the day and becomes more pronounced at night.

Many clinicians have difficulty distinguishing delirium from dementia. The symptom picture, course, and etiology of these two syndromes are distinct. In early stages of most dementia processes, consciousness is usually clear. The "clouding" phenomenon is usually absent. Changes in mental status typically occur gradually. In Alzheimer's disease, for example, the early changes occur specifically in short-term memory and constructional skills. In delirium, the patient may be able to focus attention for brief periods of time, and constructional abilities are usually intact. An exception to this distinction are patients who have a cerebral infarct (i.e., "stroke"). As noted earlier, these patients typically have histories of hypertension or other vascular risk factors. Weakness is often lateralized to one side of the body. Hallucinations are uncommon and alterations in consciousness tend to clear quickly in stroke patients. Visual hallucinations also distinguish dementias of most types from delirium.

Delirium has multiple causes. These etiologies may include infectious processes, particularly those involving the renal system. Electrolyte imbalances, medication interactions, and alcohol withdrawal are also underlying causes. Oxygen desaturation, which is often found among patients who have chronic obstructive pulmonary disease who are receiving artificial oxygen, may lead to acute confusional states.

In hospitalized patients, the "intensive care unit syndrome" has been described as causing delirium. This syndrome was probably more of an issue in the past when ICUs were much more austere and frightening settings. ICU syndrome was attributed to sensory deprivation and withdrawal of environmental stimuli. Delirium occurs in about 10% of patients in general medical hospitals with the elderly much more likely to be affected (Bross & Tatum, 1994).

Delirium is a readily treatable condition and once the diagnosis is made, the communication to the physician should include a recommendation to aggressively pursue its causes. It is likely that the psychologist who has some medical training can suggest possible contributors from the factors noted above.

SEIZURE DISORDERS

Brief Overview

Epilepsy is defined as a pattern of recurrent seizure activity that results from neuronal discharge. Seizures occur when there is an outward change in consciousness or motor sensory dysfunction associated with excess neuronal discharge (Rankin, Adams, & Jones, 1996).

In the United States, the prevalence of seizure disorders is approximately 1%. However, this figure is likely to an underestimate because a large percentage of patients with seizures are not under any form of direct treatment (McNamara, 1993). Although the population prevalence of epilepsy is relatively low, it has been estimated that up to 9% of the population will have at least one seizure during their lifetime (McLacklan, 1993). The available data suggest that after an initial seizure, the recurrence risk is about 50% over the next two to three years (Berg & Shinnar, 1991).

Generalized seizures may be of two types. Absence seizures involve disruptions in attention and small-scale movements of the limbs as well as possible blinking or upward turning of the eyes. The patient often appears to be "spacing out" or daydreaming. Odd motor movements such as blinking or lip smacking as well as an abrupt end of the episode are also characteristic of absence seizures (Rankin et al., 1996). The second type, generalized convulsive seizures, often called grand mal seizures, include several patterns. They may involve myoclonic activity including brief, repeated muscle contractions. Tonic–clonic seizures, the most prevalent generalized seizures, include loss of consciousness and muscle flexion followed by extension and jerking of the entire body. Patients often afterwards will report amnesia as well as some confusion (Rankin et al., 1996).

Partial seizures stem from localized central nervous system disturbance. Simple partial seizures may include periods of unusual motor, autonomic, or sensory activity without loss of consciousness. Patients with these seizures may have paralysis or automatic movements of a limb, visual or auditory sensory experiences, or vomiting and sweating (Rankin et al., 1996). In contrast to simple partial seizures, complex partial seizures do feature a loss of consciousness. Repetitive autonomic motor movements (e.g., lip smacking or scratching) may also occur (Rankin et al., 1996).

Pseudoseizures are nonepileptic attack disorders in which patients exhibit behavioral patterns that appear similar to seizures, but in which there is no clinical evidence (such as EEG abnormalities) of seizure activity (Rankin et al., 1996). Rankin et al. (1996) point out that the term "psychogenic seizure" should be confined to situations in which a psychological event such as a mood state or an idea elicits a seizure like pattern of behavior. EEGs during and immediately after seizure like activity are normal in patients with nonepileptic attack disorder. In cases of nonepileptic attack disorder, patients also tend not to have amnesia or confusion immediately after the episode. There is also likely to be a pattern of secondary gain.

Psychiatric Disorders among Seizure Patients

The majority of patients with ongoing seizure activity are managed by neurologists. The mental health provider working in a primary care setting should be aware, however, of the psychosocial aspects of seizure activity. There does not appear to be strong evidence of a particular personality style associated with seizure disorder (Dodrill & Batzel, 1986; Stevens, 1988).

However, there are suggestions of levels of elevated psychiatric disturbance among patients with seizure disorders. It is not clear whether the etiology of these comorbid disorders stems from abnormal central nervous system activity or whether disorders such as depression are a result of coping with a long-term chronic illness. The relationship between psychopathology and seizures appears to be more pronounced among patients with intractable and complicated seizure disorders (Blumer, Montouris, & Hermann, 1995). In a study of seizure patients on a specialized neurodiagnostic monitoring unit, it was found that nearly two-thirds exhibited a psychiatric disorder. Of these, about half had a mood disorder, with slightly over 20% exhibiting pseudoseizures (Blumer et al., 1995).

Several psychiatric syndromes are of particular concern among seizure disorder patients. Psychotic episodes are estimated to occur in about 7% of epileptic patients (McKenna, Kane, & Parrish, 1985). These patients are likely to have temporal lobe involvement. Epileptic patients with psychotic symptoms may exhibit paranoia, hallucinations, and evidence of incoherence. In contrast to schizophrenic patients, those with psychotic episodes due to seizures are more likely to have fairly abrupt changes in their functioning rather than a gradual prodrome (McKenna et al., 1985).

Depression has been the most studied psychiatric diagnosis among seizure disorder patients. Although exact prevalence rates vary considerably, it does appear that patients with seizure disorders are far more likely than the general population to have episodes of clinical depression (McKenna et al., 1985). Blumer et al. (1995) described a distinct pattern of depressive symptoms among seizure disorder patients. They noted that depressive moods may occur suddenly and with considerable intensity. These episodes of dysphoria may last from hours to a few days. There may also be episodes of euphoria as well. Angry outbursts ranging from irritability to hostile explosions may also occur. When this intermittent pattern occurs among epileptic patients, together with a loss of energy, pain, and sleep disturbance, a diagnosis of interictal dysphoric disorder may be warranted (Blumer et al., 1995). Epileptic patients appear to have a significantly higher rate of suicide attempts. It has been estimated that 30% of depressed patients with epilepsy have attempted suicide, with an effected suicide rate five times higher than the base rate in the general population (Mendez, Cummings, & Benson, 1996).

Seizure activity itself may be linked to depression. Patients who have more epileptic attacks appear to have a higher incidence of depressive symptoms (Ridsdale, Robins, Fitzgerald, Jeffrey, & McGee, 1996). A key depressive symptom leading to seizure exacerbation is sleep disturbance. (McKenna et al., 1985).

The relationship between psychological factors and seizure facilitation is not as clear. Many patients with seizure disorders report increased likelihood of seizure activity when they are anxious, sad, or tired (Fenwick, 1990). Laboratory studies, however, suggest that this relationship may be more illusory than real. Patients may make these connections from a desire to control seizure activity (Antebi & Bird, 1993).

Pseudoseizures are directly linked to psychological conflicts. Pseudoseizures have also been termed "nonepileptic seizures." In studies of specialized epilepsy treatment facilities, prevalence rates range from 10–40% (Gates, Luciano, & Devinsky, 1991).

Pseudoseizures are probably best distinguished by their pattern. For example, patients do not usually exhibit incontinence or loss of consciousness during pseudoseizure activity. In addition, there is often evidence of significant psychological distress in the patient's history. Child abuse (either sexual or physical) occurs more frequently among these patients during their earlier development (Oper, Devinsky, Perrine, Vazquez, & Luciano, 1993). Oper and colleagues found that nearly a third of patients with nonepileptic seizures had histories of physical or sexual abuse with fewer than 10% of patients with epilepsy having this history. A concern about misdiagnosis of pseudoseizures is that patients may be unnecessarily treated medically with anticonvulsive medication or a procedure such as intubation during apparent seizure activity (Oper et al., 1993).

Although depression should be seriously considered in seizure patients, some anticonvulsant medications such as phenytoin, phenobarbital, and carbamazepine may be associated with changes in mood (specifically increased irritability) as well as problems with memory and concentration. There are suggestions that long-term use of anticonvulsants in children may produce cognitive decline (McNamara, 1993).

The primary care provider should also be aware of possible behavioral affects of seizure medication toxicity. Patients may exhibit primarily cognitive symptoms such as deficits in attention, concentration, decreased motivation, as well as motor coordination difficulties and unusual eye movements.

One difficulty in treating depression among patients with seizure disorders is that many of the antidepressants lower the seizure threshold. Trazodone has been one medication that has been specifically suggested; however, patients may experience significant sedation. The newer selective serotonin re-uptake inhibitors also may reduce the seizure threshold, but tend to have fewer overall side-effects (McNamara, 1993). Supportive psychotherapy, particularly with an emphasis on helping the patient improve their quality of relationships and vocational/recreational activities, can be helpful as well. Many of these patients feel anxious or become increasingly withdrawn because of the limitations placed on some of their activities such as driving by ongoing seizure activity.

CONCLUSION

Patients with early stages of dementia are likely to initially present to their primary care provider because dementia symptoms may be nonspecific and include social and emotional changes. Therefore, there is a significant likelihood of misdiagnosis. However, depressed older patients may be misdiagnosed as demented—an error that has wide-ranging implications. Delirium may be confused as a "functional" psychotic disorder. The symptom course as well as knowledge of the patient's medical condition and medications should help clarify the diagnosis. Seizure disorder patients appear to be at greater risk for psychiatric disorder and may benefit from psychotherapy to improve coping.

Chapter 11

Psychological Aspects of Pain

Patients with various types of chronic pain are commonly seen in primary care. Psychological factors often play a significant role in exacerbation, maintenance, and coping with conditions such as headache and back pain.

CHRONIC PAIN

In the United States, it has been estimated that about 80% of patient visits to physicians are for pain-related problems (Schmitt, 1985). Over one-third of Americans have experienced partial or complete disability at some point in life in their life because of pain (Latham and Davis, 1994).

Chronic pain has been defined as pain that endures for more than a month beyond the typical course of an illness or expected healing time from an injury, or if the pain continues to recur in intervals over months to years (Portenoy, 1993). The formal *DSM–IV* (1994) diagnosis that is often employed with chronic pain patients is "pain disorder associated with psychological factors." It is estimated that up to 40% of pain patients have a significant psychological component to their pain experience (Folks et al., 1990).

Chronic pain patients are often frustrating for both medical and nonmedical providers. The average chronic pain patient has experienced pain for seven years, has spent up to one-hundred thousand dollars on medical expenses, and experiences a greater than 50% chance of drug addiction. The total cost of pain syndromes in the United States has been placed at between $60 billion and $90 billion per year including time lost from work as well as health care litigation costs (Brena, 1983; Hanson & Gerber, 1990; Turk, Meichenbaum & Genest, 1983).

The pain syndromes most commonly seen in primary care settings include headache, backache, and temporal mandibular joint pain. Pain, however, is an elusive concept. Pain is often not verifiable, and the provider must rely heavily on the provider's objective report. Like fatigue, chronic pain is often referred to as a syndrome, a constellation of symptoms without an established etiology. Over the past several decades, patients' reports of pain have also increased. In the late 1960s about 40% of Americans complained of headaches during the past two weeks. By the 1980s the comparable percentage was 70% (Blanchard & Andrasik, 1985). Reasons for this increase are not entirely clear. Certainly, it is likely that sensitivity to distress has increased. Symptoms that may have been seen as an inevitable part of life 50 years ago are now seen as medical problems requiring treatment.

It is also important for providers to recognize that in our culture, pain is also a metaphor. Verbal reports of pain often are indirect ways of describing relationships. For example, a married woman in her late 20s is sitting in her living room with her husband at about nine o'clock in the evening. As her husband yawns and stretches and says, "I'm ready for bed," she may respond with, "I have a headache." This expression may mean a range of things including report of somatic sensation, but may also express a desire not to have sex or a more symbolic statement that her marriage is emotionally painful. (Haley 1976).

The sensory value of pain is often secondary to patients' actual pain experience. Individuals' emotional involvement with their pain, their coping ability, and the social context can create major differences in how pain is actually experienced (Turk et al., 1983).

It is not uncommon for someone to sustain a traumatic injury and experience very little pain. On the other hand, it is also known that patients' emotional involvement with their pain, their coping abilities, and even their ethnic backgrounds will play a role in pain expression. In South America, there is a practice in which Indians, during Holy Week, have large hooks, similar to meat hooks, embedded in their lower back. The individual is suspended from these hooks and is elevated to bless people and animals. The subject is usually in a state of joy and religious fervor and reports no pain associated with this practice. This example highlights a finding noted by many anthropologists. Certain ethnic groups differ in their relative stoicism regarding pain. Italians often times have minimal tolerance for pain whereas individuals of Irish and German background tend to be very stoic (Zbrowski, 1969). Jewish patients may derive some meaning from the experience of suffering associated with pain (Searight, 1997c).

Psychological Perspectives on Pain

Psychologists have relied on two predominant models for understanding pain. Both models may have some limitations, particularly on neurophysiological grounds, but are very useful for intervention purposes. In addition, these models integrate both psychological and social aspects of pain and are conceptualizations readily grasped by patients. The gate control model is associated with the work of Melzack and Wall (1965), who argued that pain is not simply a function of the amount of tissue damage. They emphasize that rather than being solely a physiological phenomenon, pain is often influenced by central nervous system phenomena such as motivation, attention, and emotional states. The gate control model provides a description for the role of both peripheral and central nervous system factors in pain experience. One of the most dramatic examples of this phenomenon are chronic pain patients who are amputees. Phantom limb pain is a condition in which patients report pain emanating from the site of a now amputated arm or leg. The concept of phantom limb pain contradicts the view that pain is directly associated with a circumscribed injury.

To summarize Melzack and Wall's (1965) model, neural mechanisms in the dorsal horns of the spinal cord are seen as acting like a gate that increases or decreases the flow of nerve impulses from peripheral fibers to the spinal cord cells, which in turn, project to the brain. Somatic input is modulated by the gate before it evokes pain perception and a response. The gate is also influenced by descending influences from the brain. Of particular importance is that the gate includes the central nervous system as a modulator of pain experience. The reticulolimbic area, involving emotion, as well as the frontal cortex involved in higher cognition, can inhibit or amplify pain perception (Turk et al., 1983).

Although the anatomical and physiological basis for the gate control model has been challenged, this perspective also has support. For example, surgery or anesthetic blocks designed to reduce sensory input often do not reduce a patient's experience of pain. The model also recognizes that nonsensory dimensions such as cultural values, anxiety, depression, attention, and personality characteristics all play a role in pain experience (Turk et al., 1983).

In clinical work with patients, the gate control model is useful in that it provides a physiologically oriented explanation that is often acceptable to patients who are likely threatened by and may be defensive about a psychological interpretation of their pain. Although anchored in anatomical structures and physiological processes, gate control theory also provides an account of the role of emotional states, activity level, and attention in opening or closing the pain gate. It also provides an explanation of how pain, begun with injury or disease, may be maintained by cognitive or affective factors after tissue damage has healed.

A second explanatory perspective is the behavioral model associated with Fordyce (1976). Fordyce has used operant learning theory to explain pain. It is assumed that pain is never directly observable or measurable. In keeping with the operant perspective, pain exists within the "black box" of human experience. Pain is inherently subjective, and there is no way of genuinely knowing the extent of a patient's pain. However, "pain behavior" such as grimacing, lying down, and verbalizing about pain are observable and quantifiable. Fordyce essentially equates pain with pain behavior.

Fordyce (1976) distinguishes between respondent pain, which is attributable to tissue damage or irritation from disease processes, and chronic pain. Acute pain problems (e.g., a broken leg) are usually associated with respondent pain. Chronic pain, on the other hand, follows general principles of operant learning and is maintained by the consequences of pain behavior. Back pain, which may emerge behaviorally through complaints, grimacing, or lying down, is reinforced by attention from one's spouse or children and reduced expectations for responsibility around the house, and may also be associated with reinforcement through financial gain. In this model, there is considerable attention paid to sources of reinforcement that may seem peripheral. For example, veteran's benefits or workman's compensation, or litigation surrounding an accident, are all sources of reinforcement for pain behavior. There is evidence that patients who have litigation pending or who are seeking financial compensation report greater subjective pain experience and exhibit greater functional impairment. (Rohling, Binder, & Langhinrichsen-Rohling, 1995).

The goals of treatment are not to reduce the patient's pain experience because this dimension is subjective and can never be objectively known. Instead, the goals of treatment are to increase physical activity, increase non-pain-related social interaction, and decrease analgesic medication usage. One important step in this regard is that pain medication should be delivered on a fixed time schedule rather than on an as-needed (PRN) schedule (Fordyce, 1976). The PRN schedule sets up a reinforcement relationship for pain behavior. The fixed-interval schedule for pain medication should be incorporated into hospital care as well as into the patient's home. Spouses and other relevant adults at home should be educated in this model and encouraged to provide attention to the patient when they are not engaged in pain behavior.

Each of these models highlights an important aspect of the chronic pain experience. Gate control theory is a useful approach for patient education. As noted above, it is "physiological enough" to avoid the resistance that clinicians often encounter when discussing psychological issues with pain patients. The model also links emotional states such as depression and anxiety to pain. On the other hand, the behavioral approach is often not directly accepted by patients. However, the clinician may point out to the patient that they do indeed have pain and that the pain itself will never be completely remediated, but tolerance for the pain may be increased by engaging in productive activities. The behavioral model is also helpful in that it provides the provider and the patient with measurable objective goals that become the focus of clinical activity. Thus, walking around the block two days a week, socializing with friends at a card game, or doing the grocery shopping become behavioral goals that will not directly remediate pain, but will increase level of functioning. An often indirect side effect is that because of increased physical activity and the release of certain neurotransmitters as well as the reduced attentional focus on pain associated with increased recreational and social activity, the patient does report a decrease in their subjective pain experience. To assess this dimension assessment of chronic pain behavior, one of the most helpful questions to ask is, "What does your pain stop you from doing?"

Psychological Assessment

There are a number of self-report instruments that are used with chronic pain patients. One of the most commonly used assessment tools is the Minnesota Multiphasic Personality Inventory—(Hathaway & Mckinley, 1951). The MMPI profiles of pain patients have been grouped into several types that have distinct prognostic implications. Patients may be seen as predominantly depressed, somatically focused with little concurrent depression, or personality disordered (Armentrout, Moore, Parker, Hewett, & Feltz, 1982; Karoly & Jenson, 1987).

The McGill Pain Questionnaire (Melzack, 1975) has also been used very widely by psychologists in pain management programs. It provides information about three hypothesized dimensions of pain: sensory, affective, and evaluative. Patients review lists of adjectives divided into subclasses, with each subclass designed to reflect a particular quality of pain experience. The patient, in completing the McGill Pain Questionnaire, is asked to choose words that reflect his or her particular pain experience. The McGill questionnaire has been found useful in differentiating patients with "organic" pain from those in which psychological factors play a substantial role (Karoly & Jensen, 1987). The questionnaire also seems to be sensitive to treatment benefits (Leavitt, Garron, Whisler, & D'Angelo, 1980).

The Beck Depression Inventory (Beck, Ward, Mendelson, Mock, & Erbaugh, 1961) has also been found to be helpful for reasons noted above. It is convenient, efficient, and can be completed by patients on their own. It is often useful in eliciting depression that tends to co-exist with chronic pain syndromes.

However, the most commonly employed pain rating formats in primary care are probably simple 0–100 or 0–10 scales in which 10 or 100 is the most intense pain imaginable and 0 is no pain at all. Additionally, visual analog scales in which the patient is given a line with two end points, with one end point being "no pain" and the other end point being "the most intense pain imaginable" may be employed. The patient is asked to place a mark noting where their pain falls on this continuum (Karoly & Jensen, 1987).

A form of pain evaluation that examines behavioral aspects is the Behavioral Rating Scale, which was initially developed for head pain (Budzynski, Stoyva, Adler, & Mullaney, 1973; Karoly & Jensen, 1987). The behavioral rating scale asks patients to rate their degree of pain in relation to its disruptiveness of their daily activity. As Karoly and Jensen (1987) note, the behavior rating scale provides an indirect assessment of pain intensity. The basic rating format is no pain;

low-level pain that enters awareness only when I pay attention to it; pain exists but can be ignored at times; pain exists, but I can continue performing all the tasks I would normally; very severe pain that makes concentration difficult, but allows me to perform tasks of an undemanding nature; intense, incapacitating pain (Karoly & Jensen, 1987 adapted from Budzynski et al., 1973).

One final efficient approach for assessing pain is use of a pain diary (Blanchard & Andrasik, 1985). Patients are given a printed grid and asked to record the time spent in various physical positions: sitting, reclining, standing, and walking. They are also asked to list their daily activities and their medication usage. Patients may also rate their level of pain throughout the day. The level of pain on awakening in the morning is commonly employed as a baseline measure. Patients will then rate their pain on the hour, every two hours. The clinician can review this diary with the patient and examine types of events during the course of the day that seems to be associated with increased and decreased levels of pain. The pain diary may also include a reporting of prescription and nonprescription medication that is taken and when it is taken (Blanchard & Andrasik, 1985).

HEADACHE

Headache is one of the most common problems brought to primary care physicians. Between 7% and 10% of patients in ambulatory care have headaches as their presenting problem (Blanchard & Andrasik, 1985). In community studies, 75–80% of the population reports having a headache in the past year (Waters, 1970, 1974). Half of men and up to two-thirds of women report a significant headache in the past month (Waters, 1970, 1974). When headache is redefined as "clinically significant headache," about 8–15% of men and 15% to 30% of women have frequent headaches affecting their daily life (Leviton, 1978).

In evaluating headache patients, it is helpful to obtain a through headache history. This would include time of onset and any illnesses or injuries associated with onset (Blanchard & Andrasik, 1985). In addition, a detailed phenomenological account of the headache should be provided. This should include the site on the head where they begin and the progression of the pain. Any situations or stimuli that make the headache worse should be elicited. Time of day at which they occur should also be inquired about. Consequences of the pain as well as associated functional impairment should also be included. Family history of headache is also important to elicit. Current life stressors including marriage, friendships, and school/work issues should also be assessed.

Headache patients should be asked mental status questions with particular attention paid to symptoms of depression or anxiety. A complete picture of the patient's use of analgesic medication should be obtained (Blanchard & Andrasik, 1985).

Migraine Headaches

The overall prevalence of migraine in the general population ranges from 5–20% with the 5–10% range probably being a reasonable standard (Blanchard & Andrasik, 1985). The typical symptom picture of migraine includes unilateral pain accompanied by vomiting and nausea. The pain is often described as throbbing or pulsating. It often goes on for multiple hours to days. In the early days of behavioral medicine, "stress" was probably given an inordinate role in the etiology of migraine. In the 1940s and 1950s there was a body of clinical observation describing a "migraine personality" (Blanchard & Andrasik, 1985). One perspective was that migraine headaches represented hostility that was directed against the self rather than against a beloved person. A few recent studies have found certain emotional and personality characteristics to be more common among migraine patients (Brandt, Celentano, Stewart, Lenet, & Folstein, 1990); however, the general status of these profiles is not clear. It may be that persons who have migraines are more likely to experience anxiety and depression, exhibit less interpersonal warmth and be alienated from peers (Dalessio, 1972). However, these characteristics may result from migraine rather than be a cause.

Tension Headaches

Both stress and general psychopathology appear to be more prevalent among tension headache sufferers than among migraine patients. Although a number of studies of migraine patients have not found markedly higher levels of psychiatric symptoms than among nonpatients, tension headache patients do seem to be significantly more anxious and depressed (Blanchard & Andrasik, 1985). Tension headaches are the most prevalent type of headache. Gender differences are not usually found among tension headache sufferers. About 80% of tension headaches appear to be stress-related. However, research has found that tension headache patients do not have more objective stressors, but instead tend to perceive more stressors in their lives (Blanchard & Andrasik, 1985). In addition, research also suggests that tension headache sufferers are more likely to use less adaptive coping strategies. For example, they are more likely to engage in avoidance ("I just tried to forget the whole thing.") or self-blame ("I must have done something wrong.") rather than more adaptive strategies such as "I came up with a plan of action and followed it." In addition, patients with tension headaches seem to be less likely to rely on social support or even simple catharsis ("I just let my emotions show; I let my friends help me.").

As indicated by the following case example, patients with atypical or tension headaches often have difficulty relating physical distress to psychosocial issues:

> Julie is a 17-year-old high school senior. Her family physician has seen her in the office on an average of every six weeks for the past two years. Her primary symptoms have been "headache." Julie says that headaches are nearly always present, and they began about four years ago. Her headaches have been thoroughly "worked up." She does not respond to several analgesics, and there are consistently no other physical findings. Julie describes her headaches as starting in her scalp and spreading downwards until her whole head and neck begin to ache. There do not seem to be any variations in the headaches according to activity. On a scale from 1 to 10, (10 = extreme), they are usually a " 7." There is no nausea, vomiting, visual disturbance, or other symptoms.
>
> Julie lives with her mother. Her parents divorced when she was 11. She sees her father about once per month. For the first two years after the divorce, she saw him weekly. He remarried when Julie was 13. Julie's father and his new wife now have a baby. Julie is currently a senior in high school. Her grades are fairly good. However, she misses about 30 days of school per year because of the headaches. She may not graduate on time because of missed days. Julie is referred to a neurologist.
>
> A complete evaluation is conducted including an MRI and CT scan. All findings are negative. Julie has been tried on progressively stronger analgesics. She consistently reports that all of them reduce her pain from a "7" to a "4" for about one hour.
>
> Julie is difficult to interview. Although she is very pleasant, she does not report any stresses in her life. She says her life is basically "fine" except for the headaches. Whenever the clinician asks her about other aspects of her life, she is generally polite but not revealing. She says she and her mom get along "great." She says her relationship with her dad is "fine."

Julie's presentation is consistent with tension or atypical headache. Her symptoms are not of a classical pattern. The absence of response to typical medication as well as the negative neurological examination suggest that there are likely to be emotional factors involved. A profitable line of inquiry would be to further explore the relationship between Julie and her mother as well as Julie and her father. She might also be a good candidate for symptom-focused therapy such as biofeedback.

Psychological Treatment of Headache

For migraine sufferers, in addition to medication, thermal biofeedback has been commonly used. Digital vasodilation (hand warming) is commonly encouraged with a temperature probe. Autogenics in which verbal suggestions of warmth and heaviness in the limbs are provided is a useful induction to use for this process. Two studies found that thermal biofeedback for migraines was significantly more effective when regular home practice (Gauthier, Cote, & French, 1994) and propranolol treatment (Holroyd et al., 1995) was added.

There is also evidence that the biofeedback apparatus probably is not necessary (Blanchard, Andrasik, Aules, Teders, & O'Keefe, 1980). Relaxation training is equally effective. However, for some patients, the use of biofeedback seems to be more comfortable because it suggests a medical procedure. In addition, certain patients have considerable difficulty "reading" their internal states, and the feedback provided by the biofeedback monitor is often helpful for them. It has been useful in addressing distorted thought processes. Cognitive therapy may also be helpful in providing a patient with a grater sense of mastery over seemingly uncontrollable events.

TEMPOROMANDIBULAR JOINT PAIN (TMJ)

Temporomandibular joint pain (TMJ) usually takes the form of a clicking or popping of the jaw and may include headache as well as facial tenderness. It is estimated that 60% of the population has at least one TMJ symptom (Melamed & Williamson, 1991). Of interest, men and women seem to be equally likely to have symptoms of TMJ in the general population. However, women are about twice as likely to present for treatment of this condition (Kleinknecht, Mahoney, & Alexander, 1987). TMJ has multiple causes that include a genetic predisposition for "orofacial parafunctional behaviors" (nail biting, grinding teeth at night, or clinching of the jaw). High caffeine intake and sleep disturbance is also common among these patients.

Stress seems to play a major role. Studies in which TMJ patients wear a portable EMG device to monitor their levels of muscle tension throughout the day have found that demanding daily activities increase facial tension. The device showed increased muscle use during freeway driving, interactions with children, and stressful events such as work-related encounters (Greene, Olson, & Laskin, 1982; Rugh & Solberg, 1976).

In addition to relaxation training, treatment often includes wearing occlusal splints at night. An EMG device, functionally similar to the bell and pad for nocturnal enuresis, has also been developed. When the EMG ratings of muscle tension reach a critical value, a tone is elicited and the patient is woken. This approach is also helpful for patients who tend to grind their teeth at night (Cassisi, McGlynn, & Belles, 1987).

LOWER BACK PAIN

Low back pain is usually a self-limiting condition that resolves within several days to weeks in about 85–90% of cases (Gatchel, Polatin, Mayer, & Garcy, 1995).

The relatively small percentage of patients whose back pain does not resolve constitutes one of the largest groups of disabled patients in the United States both numerically and financially. In industrialized countries, about 3% to 4% of the general population is disabled at least temporarily by low back pain (Gatchel et al., 1995). It is estimated that about 5 million U.S. citizens currently have low back pain—about half of these qualify as "permanently disabled" (National Center for Health Statistics, 1981). Back pain alone in the United States accounts for about one third of total lost days from work. The indirect cost of back pain is estimated to be around $3–3.5 billion (Frymoyer & Cats-Varil, 1991). These figures are for lost earnings alone; the total cost of low back pain in the United States is estimated to be about $60 billion and is the syndrome associated with the largest health care costs in the U. S. (Lee, 1994).

There is evidence that back pain's prevalence is increasing. It is noted that while the U.S. population increased by 12.5% between 1971 and 1981, the number of cases of disability associated with back pain increased by 168% (National Center for Health Statistics, 1981; Gatchel, Polatin, Mayer, & Garcy, 1994).

One difficulty that physicians often encounter with low back pain patients is that there does not seem to be a relationship between established pathology and degree of distress. Radiographic findings often do not confirm or verify causes of low back pain. Similarly, many of these patients are described as having "soft tissue injuries" that cannot be verified by examination or x-ray (Gatchel et al., 1995). Many have argued that the degree of disability associated with low back pain attributed to verifiable physical pathology is very small (Jansen, Brant-Zawadzki, Obuchowski, 1994; Waddell, Main, Morris, DiPaolo, & Gray, 1984).

There does appear to be evidence of a particularly high rate of psychiatric distress among low back pain patients. Among primary care back pain patients, Coste and colleagues (1992) found that 41% had a psychiatric condition. Among these patients, depression was the most common with over 25% of the patients exhibiting depressive symptoms. Additionally, patients with psychiatric disorders were more likely to have difficulty reporting their pain intensity on a pain scale and have pain that was associated with environmental factors as well as pain that increased in intensity during domestic work (Coste, Paolaggi, & Spira, 1992). In another sample of patients in a specialized rehabilitation setting, a much higher percentage, 69%, exhibited evidence of a psychiatric disorder, even when somatoform pain syndrome was removed. Of these patients, 60% were depressed and 20% exhibited substance abuse (Gatchel et al., 1994). In this sample of patients in a specialized rehabilitation program, the presence or type of psychopathology did not affect patient's return to work. The program, however, included attention to the patient's psychiatric disorder in treating back pain. Treatment included stress management, cognitive behavioral skills, crisis intervention, as well as family counseling.

Fordyce's behavioral model of chronic pain suggests that reinforcement in the form of workmen's compensation or release from work plays a salient role in patients' recovery from chronic pain conditions. There is some support for this view in the research literature. Among patients who were referred to a low back pain clinic, Sanderson, Todd, Holt, & Getty (1995) found that unemployment as well as financial compensation were positively related to the role of psychological factors in patient's back pain. The key determinant appeared to be unemployment, with patients who were unemployed reporting greater levels of disability as compared to patients who were still employed but seeking compensation (Sanderson et al., 1995).

The pathway from acute low back pain, which is self-limiting in most patients, to chronic low back pain and subsequent disability is beginning to be established. Hadjistavropoulos & Craig (1994) suggest that immediately after acute injury, patients are generally at high levels of psychological distress and rely heavily on passive coping strategies including increased medication and reduced physical activities. With the continuation of pain, patients may adopt one of two coping styles. One subgroup will adapt to pain and use more adaptive and active coping styles with a corresponding decline in emotional distress. A second subgroup, however, probably fits the classic chronic low back pain patient. These patients tend to exhibit more catastrophic cognitions ("This pain is terrible. I can't stand it: I will never be able to work."), are of a lower socioeconomic group, and are more likely to be receiving compensation. Additionally, these patients tend to continue to focus on their pain and are often very involved with health care providers. This is consistent with the clinical course of low back pain, in that patients whose symptoms exist more than about four months will not be back at work at the end of the year. A high percentage of these patients will exhibit continued disability at two years (Gatchel et al., 1995).

In following patients over the course of a year, Gatchel & colleagues (1995) found that the degree of pain, presence of a worker's compensation or personal injury case, and female gender were more strongly associated with longer term disability. In addition, however, MMPI data suggested that patients who were more somatically focused were less likely to return to work. Of interest, severity of initial injury as well as physical demands of the patient's job were not related to return to work after one year. The longitudinal format of the study allowed the investigators to conclude that psychopathology—specifically degree of depression or substance abuse—did not precede the development of chronic pain disability but seemed to be associated with it.

As far as primary care treatment of these patients is concerned, there are several guidelines. First, evaluation of patients for depression is strongly recommended. It has been suggested that low back pain patients, particularly those with soft tissue disorders, may have better outcome with the older tricyclic antidepressants than the newer SSRIs (Gillette, 1996). Encouraging the patient to stay active will also prevent the low back pain spiral in which decreased activity causes increased pain, which in turn, caused decreased activity. Patients should be encouraged to gradually increase their level of physical activity each week. Activity may include walking for 10–15 minutes a day and also should include ongoing social activities. Again, similar to chronic fatigue sufferers, low back pain patients will often report that they "do not feel like it." The provider should emphasize the relationship between social withdrawal, inactivity, dysphoric mood, and increased disability and encourage the patient to be active anyway. Although analgesic medication may be helpful immediately after the injury, continuing use of analgesic medication may become counterproductive (Gillette, 1996). Because of the role of cognitive factors in low back pain disability, engaging the patient in a process of labeling and refuting irrational thinking may also be helpful. Relaxation training, possibly including biofeedback, is helpful in reducing exacerbations of pain that may occur through involuntary "bracing." In sum, low back pain patients respond well to a multimodal approach that should be initiated aggressively and early. As noted above, the longer the patient is inactive, the greater the likelihood of permanent inactivity and disability.

CONCLUSION

Although headache, low back pain, and other forms of chronic pain are often seen primarily as physiological or musculoskeletal in origin, the past three decades have produced a body of research emphasizing the role of psychosocial factors. Although many pain patients may not readily perceive or acknowledge the role of emotional or environmental issues in their pain experience, the clinician should always consider the interaction of these issues with medical etiologies. A key issue with pain patients is early intervention and maintenance of reasonable activity levels. Patients who respond to chronic pain by increased immobilization are likely to develop a pain-oriented lifestyle that becomes difficult to change after it has been in place for multiple months. Early and practical intervention including attention to the high rate of psychiatric disorders among these patients will be helpful to the patient as well as physicians involved in their care.

Chapter 12

Diversity Issues in Primary Care

In recent years, there has been growing attention to the role of cultural factors in medical care. There is evidence that health-seeking behavior differs among members of different cultural groups as well as by gender and sexual orientation. There is also evidence that these factors influence illness prevalence as well as the types of symptoms that are presented to providers. Lastly, there are unique syndromes associated with particular cultural groups that may be unfamiliar to the practitioner trained in traditional Western medicine including psychiatry.

CULTURAL VIEWS OF ILLNESS

Cultural norms strongly influence the labeling of experiences as "symptoms" and further, how these deviations are grouped. Etiological explanations also vary across cultures. For example, susto includes many psychiatric symptoms and is commonly found among Hispanics in the southwest as well as throughout Latin America (Broadhead, 1994). In its direct meaning, susto means "fright." Susto includes symptoms of multiple medical and mental health problems including weight loss, poor appetite, insomnia, fatigue, exaggerated startle reflex, diarrhea, and dysphoric mood. Susto may be expressed through periods of excitement and fainting. Etiologically, Susto appears to be associated with some significant trauma, as those patients who exhibit it are believed to have experienced a disconnection of the soul from the body that occurred during the frightening experience (Broadhead, 1994; Searight, 1997c).

In the southeastern United States, "nerves" is a frequent medical presentation (Broadhead, 1994). "Nerves" includes symptoms such as shaking, stomach pains, nausea, headaches, shortness of breath, dizziness, blurred vision, hot flashes, and generalized states of tension. The symptoms appear to include both depression and anxiety dimensions, but these do not fit into *DSM–IV* categories. Nerves, like susto, has also been explained in terms of recent trauma. However, nerves may also derive from ongoing psychosocial conflicts such as marital issues or difficulty with a child.

Somatic expression of psychiatric disorders appears to be prevalent among several other ethnic and cultural groups. There is some evidence that among African Americans, classical depressive symptoms may be under-reported and somatic distress may be emphasized (Broadhead, 1994). As noted earlier, somatization is characterized by a range of vague, nonspecific physical symptoms for which no organic etiology could be established. These typically include gastrointestinal, pain, cardiopulmonary, sexual, and neurological symptoms. Other ethnic groups that appear to have particularly high rates of somatization include Latinos and Asian Americans. Among Latinos, there does appear to be variability according to specific country of origin. Puerto Ricans appear to have a higher incidence of somatization than Mexican Americans. Mexican American men in particular may, because of the culture of machismo, deny and minimize physical stress (Castillo, Waitzkin, & Escobar, 1994).

Among Asian Americans, "heaviness of the chest or heart" may be a common presentation (Kleinman, 1988). This symptom has increasingly been recognized as a cultural expression of depression. Before this pattern was understood, many Asian Americans were referred to cardiologists for this presenting symptom. In Asian cultures, direct expression of emotion is discouraged, and open discussion of family conflicts is also frowned upon. Thus, when emotional distress occurs, it is more likely to take a somatic form.

There also appears to be evidence that acculturation plays a role in the expression of symptoms. Recent immigrants from Asian and Latin countries appear to be more likely to express psychological issues somatically (Angel & Thoits, 1987) than longer-term residents.

Among refugees, post-traumatic stress disorder may be particularly prominent. Many recent refugees from Central American countries such as El Salvador and Guatemala have been subjected to torture and observed a number of violent deaths. Sexual and physical abuse have also been commonly reported among Southeast Asian refugees. There is evidence of a fairly strong relationship between post-traumatic stress disorder and presentation of somatic symptoms to physicians among these individuals (Castillo et al., 1994).

HEALTH-SEEKING BEHAVIOR

Although members of different cultural groups may present with unique symptoms to their primary care physician, they may also seek help from a network of lay providers. These include herbalists, traditional healers, and nutritionists. These may be consulted instead of or in addition to traditional Western medical practitioners. There are several factors contributing to the use of indigenous healers. One issue is that the explanatory model of disorders such as susto or "nerves" may fall outside of Western medicine. In addition, in many cultures, emotional disturbances are associated with significant stigma (Castilo et al., 1994). Among many Hispanic groups, indigenous healers such as curanderos and curanderas are sought for treatment of susto and related problems.

The curandera and faith healer share an operational belief system that mind and body are unified. In addition, an imbalance between the social, physical world is seen as a contributing to these symptoms. The curandera uses a medium between the spiritual world and the individual. The healing ceremony may include chanting certain words or evoking images (Cervantes & Ramirez, 1992). Patients may also experience visual or auditory experiences that are part of the illness that should be distinguished from psychosis (Searight, 1997). Just as curanderos are common among individuals with a Mexican background, Puerto Ricans practice Santeria, which is a combination of Christian and Spanish beliefs (Cervantes & Ramirez, 1992; Searight, 1997c).

Among African Americans, faith healers and root doctors may be sought. These doctors are common among African Americans in the Southern United States. In addition, African Americans who migrated to large northern cities have continued to employ root doctors. Root doctors are seen as individuals with special powers who can perform a type of sorcery and either place or remove spells on others (Snow, 1993).

Native Americans also have a long tradition of indigenous healers. These healers are seen as being able to help the patient achieve an appropriate balance between the material and spiritual worlds. Often, these traditional healers are used as parallel providers with physicians practicing more conventional Western medicine (Carresse & Rhodes, 1995).

HEALTH CARE ETHICS

Western medicine values patient autonomy, and this emphasis on individual independence may also be affected by culture. Living wills, advanced directives, and appointing medical powers of attorney are all means of maintaining a patient's autonomy even when they are unable to make decisions for themselves. During the past 30 years, views of patient autonomy and the patient's right to know about their illness have changed dramatically (Oken, 1961). In 1961, 90% of physicians did not directly tell patients that they had a diagnosis of cancer (Oken, 1961). This paternalism has been nearly completely eradicated during the ensuing 30 years. It is now believed that patients should be told directly about illnesses and that they have a right to understand risks and benefits of treatment and make individual choices. However, this value of patient autonomy and the right to know may not be universal across cultures (Blackhall, Murphy, Frank, Michel, & Azen, 1995).

Blackhall and colleagues found that when compared with European and African Americans, Korean Americans and Mexican Americans were far less likely to believe that patients should be told the truth about a diagnosis of metastatic cancer. In addition, patients of Korean and Mexican American background were less likely to view the patient as a source for decisions about life support. Instead, family members were seen as appropriate decision makers. Specifically, 47% of Korean Americans and 65% of Mexican Americans believed that patients should be told of a diagnosis of metastatic cancer as compared with 87% of European Americans and 88% of African Americans surveyed. Among Mexican Americans, patients who were more acculturated to American society by their greater use of English and association with Anglos were more likely to believe that patients should be directly informed. However, among the majority of Mexican Americans as well as Korean Americans, it was seen as the family's responsibility to receive the information about the patient's diagnosis and prognosis and then to make medical decisions for them.

As Blackhall and colleagues (1995) note, autonomy may not be a preeminent value among many ethnic groups. Rather than being seen as providing appropriate levels of control to the individual, autonomy may be socially isolating and a burden to seriously ill patients. In clinical situations, it has been suggested that practitioners ask their patients about their desire to be informed about illness and about whether they want to make decisions or if they prefer family involvement. By asking about this issue directly, the provider can respect ethnic values around decision making and autonomy (Blackhall et al., 1995).

This emphasis on truth-telling also appears to be less valued among Native Americans (Carrese & Rhodes, 1995). Among Navahoes, advanced directives and open discussion of risks of medical treatment such as surgery were seen as "speaking in a negative way." There is a view among Navahoes that thoughts and language have considerable power in influencing reality and controlling future events. Thus, negative words may be harmful to the patient, and Native healers are very sensitive to their use of language. Because of this value of Hózhó, an emphasis on goodness, order, and harmony, implementation of advanced directives was seen as potentially harmful among the Navaho (Carrese & Rhodes, 1995).

ETHNIC AND CULTURAL ISSUES IN THE PRIMARY CARE ENCOUNTER

There are several unique issues that occur when patients of different ethnic and cultural backgrounds appear in the primary care providers' office. Language and communication barriers are certainly an obvious example of difficulties that may occur. Translators are often present in these encounters. It has been recommended that the provider continue to address his or her comments to the patient, including eye contact with the patient, when a translator is present (Fernandez, South-Paul, & Matheny, 1998). Translators may still have difficulty interpreting patients' complaints accurately, particularly when they center around more detailed medical or emotional issues. In addition, the translator may be family or a friend. In this situation, the patient may not disclose personal information to the translator. The author has observed several encounters with recent female Cambodian immigrants who were accompanied by a male translator who was a member of the local Cambodian community. There was obvious discomfort when the female patient was asked questions through the interpreter about gynecological symptoms. Similarly, reporting emotional distress may be discouraged in many cultural groups. As a result, the interpreter may downplay the significance of psychological complaints when reporting to the provider.

Because of the various meanings that may be associated with physical symptoms, it is helpful to the provider to adopt a somewhat inquisitive style in interviewing patients of different cultures. Asking a patient directly, "What do you think is causing the problem and what types of treatments have you tried?" (Fernandez et al., 1998) will help elicit patients' personal explanatory beliefs. It may be necessary to negotiate with the patient around accepting medical or psychological care. Negotiation will usually be most successful if the provider's treatment is presented as parallel with an indigenous therapy. Patients are often aware that their own explanatory models are not well received among Western practitioners. Thus, it is extremely important that the interviewer be nonjudgemental and accepting as well as somewhat persistent in eliciting these culturally based explanatory models.

SPECIFIC CULTURAL/ETHNIC GROUPS: EXAMPLES OF PRIMARY HEALTH CARE ISSUES

In the brief sections that follow, specific issues arising with different ethnic groups in the United States will be discussed.

African Americans

African Americans comprise about 12% of the U.S. population (Baker, 1995). African American men have a significantly higher mortality rate associated with violent deaths including homicide, accidents, suicide, and substance abuse. Other health problems that are common in the African American community include hypertension, cardiovascular disease, and diabetes (Baker, 1995). For primary care providers, it is important to recognize that among African Americans, extended family, including non-blood-related friends, are often considered important family members. It is also common for extended family and non-blood family such as "Godparents" to take over care of a child when a parent is unable to do so (Boyd-Franklin, 1989). This practice may be associated with procedural problems in the clinic because only parents and legal guardians may authorize medical care for minors. Thus, an aunt who brings a child in for treatment may not be able to authorize the treatment even though the child may have lived with her since he or she was an infant. The emphasis on family heritage is also evident in situations when an adolescent girl becomes pregnant. Whereas many European American providers may have strong emotional reactions to a 14-year-old girl delivering a baby, abortion is often considered inappropriate among African Americans. Aborting a child or giving a child up for adoption is seen as a disavowal of one's family heritage (Boyd-Franklin, 1989; Searight, 1997c).

HIV/AIDS is a growing health concern in the African American community. African Americans are significantly over-represented among new AIDS cases (MacQueen, 1994). African Americans now account for about one third of new AIDS cases in the United States. Intravenous drug use is a common means of transmitting the virus in the African American community. African American IV drug users have several distinctive styles of drug use that increase their risk. These include a greater frequency of injection as well as the use of drugs in "shooting galleries" (MacQueen, 1994). In "shooting galleries," drug equipment may be rented, reused, or shared among different individuals.

As noted earlier, African Americans may have specific cultural beliefs about health and illness. One example is the experience of isolated sleep paralysis, which appears to occur more commonly among African Americans and may be associated with panic disorder and hypertension (Paradis, Friedman, & Hatch, 1997). Isolated sleep paralysis occurs when a patient is falling asleep or awakening and has the experience of being unable to move. They also may experience auditory and visual illusions and panic-like symptoms including increased heart rate, difficulty breathing and fearfulness. Isolated sleep paralysis may be seen by those experiencing it as a "spell" and has been described as the "witch is riding you" (Paradis et al., 1997). It has been suggested that these episodes may be associated with a greater incidence of stress and trauma in inner city African Americans.

Snow's work (1993) emphasized that among urban African Americans, indigenous health beliefs at variance with conventional medicine are still common. For example high blood pressure is associated with blood that is "too thick" or that is rising too high in the body. Thick blood may be dangerous because it "clogs up the vessels." The blood may be "thinned" by a range of procedures including drinking prune juice or taking Epsom Salts and vinegar (Snow, 1993).

Menstruation is seen as a way that the body cleanses itself and a process that should not be impeded. Some methods of birth control may be seen as disrupting normal menstrual flow. As a result, some African American women may view methods such as IUDs as harmful. During menstruation, women are seen as having particular powers to bring about harm to others. Snow (1992) provides the example of a husband who would not allow his wife to cook during her menstrual period because the blood could be put into the food and it would make the man "go crazy" or permit her to place a spell on him. Again, the provider who is sensitive and respectful of these alternative explanations is likely to develop a better relationship with culturally diverse patients.

Native Americans

Approximately 2 million people in the United States are Native Americans. Slightly over half now live in urban areas rather than on reservations (Rousseau, 1995). Among ethnic minorities in the United States, Native Americans probably have access to more comprehensive health care than other groups because of specialized health facilities for Native Americans administered through the United States Public Health Service (Rousseau, 1995).

Among Native Americans, leading health concerns include cardiovascular disease and diabetes mellitus. Diabetes, in particular, appears to be a significant health concern, with mortality among Native Americans being greater than that for all races in the United States (Rousseau, 1995). In clinical work with Native Americans, it is important to recognize values and themes that may govern health care exchanges (Hepburn & Reed, 1995). Communication may be indirect and may be characterized by pauses that appear lengthy by European standards (Searight, 1997c). Direct eye contact for extended periods of time may be viewed as insulting by Native Americans. Autonomy is valued, but the boundaries around health care decision making include the community or immediate family or both. In addition, there may be some suspicion or hypersensitivity to external authorities, particularly those who are not native (Hepburn & Reed, 1995).

Time is viewed as circular. Because of this nonlinear perspective, future-oriented issues may not be seen as relevant or readily grasped by Native Americans. This is particularly true in mental health or medical encounters. There may even be an element of determinism in these exchanges such that future events will simply "unfold" and there is little point in predicting or discussing them (Searight, 1997c). In addition, as noted above, discussion of potentially negative events such as serious illness or death may be viewed as harmful.

The preoccupation of many professionals with formalities, including signed documents, may also be somewhat antithetical to Native American value systems. Hepburn & Reed (1995) have noted that the preoccupation with documentation may prevent the Native American's from expressing their wishes. An example of this indirect mode of communication may include talking about someone else's death rather than the patient's own. Hepburn and Reed (1995) described how the issue of advanced directives was addressed through conversations about how another member of the community had become ill and died several years earlier. Although the linkage between the patient's condition and the deceased was never made explicit, the patient later discussed the deceased tribal member in a way that indicated that they approved of the process of the previous death.

Lastly, the importance of spirituality among Native Americans should be appreciated. Native American religion emphasizes the interconnection between people and nature. Illness in an individual may be seen as a stress or imbalance in the larger community (Searight, 1997c). Spiritual belief systems may account for many psychological problems. For example, Grossman, Putsch, & Inui (1993) described spirit sickness as a mediator of death and self-destructive behavior among the Salish community of the Pacific Northwest. Spirit sickness was seen as similar to depression and often occurred because of the influence of the ghosts of deceased family and community members. Spirit sickness could cause one to become despondent and even to drink excessively. Additionally, it was believed that spirits of the dead could "snatch" the living. This explanation was often invoked for suicide and violent deaths that occurred after the death of a community or family member (Grossman et al., 1993).

Asian Americans

About 3% of the U.S. population is made up of Asians and Pacific Islanders (Lum, 1995). These include Chinese, Japanese, Koreans, Philippinos, Pacific Islanders, and other Southeast Asians such as Laotians, Vietnamese, and Cambodians. Among Asian patients, illness may be seen as emanating from supernatural forces such as the ghosts of ancestors or spirit possession as well as imbalances in bodily humors (Lum, 1995). Illness models among Asians often center around symptoms rather than underlying causes. As noted above, psychological disorders are likely to be expressed through somatic means. Asian American patients are likely to focus on fatigue, pain, or malaise.

Western providers have also been warned against over-interpretation of seemingly psychotic symptoms among these patients. It is noted that Asians may use idiosyncratic expressions such as "heaviness of the heart" to describe depression or the experience of hearing the voices of one's ancestors (Lum, 1995) to describe psychological distress. These may be mistaken as indicative of psychosis when instead they are cultural expressions.

As the study by Blackhall and colleagues (1995) underscores, Asian Americans often do not overtly address death or terminal conditions. Among Chinese families, it is unusual to have open discussions about a patient's medical condition with the patient present. Kleinman (1980) noted that in Taiwan, the primary caregiver was the family. Nearly three quarters of patients received treatment only from the family during a course of an illness. Tong and Spicer (1994) suggest that the family should be used as a colleague by health care providers. Although impending death may not be overtly acknowledged, it may be signaled indirectly (Tong & Spicer, 1994). For example, when significant narcotics are provided to the patient to relieve pain, patients are usually aware that they have a serious condition, particularly when different treatments are used in succession. Visits from family members, particularly those coming from abroad, as well as frequent and lengthy visits by closer relatives, are signals to the patient that death may be imminent. Lastly, nonverbal language including the patient's facial expression and touching of other family members may also be ways that impending death is communicated.

With the recent influx of immigrants from Southeast Asian countries such as Laos and Vietnam there have been reports of sudden death syndromes. These usually occur during sleep and are particularly common among Hmong refugees (Adler, 1995). The Hmong themselves believe that these nightmare attacks are from evil spirits. Although these experiences apparently do occur among Laotians living in their native land, the attacks did not result in death. Adler (1995) has suggested that the stresses of war, escape from Laos, difficulties occurring in refugee camps, stress of resettlement in the United States, as well as the breaking up of families and practical difficulties in maintaining religious practices may be contributing factors.

Hispanic Americans

It is estimated that about 9% of the U.S. population is of Hispanic background, coming from a range of regions including Cuba, Central America, South America, Mexico, and Puerto Rico. There is some variability regarding health beliefs among immigrants from these different locals. There are several cultural values important for health care. First, personalismo, an emphasis on individual integrity and worth rather than achievement, is an important dimension of Hispanic personality. The emphasis on personalismo is that one should be honorable and respectful rather than being evaluated in terms of achievement or material possessions (Searight, 1997c). Family is seen as very important. Extended family members and non-blood-related persons may also be included in one's kinship network. There is considerable emphasis on family hierarchies as well as respect for authority. Gender roles are often traditional and rigidly held. Men may be characterized by machismo, which emphasizes strength, emotional control, and hypersexuality. Women may be seen as spiritual and morally superior (Searight, 1997c; Vasquez, 1994) to men. These latter dimensions are often the source of considerable conflict as immigrants acculturate to a U.S. society that has increasingly emphasized more egalitarian sex roles.

The emphasis on machismo appears to be playing a role in the transmission of HIV among Hispanics. Although Hispanics only account for about 9% of the U.S. population, they have included almost 20% of new AIDS cases. About half of HIV-positive men and 40% of HIV-positive women in the Hispanic community are infected through sexual contact (Marin & Gomez, 1994). In the Latino community, sexuality is regarded with considerable ambivalence. First, there is a strong negative sanction toward homosexuality. Thus, many gay Latino men do not label themselves as such, and safe sex educational messages directed toward gays may not be seen as relevant. Sexuality, in general, in the Latino community is regarded with considerable ambivalence. Open discussion of sexual matters is not culturally accepted. At the same time, there is a cultural view of Hispanic men as being very sexually active (Marin & Gomez, 1994). There is some empirical support for this "myth." Among married men, it was found that about twice as many married Hispanic men as compared to White men reported having multiple sexual partners in the previous year (Marin & Gomez, 1994; Searight & McLaren, 1997). Once they are infected, the strong sense of loyalty and responsibility to the family may prevent Latino men from disclosing their HIV status (Mason, Marks, Simoni, Ruiz, & Richardson, 1995). Mason and colleagues (1995) found that when compared with English-speaking Latinos, Spanish-speaking Latin men were much less likely to disclose their HIV positive status as well as their gay or bisexual orientation to family members.

Latino women have also been found to hold distinct beliefs regarding breast cancer risks and symptoms as compared with the prevailing biomedical model. Chavez and colleagues (Chavez, Hubbell, McMullin, Martinez, & Mishira, 1995) found that Latino women viewed primary breast cancer risks as physical trauma to the breast itself, as well as drinking and using illegal drugs. Anglo American women were much more likely to adopt a biomedical model, which includes age and family history. The emphasis on family also extends to caring for elderly individuals. Respect for the elderly is a strong value in the Hispanic community. Cox and Monk (1993) found that Hispanic caregivers of the elderly almost unanimously believed that married children should live close to parents in order to provide care and saw it is a child's duty to assist their parents. There was a very strong negative sanction about hiring professionals to provide care for the elderly. At the same time, the caregivers reported considerable strain in the caregiver role. These included physical symptoms, depression, and stress (Fox & Monk, 1993). However, although adult children were aware of community-based sources of assistance, they did not rely on them. A common form that this stress took was as somatic symptoms. Primary care mental health providers should be aware that a cultural value stressing responsibility towards one's family may result in a higher incidence of psychological and nonspecific somatic symptoms among caregivers, particularly in persons acculturating to European standards.

GENDER AND HEALTH CARE

Mental health professionals are well aware of gender differences in identity development as well as in the prevalence of different psychiatric disorders. Gilligan's (1982) work highlighted the role that relational factors played in the development of identity among women, whereas men's identity was often rooted in achievement. Similarly, moral and ethical dilemmas are often addressed from a contextual perspective by women, who attempt to meet the needs of those involved while simultaneously attending to a value of equity. Men, in contrast, make these decisions based on impartial, abstract standards.

With respect to the medical setting, men are more likely to have cardiovascular disorders including hypertension and myocardial infarctions. Women, on the other hand, are more likely to have chronic conditions such as diabetes, rheumatoid arthritis, or gastrointestinal problems (Mann, 1996). Most disorders associated with high-risk behavior including lung cancer, heart disease, and stroke are more common among men. In addition, men are much more likely to be hospitalized for physical trauma (Mann, 1996). At the same time, however, women have a longer lifespan. There are some suggestions that women are more likely to be sick, but with less severe illnesses (Verbrugge, 1989).

Although risk factors are generally more common among men, it is important to note that smoking has increased fairly dramatically among women over the last 25 to 30 years. In 1955, about 25% of American women and 52% of American men smoked. By 1977, the rate of smoking by women was at 40% (Chesney & Nealey, 1996). Women begin smoking at a somewhat younger age and also appear to have a lower rate of smoking cessation. There is some research suggesting that women who smoke are viewed as somewhat more glamorous and attractive. This perspective may be fueled by cigarette advertising directed toward women, both in terms of female models as well as in female-oriented media, such as women's magazines (Chesney & Nealey, 1996). It is also possible that weight gain that is commonly experienced when smoking cessation is initiated is particularly distressing to women and conflicts with strong social messages directed toward slenderness as attractive among females.

Among men, there are suggestions that adherence to traditional gender roles may be indirectly associated with greater health risks. Men who perceive greater threats to their masculinity appear to respond with greater systolic blood pressure reactivity to these threats. Excessive self-reliance, a highly competitive approach to personal interactions, and self-monitoring around masculinity all are contributors to traditional masculine gender role. Masculine gender role has been associated with higher levels of anger and, in turn, could be a mediating factor involving type A personality and cardiac conditions (Copenhaver & Eisler, 1996).

These differences in gender socialization appear to influence help-seeking behavior. Women are much more likely to visit health care providers. This pattern occurs even when gynecological and obstetric visits are controlled (Copenhaver & Eisler, 1996). Gender roles are such that men appear to have much more difficulty acknowledging distress, including physical symptoms. Men also may not be well aware of their internal distress. Men's stoicism is likely to extend to both psychological and physical symptoms. The degree of dependence and vulnerability in taking on the "sick role" even for a brief office visit may be particularly incongruent for men (Copenhaver & Eisler, 1996).

Clinically, the author emphasizes to physicians that when men (particularly those in the 20 to 45 age group) appear with a seemingly "minor" complaint, the provider should be particularly aggressive about looking for other issues including psychosocial conflicts. It is extremely unusual for young and middle-age males to present to their physician for "routine health maintenance" or nonspecific symptoms such as fatigue. There is often an underlying agenda such as a desire for a test for a sexually transmitted disease or concern about more serious health-related symptoms (blood in one's stool). Psychological problems such as depression may be minimized with symptoms being vague or downplayed in their significance.

All providers in primary care settings should be aware of domestic violence. The research of Strauss and colleagues (Straus, Gelles & Steinmetz, 1980) found that at least 16% of couples had at least one violent episode during the past year. Close to one third of couples report physical violence at some point in the history of their relationship. There is considerable evidence that primary care physicians underdetect violence. Goldberg and Tomlanovich (1984) found that in a survey of emergency room patients, 22% reported being victims of domestic violence, with only 5% of these patients having actually been detected by their physicians. Similar to the issues raised with child abuse, whenever the provider is confronted with suspicious injuries in an adult, domestic violence should always be considered. The provider should interview the patient alone and ask directly about current or past episodes. Developing a "safe" plan including information about women's shelters and how to obtain legal support for restraining orders should also be included. It is also important for providers to recognize that for women who have been battered by their partner, there are often long-term emotional sequelae. These include depression and increased somatic distress, as well as flash backs, sleeping problems, hypervigilance, and other symptoms associated with post-traumatic stress disorder. Conversely, when the provider is seeing a woman with many of these symptoms, the possibility of partner or spousal abuse should be seriously considered. It may take some time and multiple contacts before the woman will disclose the history to the mental health professional or physician.

GAY AND LESBIAN RELATIONSHIPS

Recent estimates suggest that about 5% of the U.S. population identifies themselves as gay with approximately 2% self-identified as lesbian (Diamond, 1993; Janus & Janus, 1993). When surveys ask about both homosexual and heterosexual activity in adulthood, figures rise to about 9% of men and about 5–6% of women (Seidman & Rieder, 1995). A significant proportion of gays and lesbians are in long-term relationships. Among lesbians, a significant percentage of long-term relationships include children. These are children either from prior heterosexual relationships or children who have been adopted or conceived through artificial insemination (Patterson, 1992).

The health care system has been found to be an inhospitable environment for gays and lesbians. One survey of physicians reported that about 40% indicated that they were "sometimes or often" uncomfortable treating gay or lesbian patients. Additionally, nearly one third would not admit a qualified gay or lesbian applicant to medical school and slightly less than one half would stop referring patients to a colleague if they learned they were gay or lesbian (Matthews, Booth, Turner, & Kessler, 1986; Rankow, 1995). In a more recent survey of primary care physicians, over one third said they would feel "nervous" among a group of homosexuals, and one third indicated that homosexuality is a threat to many basic social institutions (Harrison, 1996; Murphy, 1991).

Both mental health professionals as well as medical practitioners tend to receive little formal training regarding gay and lesbian patients. There is often an assumption during the clinical history that the patient is heterosexual. Patients are routinely asked about sexual intercourse and contraception or about their husband or wife. Gay and lesbian patients themselves often are reluctant to disclose their sexual identity to healthcare providers. Given the attitudes of many health care providers noted above, this reluctance is understandable. The practical result may be that both gays and lesbians do not seek appropriate routine care. For example, lesbians are much less likely to have PAP smears and when they do, they obtain them less frequently (Harrison, 1996). O'Hanlan (1996) notes that breast, ovarian, and endometrial cancers may be more frequent in lesbians than among heterosexual women. Among gay men, HIV infection is more prevalent that in heterosexual males. Other sexually transmitted diseases may be more common among gay men.

With respect to mental health concerns, providers should be aware that lesbian and gay adolescents are at particularly high risk for suicide. They are also at greater risk for running away from home or being put out of their home by parents (Rankow, 1995). There continues to be homophobia among high school age teenagers, making it difficult for gay and lesbian teenagers to internalize and accept their sexual orientation. There is evidence that this psychological distress does not necessarily resolve with age. Rankow's (1995) review indicates that about

40% of adult lesbians have considered suicide with 18% attempting it. Although heterosexual women are at higher risk for eating disorders such as bulimia and anorexia, homosexual men are more likely to develop eating disorders than heterosexual males (Mann, 1996). Additionally, there appears to be a greater use of alcohol, marijuana, and cocaine among lesbians and gay men than in the general population (Mann, 1996). There are also some suggestions that partner abuse may be as common in lesbian couples as heterosexuals. However, because of societal homophobia, reporting abuse by a same-gender partner may be much more problematic than among heterosexual women.

Providers should openly discuss with gay and lesbian patients their documentation in the medical record. The patient should be asked directly if they would want their sexual orientation recorded. Although some of the health risks associated with gay or lesbians are important for providers to know, patients may have concerns about information being disclosed to third parties as well as to other office staff and physicians (Rankow, 1995).

CONCLUSION

Increased attention to gender issues, cultural/ethnic diversity, and gender orientation in mental health care has yet to completely "filter down" to medicine. Mental health professionals are most likely to be sensitive to these issues and can provide significant contributions to health care teams by sensitizing physicians, nurses, and other providers to diversity issues. At present, there has been relatively little research devoted to the interactions between ethnicity and gay and lesbian patients in primary health care. There is more extensive background information about gender, particularly around domestic violence and obstetrics, which has highlighted unique issues and behavioral aspects of health care for women. However, while men are often highlighted in acute care and research on health risks, there is less known about issues surrounding men's reluctance to utilize medical care. Additional research and clinical writing in this area is likely to be forthcoming in years ahead and will be particularly helpful to mental health providers working in this setting.

Chapter 13

Ethical Dilemmas in Primary Care

Mental health professionals are generally well-trained in ethics. Psychotherapy and psychological evaluation require frequent critical reflections around legal and philosophical issues as well as application of ethical principles to ongoing practice. Primary medical care, although often involving mental health treatment, has not devoted the same degree of attention to many of these dilemmas. Medical practice also presents unique dilemmas to most psychological providers. Issues include informed consent, competence, distinct applications of the duty to warn, end-of-life decision making, and genetic counseling.

INFORMED CONSENT

The issue of informed consent has become more salient in medicine than in mental health care. Physicians are required to disclose relevant information and obtain the patient's signature as well as verbal consent prior to performing nearly all procedures as well as diagnostic tests. Although there is some legal debate about the requirements for disclosure, there is agreement around five basic elements: (1) purpose of the procedure, (2) potential risks, (3) anticipated benefits, (4) alternative procedures, and (5) patient's voluntariness.

With respect to purpose, patients should receive information about whether a procedure is diagnostic versus therapeutic as well as the anticipated length of treatment and body systems or anatomical regions involved (Searight & Barbarash, 1994). Risks have been highlighted in discussions of informed consent. In addition to a description of possible risks, patients should be made aware of the likely magnitude or seriousness of risks. Risks are also relative to a patient's value system and life style (Searight & Barbarash, 1994). An example provided by Appelbaum, Lidz, & Meisel (1987) is that a medical procedure that leads to possible minor sensory loss in the hands may be of little importance to a retiree who spends his days watching television, but may be of much greater significance to someone who repairs watches for a living. The actual likelihood of a particular risk occurring has not been well incorporated into consent disclosure. Legally, there have been distinctions made between material, substantial, probable, and significant risks (Appelbaum et al., 1987; Searight & Barbarash, 1994). However, these categories are usually not well grasped by providers. Legal cases have arisen surrounding whether or not low probability risks should have been disclosed to a patient.

Benefits are usually apparent to the patient. However, patients may be confused about procedures that are diagnostic rather than therapeutic and also between treatments that are palliative versus curative. These distinctions should be formally explained to the patient (Searight & Barbarash, 1994; Appelbaum et al., 1987).

Treatment alternatives are not consistently presented to patients. Although there are certain illnesses for which there are no treatment options, most medical conditions can be treated with relative degrees of efficacy with a range of therapies. Patients' consent must be voluntary. Communication styles of providers often convey subtle pressure or preferences for a particular treatment. Although it is not inappropriate for a provider to indicate his or her view that a treatment is an optimal fit for a patient, the provider should clearly state this bias and be particularly explicit about this viewpoint when there are several established treatments of relatively equal effectiveness (Searight & Barbarash, 1994; Macklin, 1991).

Informed consent tends to be carried out as a procedure (Appelbaum et al., 1987). The patient is provided with a consent form, the highlights are covered verbally by the physician or their representative, and the patient is then asked to sign. Patients may be invited to ask questions prior to signing the consent form. However, these inquiries are relatively rare. This event-oriented model stands in contrast to an alternative, process approach to informed consent. The process model emphasizes the gradual presentation of relevant information over periods of time between the physician and patient (Appelbaum et al., 1987). The process approach also involves a greater sense of "negotiation" between the provider and patient.

Mental health providers can facilitate informed consent by encouraging patients to articulate their own understanding of a proposed procedure. Patients can be encouraged to describe their personally held belief model about their illness and their view of proposed treatment. These patient explanatory models are often strongly influenced by cultural and familial values. However, they often play a significant role in the frustrating encounters that occur between physician and patient around issues such as noncompliance (Searight & Noce, 1988). For example, a patient who views their diabetes as "just a touch of sugar" often will not use insulin on a consistent basis but only when they "feel" that their blood sugars are particularly high.

CONFIDENTIALITY

Confidentiality and privileged communication frequently become more challenging in medical settings than in traditional mental health settings. In inpatient settings, patients are frequently cared for by a team of professionals, all of whom have access to the patient's record. The team as well as any consultants on the case will all be able to read any information about the patient that has been put into the record. In addition, this information may be readily disclosed to an outside source. The mental health professional will have little control over these disclosures (Belar & Deardorff, 1995). At a practical level, evaluating patients in the hospital setting may pose challenges to confidentiality because of the proximity of other patients and health care professionals. For example, patients who are in multipatient bedrooms and who cannot walk or sit up in a wheelchair, may have to undergo assessment in the presence of roommates and nursing staff. Belar and Deardorff (1995) indicate that patients should be given explicit instructions that they may decline services if they are not comfortable with the situation.

Another challenge to confidentiality is that patients' relatives may often make direct contact with the provider seeking information about the patient. The author has been in a number of situations in which a physician disclosed information to the adult children of elderly patients without the patient's explicit consent. Additionally, adult children of geriatric patients will frequently attempt to make direct, private contact with a provider seeking information about their parent. Unless the patient has been adjudicated incompetent with a guardian appointed or power-of-attorney and the patient indicates that the adult child is making medical decisions on the patient's behalf, disclosure to these third parties without the patient's explicit consent is not strictly appropriate from an ethical–legal perspective.

DUTY-TO-WARN AND VIOLENCE

Confidentiality is maintained between the provider and adult patients except in situations where potential harm can arise to the patient or others. The duty-to-warn, which is familiar to most mental health professionals, has often been presented as a logical extension of a physician's obligation to warn and protect innocent parties from a patient with infectious disease (Falk, 1988). This issue was discussed earlier in the application to HIV positive patients.

Patients presenting risks for assaulting others are often encountered in the emergency room. Primary care medical providers may not be familiar with the ethical and legal issues involved with patients posing risks to others. These providers also do not customarily employ the framework that mental health professionals have developed for evaluating dangerousness patients and protecting others (Searight,

1997). In assessing violence-prone patients, clinicians need to be aware of risk factors. Demographically, patients with higher rates of aggression toward others are likely to be young adult men (Searight, 1997b; Simon, 1992). Psychiatric diagnoses associated with elevated violence risk include antisocial personality disorder, substance abuse, and possibly, paranoid schizophrenia (Simon, 1992; Swanson, Holzer, Ganju, & Jono, 1990). More imminent predictors of violence include loss or threatened loss of a valued role (e.g., job) or relationship, as well as the availability of a weapon (Searight, 1997b; Wilson & Daly, 1993).

If the provider determines that future violence is likely, the clinician should ask the patient directly about recent acts of violence as well as about their past history of violence ("What's the most harm you've ever done to anyone?") (Searight, 1997b). If it is determined that the patient does pose an imminent threat to others, a duty to protect should be implemented. This duty usually includes warning both an intended victim and the authorities. The only exception to this guideline would be a situation in which direct warning of a potential victim might actually increase the likelihood of violence. Although notification effectively enacts a duty to warn, it may be not adequate as a duty to protect. Protection may include evaluation of the patient for possible psychiatric inpatient admission.

Although mental health professionals are generally well-versed in situations such as those described above, there are several variations on the duty to protect that may arise in primary medical care settings. Recently, there has been concern about physicians' responsibilities when patients who are driving exhibit evidence of medical or psychiatric conditions that could result in accidents. Several years ago, there was a publicized case in which a school bus driver had sustained a myocardial infarction and had plunged his bus into New York City's East River killing 30 passengers (Simon, 1992). Apparently, the physician knew of the patient's medical status and of his occupation. The physician did not report the patient's medical history to the bus company because of fears that the patient could lose his job. Patients with significant substance abuse histories as well as patients with cognitive impairment such as dementia or episodes of psychosis are also likely to pose driving risks (Godard & Bloom, 1990). Although some states encourage the reporting of these patients to the local motor vehicle bureau, state laws have often not required physicians to make an absolute judgement about driving ability. Instead, descriptive information about the patient's medical condition is conveyed to state motor vehicle authorities who, in turn, make final decisions (Godard & Bloom, 1990).

MANAGED CARE

Nearly all health care providers, including mental health specialists, will have contact with patients in managed care plans. Even government programs such as

Medicare and Medicaid have, over the past five years, shifted into managed care plans. Appelbaum (1993) notes that all managed care approaches share several common elements:

1. Prospective or concurrent review of care.
2. Frequent economic incentives to reduce utilization.
3. Denial of payment for care not pre-approved or not determined to be medically necessary.

Although there has been considerable interest in integrated service organizations in which mental health providers see patients as part of the same system as medical providers, managed care plans have often established rules to prevent this type of integration (Seaburn et al., 1996). The most common form is the "carve out" of mental health services such that mental health services are treated differently than medical services. Many plans subcontract with particular managed mental health care organizations to provide psychiatric and substance abuse services. These mental health organizations may include a particular panel of providers in the geographic area, may operate their own mental health services, or may provide some combination of these two models. One effect of the increased movement toward managed care has been the ascendance of primary medical care. In the past, many patients self-referred to a range of specialists without having a personal or family physician. Most managed care entities require that the patient have a primary care physician and that this provider serve as the "gatekeeper" for other medical tests as well as access to specialists. In some plans, the primary care physician is also the gatekeeper for access to mental health care.

Managed care has brought with it several unique ethical and legal dilemmas. As Appelbaum (1993) notes, one fundamental issue is that providers are often not able to provide or obtain access to the level of mental health services that they believe many patients need. There has been a major emphasis placed on brief therapy with frequent reviews and justification of treatment needed often after as few as two to three sessions. In addition, although patients usually have a reasonable number of sessions included in their plan (20–25 per year), a reviewer may determine that a depressed patient may not require more than 10 sessions. A major conflict arises for practitioners when the level of service necessary to meet the consensually accepted standard of care for a particular disorder is not covered by the insurer. For example, considerable pressure is placed on clinicians to maintain hospitalizations for the briefest period of time possible and to rely heavily on outpatient over inpatient care. In treating patients who are suicidal or homicidal, this policy could potentially result in patients being released from a protected environment prematurely, so that harm to self or others occurs. In addition, the level of the professional's responsibility to a patient who has been treated for a period of time yet continues to have acute psychiatric symptomatology, but whose insurer will no longer pay for further treatment, raises a particularly difficult set of issues.

In this latter situation, the recommended response by the practitioner is to appeal the decision within the framework of the insurance company's policies. An early legal case that generated the standard of appeal is *Wickline v. State* (1986). In this case, the patient was hospitalized for vascular surgery. The physician's request for additional hospital days was denied. The patient was discharged, but later the condition of her leg deteriorated and amputation was required. The resulting ruling emphasized the physician's responsibility to the patient independent of the managed care company's policies (Appelbaum, 1993). The general recommendation in these situations is to initiate an appeal process through the managed mental health care company. It has been suggested that managed care companies have become increasingly concerned about liability. As a result, if an appeal for additional care is initiated, ongoing treatment is often covered during the time period until the dispute is resolved.

As a general rule, patients who have acute symptomatology should receive continued treatment by the mental health provider until their symptoms resolve. After the acute episode has resolved and if treatment has not been authorized by the managed care company, the patient may be referred to public mental health resources or to their new provider.

A final concern that probably arises more in medical practice than in mental health care is the issue of "gag" clauses. Gag clauses are written statements in the managed care contract preventing the provider from discussing reasonable alternative treatments that may not be covered by the patient's plan. For example, long-term psychotherapy groups may be appropriate for children with overanxious disorder and social skills deficits. However, many managed care plans will not cover these services. An additional example is that many managed mental health care plans place significant restrictions and require very intensive review for psychological testing. Even in situations in which a child presents with considerable evidence of a learning disability, the managed mental health care representative may not authorize testing to assess for learning difficulties. Gag rules prevent the provider from discussing these limitations directly with patients. Recently, there have been several legal challenges as well as legislation intended to abolish gag rules.

COMPETENCE AND CAPACITY

Legal Aspects

Questions about a patient's capacity for medical decisions frequently arise in hospital care. Although medical personnel typically request "competence evaluations" when patients refuse needed surgery or diagnostic procedures, or wish to return to independent living against medical advice, this terminology is not strictly correct. "Competence" is a legal term. A patient's incompetence can only be established through a legal proceeding. The psychological or cognitive analog to competence is "decision-making capacity." The courts rely heavily upon the health care provider's evaluations of patient's decisional abilities in determining competence. Relatives may request an evaluation of a patient's capacity for financial management if the individual appears to be using their economic resources in a frivolous or irresponsible manner.

With respect to medical care, physicians often find themselves in difficult situations. A provider may be found negligent if they comply with an incompetent patient's refusal to receive treatment. On the other hand, they can be held liable for battery if they proceed with treatment against the wishes of the competent patient (Searight, 1992a). Grisso (1994) notes that competence is a "threshold" legal dimension that needs to be addressed before guardianship and other forms of surrogate decision making are put into place. Legally, the standards for competence have become more differentiated with time. Historically, involuntary psychiatric hospitalization and "senility" have both carried the automatic presumption of incompetence. In the 1970s, however, state statutes began including more behaviorally specific wording to describe competence (Grisso, 1994).

Decisional Capacity

Mental health professionals often receive consultation requests worded globally (e.g., "assess patient's competence"). The wording of these requests implies that decisional capacity is a pervasive skill or trait. Capacity can only be validly assessed relative to a particular context (Searight, 1992). For example, a mildly mentally retarded patient might be quite capable of choosing between two nursing home placements, but may not have the capacity to consent to surgery to remove an intrauterine tumor. On the other hand, a 12-year-old boy may be able to give meaningful consent to a sports physical but not to a hernia repair. From a strictly legal perspective, a minor cannot give consent to medical procedure; however, cognitively they may well have the capacity to assent to certain medical procedures with low levels of risk (Miller & Searight, in press). In clinical practice, requests to evaluate a patient's capacity for decision making are usually triggered when a patient refuses to follow medical advice. These patients may include those with psychiatric disorder, delirium, or dementia, or patients who have values or a religious system that places limits on medical care such as when a member of the Jehovah's Witness faith refuses blood transfusions.

Assessment of cognitive functioning is certainly relevant to capacity. A neuro-logically oriented mental status examination, such as that described by Strubb and Black (1993), is a useful place to begin the process.

Attention to the presence of psychiatric symptoms, such as delusions and hal-lucinations, should also be part of the assessment. However, clinicians should recognize that patients with impaired decisional capacity may well have normal mental status. Conversely, patients with some fluctuation in their mental status may be capable of making medical decisions for themselves. The relevant dimen-sions of determining a patient's capacity for decision making center around his or her understanding of the illness and the proposed medical treatment (Appelbaum & Grisso, 1989). Appelbaum and Grisso (1989) highlight four basic functional skills: communicating choices, understanding relevant information, appreciating the situation and its consequences, and rational manipulation of information. Com-municating a consistent choice can be directly assessed by asking patients about the proposed treatment and their decision. Asking the patient again after a rea-sonable period of time will help the physician assess the stability of the decision. Patients who provide consent and then withdraw it in a "flip-flop" process may be experiencing significant anxiety or possibly some underlying process such as delirium or psychosis. Patients' capacity for understanding relevant information is best evaluated by having them paraphrase in their own words information given to them by their physician. Understanding should include a description of their condi-tion as well as proposed treatment. Appreciating the illness and its consequences is assessed through asking patients what they understand about the short- and long-term implications or prognosis of their disorder. In addition, this dimension includes attention to a patient's capacity to informally evaluate risks and bene-fits of various treatment options. Lastly, rational manipulation of information re-flects a systematic process of weighing pros and cons of various therapies including no treatment and arriving at a decision. Conceptually, the provider should focus on the process by which the patient reaches a decision rather than the outcome itself.

Although these dimensions provide general guidance for the assessment, the interview content should focus on the following: (1) a description of the illness, (2) comprehension of the course of the illness, (3) description of treatment op-tions, (4) description of the consequences of treatment, (5) explanation of the risks and benefits of treatment, and (6) an articulated account of the decision-making process regarding the treatment choice (Searight, 1992a). When patients refuse recommended treatment for a life-threatening or significantly disabling condition, they should be able to articulate a personal belief system that is internally consistent for their treatment refusal.

One option that is often not considered in performing capacity evaluations is the availability of alternative treatments. One recent study (Katz, Abbey, &

Rydall, 1995) noted that about 50% of patients who initially refused treatment later accepted it and about 19% of patients accepted another treatment option. It is important to recognize that treatment alternatives are often not presented to patients. Health care providers often become narrowly focused on a singular recommended treatment and do not consider alternatives. Although there may be some alternatives that are less efficacious clinically, they may be more acceptable to patients' personal values.

ADVANCED DIRECTIVES

Patient self-determination has become a preeminent value in American health care. This emphasis on patient autonomy has been extended to situations in which patients are no longer able to make decisions about their own care. Advanced directives are a set of guidelines drawn up by the patient when they are legally competent and presumably have intact decisional capacity. These guidelines take the form of a document that specifies the degree and type of life-sustaining treatment as well as general medical care that the patient will receive if they become incapacitated and are no longer able to make or indicate these choices for themselves. The primary objective of advanced directives is to prevent implementation of treatment that contradicts the patient's own wishes.

In the United States, advanced directives have been supported through state legislation. The Patient Self-Determination Act, a federal law, was passed in 1990. This law requires health care facilities receiving federal funds to inform patients of their right to refuse medical treatment. In addition, it also includes a provision for patients to complete an advanced directive upon hospital admission (Reconciliation Act, 1990).

As noted above, advanced directives take two basic forms. The first is a document drawn up by the patient. These are often known as "living wills." Living wills provide written direction to family members as well as physicians about the patient's care—specifically about the use of varying degrees of life support. The second form, durable power of attorney, appoints an individual, usually a family member, to make decisions on the patient's behalf. Durable powers of attorney have a relatively long history as a vehicle for managing patient's finances should they become incapacitated. In the past two decades, they have become increasingly advocated as a legal mechanism for making medical decisions. Although there are different degrees of specificity surrounding advanced directives, the general intent with both written advanced directives and durable powers of attorney is to express the genuine wishes of the incompetent patient.

Although the intent of advanced directives is to clarify patient's wishes regarding life support and related medical treatment, the actual implementation of these guidelines has raised several difficulties. In actual practice, many patients do not specify their wishes until they enter the hospital with an acute or life-threatening condition. Because of physical and emotional distress as well as frequent cognitive compromise associated with delirium or dementia, this is probably not the optimal time at which to address these issues. Ideally, patients should discuss their wishes regarding life support, nursing home placement, and who they would like to make decisions on their behalf with their primary care provider when they are healthy. Family physicians are likely to know the patient better and also have an understanding of the patient's religious beliefs and values. In addition, family physicians are also likely to know the patient's family as well. Kohut & Singer (1993) note that these conversations should emphasize the physician's desire to follow the patient's wishes rather than emphasizing the patient's death. They suggest asking patients directly about whether they want to be informed about all medical findings, whether the patient wants input on all medical decisions and who they would like to have make decisions on their behalf.

As noted in an earlier chapter, culture plays a role in whether patients wish to be directly informed about life-threatening illness and whether the patient versus their family should make the decisions about treatment. Thus, these "meta-questions" respect these differences around ethics and values. Additionally, as mentioned in the chapter on infectious disease, appointing a durable power of attorney is particularly helpful in situations involving relationships that are not legally sanctioned. Couples who have cohabitated for a number of years, patients who have a close friendship, or gay and lesbian couples who are not legally married should seriously consider appointing a durable power of attorney. Having the patient select a surrogate decision-maker will hopefully prevent family members from automatically making unwanted decisions on the patient's behalf should they become incapacitated.

The majority of patients want to discuss life support issues with their physician. Nearly 90% of the general public expresses a desire to have an advanced directive (Emanuel, Barry, Stoeckle, Ettelson & Emanuel, 1991). However, fewer than 20% of U.S. citizens have completed living wills. This roughly corresponds with the percentage of patients indicating that they have discussed life support with their physicians (Kohut & Singer, 1993). There does appear to be an expectation on the part of patients that physicians will initiate these discussions. Although health care providers are often concerned about the adverse emotional impact of explaining advanced directives to patients, patients do not appear to be particularly disturbed about these discussions (Emanuel et al., 1991). A concern that has been raised about advanced directives is that it asks the individual to forecast their future wishes. With the currently healthy patient, it asks them to essentially predict what their desires would be regarding life support when they are in a much different emotional state and may be experiencing considerable physical distress. Particularly with young adults, considerable time may elapse between enacting the advance directive and onset of life-threatening illness.

Emanuel and colleagues (1994) examined the stability of patient's treatment choices. Patients were interviewed twice so that stability over a two-year period could be assessed. Overall, patients' choices were stable over time. There also appeared to be a pattern in which patients developed greater stability of their choice with repeated questioning. In the study, 7% of the patients who initially declined life-sustaining treatment accepted the treatment later between the first and second interview. The same pattern emerged in 3% of choices between the second and third interview. Interestingly, the authors note that these rates are comparable to the 1975 divorce rate in the United States at the beginning of the second year of marriage. The authors note that patients who do change their minds should usually be more skeptically evaluated regarding their decision-making capacity.

Another disadvantage of written advanced directives is that no matter how detailed, it is unlikely that all possible clinical, social, and emotional situations can be predicted. Many of these documents are written in nonspecific language. Kohut & Singer (1993) note that common wording includes "there is no reasonable expectation of ... recovery from extreme physical or mental disability" or "not to be kept alive by ... heroic measures" (p. 1091). In both of these phrases, terms such as "reasonable expectations" as well as "heroic measures" can be interpreted very differently. Another approach to this dilemma has been the use of the medical directive. The medical directive includes clinical scenarios or vignettes. Patients are asked about various treatment options such as tube feeding, cardiopulmonary resuscitation, mechanical ventilation, and antibiotics. In studies involving these scenarios, patients often do not discriminate between highly intrusive and less invasive interventions. Suhl and colleagues (Suhl, Simons, Reedy, & Garrick, 1994) found that patients were equally likely to reject tube feeding, cardiopulmonary resuscitation, and ventilation. Also of note, patients were equally likely to reject life support when faced with coma, terminal cancer, severe emphysema, and progressive paralysis. There was a tendency to desire life support somewhat more in situations of coma or emphysema than in terminal cancer or paralysis (Suhl et al., 1994); however, the percentages of those desiring treatment ranged from 23% to 44%.

An alternative to written advanced directives is to appoint a proxy decision maker. The proxy's duty is to represent the patient's wishes should the patient themselves become incapacitated. Although proxy decision making allows for greater flexibility in the face of changing health status and in theory allows for the patient's wishes to be represented in medical situations that could not be predicted in advance or through a written advanced directive. Proxies may not in practice actually represent the patient's wishes. Several studies have shown that health care providers as well as family members do not consistently predict patient preferences for life support (Suhl et al., 1994; Uhlman, Pearlman, & Cain, 1988). Although spouses would typically be seen as understanding a patient's wishes better than anyone else, research has found that they are not particularly knowledgeable about patients' desires for life support and associated treatment. Suhl et al. (1994) found that surrogates—the majority of whom were spouses—were unable to predict a patient's wishes regarding life support across several medical scenarios. Of particular note was that the surrogates had lived with the patients for an average 21 years and believed that they were able to predict their partner's wishes with considerable confidence. In about half the dyads, the patients had had some discussion about life support with their surrogate. The amount of discussion between the patient and the surrogate was found to be predictive of the surrogate's ability to accurately predict the patient's choice. Surrogates were twice as likely to favor life support when the patient did not wish treatment. This pattern is commonly found in clinical practice. It may be that surrogates experienced considerable turmoil and guilt about having the final decision in a process that would end the patient's life.

In order for advanced directives to be implemented, the patient must be determined to be incompetent. Additionally, many states that permit living wills or durable powers of attorney require that the patient have a "terminal condition" (Loue, 1995). As Loue (1995) notes, a "terminal condition" is defined differently by various states. For example, Louisiana requires that living wills are only enacted if the patient has a condition that is "both terminal and irreversible," while North Dakota specifically excludes "senility, Alzheimer's disease, mental retardation, mental illness, or chronic mental or physical impairment including comatose conditions" (Loue, 1995, p. 470) that do not necessarily result in the patient's death.

Because of these varying definitions, family members appointed as surrogates may be reluctant to take over decision-making duties with patients exhibiting cognitive fluctuations. Typically, the physician or mental health professional conducts a clinical capacity evaluation either formally or informally, and based on this assessment, the surrogate will begin making medical decisions.

Because of the rapid technological advances in medicine in the past few decades, there are a much larger number of incapacitated seriously and terminally ill patients in hospital and nursing home care. The legal and ethical parameters surrounding advanced directives have not been well-established. A common clinical dilemma is that family members of an incapacitated patient may wish more aggressive treatment than the patient's own written advanced directive request. Clinically, there are suggestions that physicians will follow family members' requests rather than the patient's own written directive, in part, because of concerns about litigation.

GENETIC DISEASES AND COUNSELING

In the past decade, knowledge about genetically related illnesses has accelerated. The Human Genome project is an ambitious effort to map out the entire DNA sequence (Shiloh, 1996). Genetic counseling is an established subspecialty within medicine. However, research on psychological aspects of genetic testing and diseases is only beginning to be conducted. Even less information is available about processes and outcomes of genetic counseling. Genetic counseling is, however, likely to become an activity conducted in primary care (Geller, Tambor, Chaese, Hofman, Faden, & Holtzman, 1993). About half of a sample of family physicians indicated that they would counsel a couple about genetic testing when one parent was a carrier of cystic fibrosis.

Geneticists use the term "heritable" to describe predispositions that are passed from parent to children. Genetic testing makes these predictions of inheritability more specific (Baum, Friedman, & Zabowski, 1997). Monogenic disorders involving a single gene that would be inherited in a recessive, autosomal dominant, or sex-linked pattern were the first sequences to be identified. Recessive disorders require two copies of the gene for the disease to develop. In the autosomal dominant pattern, a single copy of the altered gene will produce the illness. Examples of recessive disorders include sickle cell anemia and cystic fibrosis, whereas autosomal dominant diseases include neurofibromatosis and Huntington's disease (Lerman, 1997). Another pattern is that of reduced penetrance—monogenic conditions in which environmental or other genetic contributors influence the expression of the gene. The recently discovered breast cancer gene, BRCAI, is an example of this pattern.

The objectives of genetic counseling are summarized by Alysworth (1992) and include helping the patient or family to: "(1) comprehend the medical facts including the diagnosis, probability, course of the disorder, and the available management; (2) appreciate the way heredity contributes to the disorder, and the risk of recurrence in specified relatives; (3) understand the alternatives for dealing with the risk of recurrence; (4) choose the course of action that seems to them appropriate in view of their risk, their family goals, and their ethical and religious standards, and to act in accordance with that decision; and (5) to make the best possible adjustment to the disorder in an affected family and/or to the risk of recurrence of that disorder" (pp. 229–230).

The psychological issues involved in genetic disorders are unique. Disease likelihood is often not definitively diagnosed but can only be understood in terms of probabilities (Lerman, 1997). For breast cancer, genetic testing can only provide data about the likelihood that a condition can develop, whereas for Huntington's disease, the time of onset is unknown. The time element adds another layer of uncertainty because the patient with an autosomal dominant condition does not know when they will manifest the illness. These disorders are transmitted by families, and members with a negative test result may experience guilt because a sibling is a carrier (Lerman, 1997). Additionally, ethical concerns are raised around genetic testing with children and young adults who have not developed symptoms of the disease. Anxiety, depression, and denial, including risky sexual behavior and substance abuse in adolescents, may be reactions to positive or equivocal test results (Shiloh, 1996).

Persons undergoing genetic counseling appear to have difficulty in cognitively assimilating percentage and probablistic data. Counselees appear to reduce this information to a yes–no dichotomy; the disease will or will not arise. Interestingly, when risk is presented in "a ___ of 10 format," the magnitude of risk was interpreted as greater than when equivalent percentages were communicated (e.g., 2 out of 10 versus 20%). Kessler and Levine (1987) suggest that this is because the 2-of-10 format tends to evoke personalized images. Genetic counseling regarding recurrence risks seems to be incorporated into individuals' pre-existing risk schemes. Perceptions of risk after counseling seem to be most strongly related to appraisals prior to counseling than to information provided by the professional (Shiloh, 1996). Although relatively little research has been conducted on genetic counseling as a process, a study by Shiloh and Saxe (1989) found that counselors perceived as "more neutral" were seen as conveying greater degrees of risk. This pattern was interpreted as suggesting that professional neutrality often implicitly conveys "bad news." Genetic counseling is a new field for mental health professionals. At present, there is little research to guide practice. With the increased knowledge about genetic predisposition for disease, the demand for these skills will undoubtedly increase.

CONCLUSION

The mental health professional who is providing services in a primary care setting will encounter a range of dilemmas that their training in ethics has not addressed. The primary medical setting raises unique variations on issues surrounding confidentiality as well as the duty-to-warn. Because of the aging of the general population, the clinician is increasingly likely to be called on to evaluate a patient's decisional capacity. Knowledge of state law as well as hospital policy surrounding advanced directives and surrogate decision makers and state definitions of incapacity will be particularly helpful in this process. As will be discussed in more detail in the final chapter, managed care programs will increasingly exert control over how mental health care is delivered. At present, many of these plans, which carve out mental health care, present particular challenges to mental health providers attempting to address patients' psychological needs in the context of their ongoing medical care. Rapid technological advances in medicine have also increased our knowledge of genetic diseases. Although the psychological issues surrounding genetic counseling have not been thoroughly studied, this is a newly evolving area for psychologists and other mental health professionals.

Chapter 14

Conclusion

In the past five years, our health care system has changed dramatically. Previously both physicians and most mental health professionals functioned in independent private practices. Reimbursement was consistently on a fee-for-service basis, with many patients receiving compensation through their insurance companies. Mental health professionals who have grown accustomed to this autonomy rapidly became aware of its loss as third parties began placing parameters on types of care provided. One form of practice that began to evolve coincident with managed care has been group practice. This has included mental health professionals in interdisciplinary group practices such as psychologists, social workers, licensed professional counselors, and psychiatrists all sharing office space as well as commonly sharing patients and administrative costs. A more recent and newly emerging practice model is the mental health professional developing a collaborative practice with primary care medical providers.

MANAGED CARE: A BRIEF OVERVIEW

In the United States, managed care is generally traced to the 1930s (Scherger, 1988). As that time, Kaiser created a health care plan to care for construction workers and their families. At about the same time, several physicians in the Los Angeles area entered into prepaid contracts to provide medical care to water company employees. At that time, these contractually based physicians were looked down on by their peers. Starr (1982) emphasizes that these contract-based physicians were often seen as emulating a form of socialism that was not well received by the medical establishment.

During the 1970s however, health care costs began rising dramatically, and health maintenance organizations were developed. With continuing increases in health care expenditures, health maintenance organizations, which included controlled access to specialty services and discounts for many health care services through guaranteed large volume, became more predominant (Scherger, 1998).

Financially, the model of many of these health organizations changed the standard practice of providers from a fee for service model to a salary. Both physicians as well as mental health professionals working within these systems essentially became employees.

There have been several forms of managed care organization. One model is the "staff model" (Scherger, 1998). In this approach, providers are essentially employees of an organization that contracts with a specific population—usually employees of particularly large companies. Independent associations are a second model, in which providers are usually paid a particular amount for each insured patient or provide discounted fee for service—often about 20% to 30% less than normal fees. In this model, the providers are often not situated in the same entity but are part of a network that may be geographically quite diverse (Scherger, 1998).

With the development of managed care, primary care providers who had receded both in numbers and visibility during the 1970s became much more prominent. In most health maintenance organizations, a patient must have a primary physician who will then refer them to any necessary specialist. In addition to providing care for a large range of conditions, the primary care physician also serves as a case manager.

At present, there may be too few primary care physicians to meet current needs. Whereas half of all physicians in 1961 were generalists, this figure fell to about 35% by 1990. Between 1980 and 1990, there were major increases in specialists and subspecialists with emergency medicine growing 150%, radiology 118%, anesthesiology 63%, and pediatric subspecialties 117% (Frank & Johnstone, 1996). Frank and Johnstone (1996) note that there do appear to be shortages of primary care physicians in many geographic areas, particularly less populated regions.

Although the rise in primary care and the high prevalence of mental health conditions among patients seen in these settings would seem to lead to a natural alliance between mental health professionals and primary care physicians, the health care funding system has often prevented such collaboration.

There are several "roadblocks" to effective linkage between medical and mental health care. First, as noted in the chapters on pediatric problems and mood disorders, a significant number of primary care mental health problems are "subclinical." These may include difficulties with child rearing, developmental issues such as poor academic performance, enuresis, "minor depression," or bereavement. Additionally, as suggested in the discussion of the family life cycle, normal family transitions may be particularly stressful for families with poor pre-existing coping skills. Many managed mental health care plans require that "medical necessity" be established in order for services to be compensated (Barrett, Detre, Pincus, Traugott, & Moyer, 1997). It is not uncommon for many of the problems that are brought to primary care providers to be relatively minor variations on normal development. This may conflict with managed care requirements that the mental health provider must have a behaviorally specific and typically quantifiable treatment plan directed toward a clearly diagnosed mental disorder.

As noted earlier, a common practice among managed health care organizations has been to "carve out" mental health services such that they are provided by a different company. This practice has also created obstacles to integrated care.

IMPLICATIONS OF "CARVED-OUT" MENTAL HEALTH CARE

Fisher and Ransom (1997) have raised a number of concerns about the rise of "carve outs" for mental health services. They cite a 1996 poll indicating that of those Americans with health insurance, approximately 68% were enrolled in some type of specialty behavioral health program with 21% covered by risk-based, managed behavioral health care plans independently serviced by "carve out" companies. This latter group is expected to increase through the next few years. They note that this segregation of mental health from general medical care occurred in part as a result of poor cost control and the absence of quality assurance standards in mental health. Mental health spending by employers for mental health coverage reportedly increased by 50% during a four-year period from 1996 to 1990. A primary force for this increase was increased use of psychiatric hospitalization, particularly for adolescents. Early health maintenance organizations strictly controlled access to services. Because of this restriction, some companies chose to sign independent contracts with managed mental health concerns so that these services were provided separately from medical care. Additionally, some HMOs carved out mental health services because of their cost.

Primary care providers have continued to diagnose and treat mental health conditions. Some of these are reimbursed through general medical insurance. However, because of concerns about payment, physicians have been giving nonpsychiatric diagnoses. As Fisher and Ransom (1997) note, primary care physicians have been providers for a vast array of mental health services without compensation. Those services include supportive counseling, prescriptions for psychotropic medication, and advising parents about psychosocial issues of childhood.

The additional development of independent sources of funding for medical and mental health care prevent optimal patient care because flexibility for meeting individual patient needs is reduced. Additionally, evaluation of the true cost benefits of different HMOs or medical health insurance plans is difficult to evaluate because of the independence of physicians and mental health systems.

The American Academy of Family Physicians White Paper on the Provision of Mental Health Services by Family Physicians notes that mental health and pay-for-fee services should remain within a centralized insurance plan so that the primary care provider can continue to provide mental health services (Fisher & Ransom, 1997). Communication between primary physicians and the mental health professional is impeded under current practice patterns. Physicians may be required to refer to mental health providers that they do not know or they may find that a provider with which they have a relationship is no longer in that managed care organization.

POTENTIAL SOLUTIONS

Many patients can be managed successfully through collaboration between a primary care physician and a mental health professional. These patients include those with most mood and anxiety disorders as well as childhood problems such as attention-deficit hyperactivity disorder. However, managed mental health care organizations may have policies that preclude this type of collaboration. For example, psychotropic medications may only be reimbursed if they are prescribed by a psychiatrist (Barrett et al., 1997). Additionally, separating treatments in this manner is actually less cost effective. At an organizational level, one solution has been to include both mental health and medical services in the same contracted managed care organization. One example of an integrated system described by Seaburn and colleagues (1996) is the Northcoast Faculty Medical Group in California. The group controls all primary and secondary care of fees and includes a group of family physicians as well as psychologists. The group has managed to maintain flexibility in providing both medical and behavioral services. In addition, it includes a large number of contracted medical specialists. Because health care funds for both mental health care and medical care are pooled, there is greater flexibility in meeting patients' needs. Additionally, collaboration between mental health providers and physician providers seems to result in a reduction in hospitalizations—a large proportion of health care costs.

At a legislative level, Congress last year passed a mental health parity act. The act required that by January 1998, a plan that offers any mental health benefit must provide equal payment limits for mental health and medical care. There are some exemptions to this plan. Health care plans are not required to cover mental health care. However, if they do cover psychiatric services, the above regulation is in effect. At the state level, a number of states have legislation in differing stages devoted to the same end.

CONCLUSION

Given the high prevalence of mental health conditions as presenting problems or as contributors to significant medical problems, the role of mental health specialists in the primary care sector is only likely to increase. Another factor contributing to this need is a relative shortage of primary care physicians themselves. These medical providers are eager to share patient care responsibilities with knowledgeable mental health professionals who can effectively function in these settings. The core values and skills described in the first chapter will be essential to the success of mental health professionals in this arena. Flexibility, tolerance for ambiguity, pragmatism, efficiency, and a respect for medical illness and psychotropic medication will greatly enhance the receptiveness of physicians to mental health collaboration.

References

Abramowitz, J. S. (1997). Effectiveness of psychological and pharmacological treatments for obsessive compulsive disorder: A quantitative review. *Journal of Consulting & Clinical Psychology, 65*, 44–52.

Adler, S. R. (1995). Refugee stress and folk beliefs: Hmong sudden deaths. *Social Science and Medicine, 40*, 1623–1629.

Alexander, F. (1950). *Psychosomatic medicine.* New York: Norton.

Alysworth, A. S. (1992). Genetic counseling in patients with birth defects. *Pediatric Clinics of North America, 39*, 229–253.

American Psychiatric Association. (1994). *Diagnostic and statistical manual of mental disorders* (4th ed.). Washington, DC: Author.

American Psychological Association, Council of Representatives. (1991, February 8). *Statement on the use of anatomically detailed dolls in forensic evaluations.* Washington, DC: Author.

Anda, R. F., Remington, P. L., Sinenko, B. G., & Davis, R. M. (1987). Are physicians advising smokers to quit? The patient's perspective. *Journal of the American Medical Association, 257*, 1916–1919.

Anfinson, T. J. (1995). Diagnostic assessment of chronic fatigue syndrome. In A. Stoudemire & B. S. Fogel (Eds.), *Medical-psychiatric practice: Vol. 3* (pp. 215–256). Washington, DC: *American Psychiatric Association.*

Angel, R., & Thoits, P. (1987). The impact of culture on the cognitive structure of illness. *Culture, Medicine & Psychiatry, 11*, 465–494.

Antebi, D., & Bird, J. (1993). The facilitation and evocation of seizures: A questionnaire study of awareness and control. *British Journal of Psychiatry, 162*, 759–764.

Appelbaum, P. S. (1993). Legal liability in managed care. *American Psychologist, 48*, 251–257.

Appelbaum, P. S., & Grisso, T. (1989). Assessing patients' capacity to consent to treatment. *New England Journal of Medicine, 319*, 1635–1638.

Appelbaum, P. S., Lidz, C. W., & Meisel, A. (1987). *Informed consent: Legal theory in clinical practice.* New York: Oxford University Press.

Argas, W. S. (1987). *Eating disorders: Management of obesity, bulimia, and anorexia nervosa.* New York: Pergamon Press.

Armentrout, D. P., Moore, J. E., Parker, J. C., Hewett, J. E., & Feltz, C. (1982). Pain-patient MMPI subgroups: The psychological dimensions of pain. *Journal of Behavioral Medicine, 5*, 201–211.

Baker, F. N. (1995). Mental health issues in elderly African-Americans. *Clinics in Geriatric Medicine, 11*, 1–13.

Barkley, R. A. (1991). *Attention-deficit hyperactivity disorder: A handbook for diagnosis and treatment.* New York: Guilford Press.

Barkley, R. A. (1994). Can neuropsychological tests help diagnose ADD/ADHD? *ADHD Report, 2*(1), 1–3.

Baron, C., Lamarre, A., Veilleux, P., Ducharme, G., Spier, S., & Lapierre, J. G. (1986). Psychomaintenance of childhood asthma: A study of 34 children. *Journal of Asthma, 23*, 69–79.

Barrett, J. E., Barrett, J. A., Oxman, T. E., & Gerber, P. D. (1988). The prevalence of psychiatric disorders in a primary care practice. *Archives of General Psychiatry, 45*, 1100–1106.

Barrett, J., Detre, T., Pincus, H. A., Traugott, & Moyer, P. (1997). Mental health benefits in the era of managed care. *Patient Care* (September), 76–84.

Barsky, A. J., Ahern, D. K., Bailey, E. D., & Delameter, B. A. (1996). Predictors of persistent palpitations and continued medical utilization. *Journal of Family Practice, 42*, 465–471.

Barsky, A. J., & Borus, J. F. (1995). Somatization and medicalization in the era of managed care. *Journal of the American Medical Association, 274*, 1931–1934.

Baum, A., Friedman, A. L., & Zakowski, S. G. (1997). Stress and genetic testing for disease risk. *Health Psychology, 16*, 8–19.

Beck, A. T., Rush, A., Shaw, B., & Emery, G. (1979). *Cognitive Therapy of Depression.* New York: Guilford Press.

Beck, A. T., Ward, C. H., Mendelson, M., Mock, J., & Erbaugh, J. (1961). An inventory for measuring depression. *Archives of General Psychiatry, 4*, 561–571.

Beck, D. A. & Koenig, H. G. (1996). Minor depression: A review of the literature. *International Journal of Psychiatry in Medicine, 26*, 177–209.

Belar, C. D., & Deardorff, W. W. (1995). *Clinical health psychology in medical settings: A practitioners guidebook.* Washington, DC: American Psychological Association.

Belsky, J., Perry-Jenkins, M., & Crouter, A. (1985). The work–family interface and marital change across the transition of parenthood. *Journal of Family Issues, 6*, 205–220.

Bender, B. G. (1996). Establishing a role for psychology in respiratory medicine. In R. J. Resnick & R. H. Rozensky (Eds.), *Health psychology through the life span: Practice and research opportunities* (pp. 227–238). Washington, DC: American Psychological Association.

Berg, A. T., & Shinnar, S. (1991). The risk of seizure recurrence following a first time provoked procedure: A quantitative review. *Neurology, 41*, 965–972.

Berkman, L. S. (1986). Social networks, support and health: Taking the next step forward. *American Journal of Epidemiology, 123*, 559–562.

Berliner, L., & Conte, J. R. (1993). Sexual abuse evaluations: Conceptual and empirical obstacles. *Child Abuse and Neglect, 17*, 111–125.

Blackhall, L. J., Murphy, S. T., Frank, G., Michel, V., & Azen, S. (1995). Ethnicity and attitudes toward patient autonomy. *Journal of the American Medical Association, 274*, 820–825.

Blair, S. N., Goodyear, N. N., Gibbons, O. W., & Cooper, K. H. (1994). Physical fitness and incidence of hypertension in healthy normotensive men and women. *Journal of the American Medical Association, 252*, 487–490.

Blake, R. L., Roberts, C., Mackey, T., & Hosokawa, M. (1980). Social support and utilization of medical care. *Journal of Family Practice, 11*, 810.

Blanchard, E. B., & Andrasik, F. (1985). *Management of chronic headaches: A psychological approach.* New York: Pergamon Press.

Blanchard, E. B., Andrasik, F., Ahles, T. A., Teders, S. J., & O'Keefe, D. (1980). Migraine and tension headache: A meta-analytic review. *Behavior Therapy, 11*, 613–631.

Blumer, D., Montouris, G., & Hermann, B. (1995). Psychiatric morbidity in seizure patients on a neurodiagnostic monitoring unit. *Journal of Neuropsychiatry and Clinical Neuroscience, 7*, 445–456.

Borkovec, T. D., & Costello, E. (1993). Efficacy of applied relaxation and cognitive behavioral therapy in the treatment of generalized anxiety disorder. *Journal of Consulting and Clinical Psychology, 61*, 611–619.

Boscolo, L., Cecchin, G., Hoffman, L., & Penn, P. (1987). *Milan systemic family therapy.* New York: Basic Books.

Boyce, W. T., Jensen, E. W., & Cassel, J. C. (1977). Influence of life events and family routines on childhood respiratory illness. *Pediatrics, 660*, 609–615.

Boyd-Franklin, N. (1989). *Black families in therapy: A multisystems approach.* New York: Guilford Press.

Bracke, P. A., & Toheresen, C. E. (1996). Reducing type A behavior patterns: A structured group approach. In R. Allan & S. Scheidt (Eds.), *Heart and mind: The practice of cardiac psychology* (pp. 255–290). Washington, DC: American Psychological Association.

Brandt, J., Celentano, D., Stewart, W., Linet, M., & Folstein, M. (1990). Personality and emotional disorder in a community sample of migraine headache sufferers. *American Journal of Psychiatry, 147*, 303–308.

Brena, S. F. (1983). Pain control facilities: Roots, organization, and function. In S. F. Brena & S. L. Chapman (Eds.), *Management of patients with chronic pain* (pp. 11–20). New York: SP Medical and Scientific Books.

Broadhead, W. E. (1994). Presentation of psychiatric symptomatology in primary care. In J. Miranda, A. A. Hohmann, C. C. Attkisson, & D. P. Larson (Eds.), *Mental disorders in primary care* (pp. 139–162). San Francisco: Jossey-Bass.

Bross, M. H., & Tatum, N. O. (1994). Delirium in the elderly patient. *American Family Physician, 50*, 1325–1332.

Brown, G., & Harris, T. (1978). *Social origins of depression.* London: Tavistock.

Brown, R. O., Leonard, T., Saunders, L. A., & Papasouliotis, O. (1997). A two item screening test for alcohol and other drug problems. *Journal of Family Practice, 44*, 151–160.

Brown, S. W., & Smith, C. R. (1991). Diagnostic concordance in primary care somatization disorder. *Psychosomatics, 32*, 191–195.

Brown, T. A., Antony, M. M., & Barlow, D. H. (1995). Diagnostic co-morbidity in panic disorder: The effect on treatment outcome and course of co-morbid diagnoses. *Journal of Consulting and Clinical Psychology, 63*, 408–418.

Brown, T. A., & Barlow, D. M. (1992). Co-morbidity among anxiety disorders: Implications for treatment and DSM–IV. *Journal of Consulting and Clinical Psychology, 60*, 835–844.

Brownell, K. D., & Wadden, T. A. (1992). Etiology and treatment of obesity: Understanding a serious, prevalent, and refractory disorder. *Journal of Consulting and Clinical Psychology, 60*, 505–517.

Budzynski, T. H., Stoyva, J. N., Adler, C. S., & Mullaney, D. J. (1973). EMG biofeedback and tension headache: A controlled outcome study. *Psychosomatic Medicine, 35*, 504–514.

Buelow, G. D., & Chafetz, A. D. (1996). Proposed ethical practice guidelines for clinical pharmaco-psychology: Sharpening a new focus in psychology. *Professional Psychology: Research and Practice, 27*, 53–58.

Butters, N. A., Salmon, D. P., & Butters, M. (1994). Neuropsychological assessment of dementia. In M. Storandt & G. R. Vandenbos (Eds.), *Neuropsychological assessment of dementia and depression in older adults: A clinician's guide* (pp. 33–60). Washington, DC: American Psychological Association.

Caine, E. D., Lyness, J. M., Caine, D. A., & Connors, R. (1994). Clinical and etiological heterogeneity of mood disorders in elderly patients. In C. S. Schneider, C. S. Reynolds, B. D. Lebowitz, & A. J. Freidhoff (Eds.), *Diagnosis and treatment of depression in late life* (pp. 21–54). Washington, DC: American Psychiatric Press.

Callahan, C. N., Hendrie, H. C., & Tierney, W. M. (1996). The recognition and treatment of late life depression: A view from primary care. *International Journal of Psychiatry in Medicine, 26*, 155–171.

Campbell, T., & Patterson, J. M. (1995). The effectiveness of family intervention in the treatment of physical illness. *Journal of Marital & Family Therapy, 21*, 545–583.

Cantwell, D. P. (1996). Attention deficit disorder: A review of the past ten years. *Journal of the American Academy of Child and Adolescent Psychiatry, 35*, 978–987.

Carek, P. J., Sherer, J. T., & Carson, D. S. (1997). Management of obesity: Medical treatment options. *American Family Physician, 55*, 551–558.

Carney, R. M., Freedland, K. E., Eisen, S. A., Rich, N. W., & Jaffe, A. S. (1995). Major depression and medication adherence in elderly patients with coronary artery disease. *Health Psychology, 14*, 88–90.

Carrese, J. A., & Rhodes, L. A. (1995). Western bioethics on the Navaho reservation: Benefit or harm? *Journal of American Medical Association, 274*, 826–829.

Carter, B., & McGoldrick, M. (1989). Overview: The changing family life cycle: A framework for family therapy. In B. Carter & M. McGoldrick (Eds.), *The changing family life cycle: A framework for family therapy* (2nd ed., pp. 3–28). Boston: Allyn & Bacon.

Casey, D. A. (1994). Depression in the elderly. *Southern Medical Journal, 67*, 559–563.

Casey, P. R., & Tyrer, P. (1990). Personality disorder and psychiatric illness in general practice. *British Journal of Psychiatry, 156*, 261–265.

Cassisi, J. E., McGlynn, F. P., & Belles, D. R. (1987). EMG-activated feedback alarms for the treatment of nocturnal bruxism: Current status and future directions. *Biofeedback and Self Regulation, 12*, 13–30.

Castillo, R., Waitzkin, H., & Escobar, J. I. (1994). Somatic symptoms and mental health disorders in immigrant and refugee populations. In J. Miranda, A. A. Hohmann, C. C. Attkisson, & D. V. Larson (Eds.), *Mental disorders in primary care* (pp. 163–185). San Francisco: Jossey-Bass.

Cervantes, J. M., & Ramirez, O. (1992). Spirituality and family dynamics in psychotherapy with Latino children. In L. A. Vargas & J. D. Koss-Chioino (Eds.), *Working with culture: Psychotherapeutic interventions with ethnic minority children and adolescents* (pp. 103–128). San Francisco: Jossey-Bass.

Chamberlain, P., & Rosicky, J. G. (1995). The effectiveness of family therapy in the treatment of adolescents with conduct disorders and delinquency. *Journal of Marital and Family Therapy, 21*, 441–459.

Chavez, L. R., Hubbell, F. A., McMullin, J. N., Martinez, R. G., & Mishara, S. I. (1995). Understanding knowledge and attitudes about breast cancer: A cultural analysis. *Archives of Family Medicine, 4*, 145–152.

Chesney, M. A., & Nealey, J. B. (1996). Smoking and cardiovascular disease risk in women: Issues for prevention in women's health. In P. N. Kato & T. Mann (Eds.), *Handbook of diversity issues in health psychology* (pp. 199–218). New York: Plenum Press.

Chistensen, N. K., Terry, R. D., Wyatt, S., Pichert, J. W., & Lorenz, R. A. (1983). Quantitative assessment of dietary adherence in patients with insulin dependent diabetes mellitus. *Diabetes Care, 6*, 245–250.

Clark, D. M., Salkovskis, P. M., Ost, L., Vrietholtz, E., Koehler, K. A., Westling, B. E., Jeavons, A., & Gelder, M. (1997). Misinterpretation of body sensations in panic disorder. *Journal of Consulting & Clinical Psychology, 65*, 203–213.

Clark, W. B., & Midanik, L. (1981). *Alcohol use and alcohol problems among U.S. adults: Results of the 1979 national survey.* Washington, DC: NIAAA.

Cleckley, H. N. (1978). *The mask of sanity.* St. Louis: Mosby.

Clover, R. D., Abell, T., Becker, L. A., Crawford, S., & Ramsey, C. N. (1989). Family functioning and stress as predictors of influenza B infection. *Journal of Family Practice, 28*, 535–539.

Cohen-Cole, S. A., Brown, F. W., & McDaniel, J. S. (1993). Assessment of depression and grief reactions in the medically ill. In A. Stoudemire & B. S. Fogel (Eds.), *Psychiatric care of the medical patient* (pp. 53–70). New York: Oxford University Press.

Cohen-Cole, S. A., & Stoudemire, A. (1987). Major depression and physical illness: Special considerations in diagnosis and biologic treatment. *Psychiatric Clinics of North America, 10*, 1–17.

Collyer, J. A. (1979). Psychosomatic illness in a solo family practice. *Psychosomatics, 20*, 762–767.

Comer, R. J. (1995). *Abnormal psychology* (2nd ed.). New York: Freeman.

Comley, A. (1973). Family therapy and the family physician. *Canadian Family Physician, 19*, 78–85.

Connors, C. K. (1989). *Connors rating scale manual.* North Tonawanda, NY: Multiple-Health Systems.

Copenhaver, M. N., & Eisler, R. N. (1996). Masculine gender role stress: A perspective on men's health. In P. N. Kato & T. Mann (Eds.), *Handbook of diversity issues in health psychology* (pp. 219–236). New York: Plenum Press.

Coste, J., Paolaggi, J. B., & Spira, A. (1992). Classification of non-specific back pain, I. Psychological involvement in low back pain. *Spine, 17*, 1028–1037.

Coulehan, J. L., Schulberg, H. C., Block, N. R., & Zettler-Segal, N. (1988). Symptom patterns of depression in ambulatory medical and psychiatric patients. *Journal of Nervous and Mental Disease, 176*, 284–288.

Council on Ethical and Judicial Affairs (1987). *Ethical issues involved in the growing AIDS crisis* (Report A). Chicago: American Medical Association.

Cox, C., & Monk, A. (1993). Hispanic culture and family care of Alzheimer patients. *Health and Social Work, 18*, 92–100.

Cox, D. J., Gonder-Frederick, L., & Saunders, J. T. (1991). Diabetes: Clinical issues in management. In J. J. Sweet, R. H. Rozensky, & S. M. Tovian (Eds.), *Handbook of clinical psychology in medical settings* (pp. 473–496). New York: Plenum Press.

Coyne, J. C., & Anderson, B. J. (1988). The "psychosomatic" family reconsidered: Diabetes in context. *Journal of Marital and Family Therapy, 14*, 113–123.

Coyne, J. C., & Schwenk, T. L. (1997). The relationship of distress to mood disturbance in primary care and psychiatric populations. *Journal of Consulting and Clinical Psychology, 65*, 161–168.

Creer, T. L., Reynolds, R. V., & Kotses, H. (1991). Psychological theory, assessment, and interventions for adult and childhood asthma. In J. J. Sweet, R. H. Rozensky, & S. M.

Tovian (Eds.), *Handbook of clinical psychology and medical settings* (pp. 497–516). New York: Plenum Press.

Cross, G. M., & Hennessey, P. T. (1993). Principles and practice of detoxification. *Primary Care, 20*, 81–93.

Crum, R. M., Anthony, J. C., Bassett, S. S., & Folstein, M. F. (1993). Population-based norms for the mini mental state examination by age and educational level. *Journal of the American Medical Association, 269*, 2386–2391.

Cummings, E. M., & Davies, P. (1994). *Children and marital conflict: Impact of family dispute and resolution.* New York: Guilford Press.

Cummings, J. L. (1987). Dementia syndromes: Neurobehavioral and neuropsychiatric features. *Journal of Clinical Psychiatry, 48*(Suppl. 5), 3–8.

Dalessio, D. J. (1972). *Wolff's headache and other head pain* (3rd ed.). New York: Oxford University Press.

Dare, C., Eisler, I., Russell, T. F. M., & Szmukler, T. I. (1990). The clinical and theoretical impact of a controlled trial of family therapy and anorexia nervosa. *Journal of Marital and Family Therapy, 16*, 39–57.

Daughton, D. M., Heatley, S. A., Prendergast, J. J., Causey, D. M., Knowles, M., Rolf, C., Cheney, R., Hatelid, K., Thompson, A. B., & Rennard, S. (1991). Effect of transdermal nicotine delivery as an adjunct to low-intervention smoking cessation therapy. *Archives of Internal Medicine, 151*, 749–752.

Davis, K. L., Thal, L. J., Gamzu, E. R., Davis, C. S., Woolson, R. F., Gracon, S. I., Drachman, D. A., Schneider, L. S., Whitehouse, P. J., Hoover, T. M., Morris, J. C., Kawas, C. H., Knopman, D. S., Earl, N. L., Kumar, V., Doody, R. S., & the Tacrine Study Group (1992). A double blind placebo controlled multicenter study of Tacrine for Alzheimer's disease. *New England Journal of Medicine, 327*, 1253–1259.

Davison, G. C., & Neale, J. M. (1994). *Abnormal psychology* (6th ed.). New York: Wiley.

DeGood, D. E. (1983). Reducing medical patients' reluctance to participate in psychological therapies: The initial session. *Professional Psychology: Research and Practice, 14*, 570–579.

DeGruy, S. (1994). Management of mixed anxiety and depression. *American Family Physician, 49*, 860–866.

de Shazer, S. (1985). *Keys to solutions in brief therapy.* New York: Norton.

Delameter, A. N. (1995). Cardiovascular disease. In M. ·C. Roberts (Ed.), *Handbook of pediatric psychology* (2nd ed., pp. 403–424). New York: Guilford Press.

Delbanco, T. L., & Barnes, H. N. (1987). The epidemiology of alcohol abuse and the response of physicians. In H. N. Barnes, M. D. Aronson, & T. L. Delbanco (Eds.), *Alcoholism: A guide for the primary cure physician* (pp. 3–8). New York: Springer-Verlag.

Diamond, N. (1993). Homosexuality and bisexuality in different populations. *Archives of Sexual Behavior, 22*, 291–310.

Dickson, L. R., & Neill, J. R. (1987). When schizophrenia complicates medical care. *American Family Physician, 35*, 153–159.

Dodrill, C. B., & Batzel, L. W. (1986). Interictal behavioral features of patients with epilepsy. *Epilepsia, 27*(Suppl. 2), 564–576.

Drewnowski, A., Hopkins, S. A., & Kessler, R. C. (1988). The prevalence of bulimia nervosa in the U.S. college student population. *American Journal of Public Health, 78*, 132–135.

Elks, N. L. (1996). Appetite suppressants as adjuncts in the treatment of obesity. *Journal of Family Practice, 42*, 287–292.

Ellenberg, N. (1983). Diabetic neuropathy. In N. Ellenberg & H. Rifkin (Eds.), *Diabetes mellitus theory and practice* (3rd ed., Vol. 2, pp. 777–801). New Hyde Park, NY: Medical Examination Publishing.

Emanuel, L. L., Emanuel, E. J., Stoeckle, J. D., Hummel, L. R., & Barry, M. J. (1994). Advanced directives: Stability of patients' treatment choices. *Archives of Internal Medicine, 154,* 209–217.

Emanuel, L. L., Barry, M. J., Stoeckle, J. D., Ettelson, L. M., & Emanuel, E. J. (1991). Advance directives for medical care: A case for greater use. *New England Journal of Medicine, 324,* 889–895.

Endicott, J. (1984). Measurement of depression in patients with cancer. *Cancer, 53,* 2243–2248.

Erker, G. J., Searight, H. R., & Peterson, P. (1995). Patterns of neuropsychological functioning among patients with multi-infarct and Alzheimer's dementia: A comparative analysis. *International Psychogeriatrics, 2,* 393–406.

Escobedo, L. G., Anda, R. F., Smith, P. F., Remington, P. L., & Mast, E. E. (1990). Sociodemographic characteristics of cigarette smoking initiation in the United States: Implications for smoking prevention policy. *Journal of the American Medical Association, 264,* 1550–1555.

Fairburn, C. T., Norman, P. A., Welch, S. L., O'Connor, N. E., Doll, H. A., & Peveler, R. C. (1995). A prospective study of outcome in bulimia nervosa and the long term effects of three psychological treatments. *Archives of General Psychiatry, 52,* 304–312.

Fairburn, C. T., & Peveler, R. C. (1990). Bulimia nervosa and a stepped care approach to management. *Gut, 31,* 1220–1222.

Falk, T. C. (1988). AIDS and public health law. *Journal of Legal Medicine, 9,* 529–546.

Fawzy, F. I., Namir, S., & Wolcott, D. O. (1989). Structured group intervention for AIDS patients. *Psychiatric Medicine, 7,* 35–45.

Fenwick, P. B. C. (1990). Behavioral treatment of epilepsy. *Postgraduate Medical Journal, 66,* 336–338.

Fernandez, E. S., South-Paul, J. E., & Matheny, S. C. (1998). Sociocultural issues in health care. In R. B. Taylor (Ed.), *Family medicine: Principles and practice* (pp. 19–25). New York: Springer-Verlag.

Fisch, R., Weakland, J., & Segal, L. (1982). *The tactics of change: Doing therapy briefly.* San Francisco: Jossey-Bass.

Fischer, L., & Ransom, D. C. (1997). Developing a strategy for managing behavioral healthcare within the context of primary care. *Archives of Family Medicine, 6,* 324–333.

Fleury, J. (1993). An exploration of the role of social networks in cardiovascular risk reduction. *Heart and Lung, 22,* 134–144.

Fogel, B. S. (1993). Personality disorders in a medical setting, In A. Stoudemire & B. S. Fogel (Eds.), *Psychiatric care of the medical patient* (pp. 289–305). Washington, DC: American Psychiatric Press.

Fogel, B. S., & Mor, V. (1993). Depressed mood and care preferences in patients with AIDS. *General Hospital Psychiatry, 50,* 203–207.

Folks, D. G., Ford, C. V., & Houck, C. A. (1990). Somatoform disorders, factitious disorders and malingering. In A. Stoudemire (Ed.), *Clinical psychiatry for medical students* (pp. 237–268). Philadelphia: J. B. Lippincott.

Folks, D. G., & Houck, C. A. (1993). Somatoform disorders, factitious disorders and malingering. In A. Stoudemire & B. S. Fogel (Eds.), *Psychiatric care of the medical patient* (pp. 267–288). New York: Oxford University Press.

Folstein, M. F., Folstein, S. E., & McHugh, P. R. (1975). Mini mental state: A practical method for grading the cognitive state of patients for the clinician. *Journal of Psychiatric Research, 12,* 189–198.

Ford, C. Z., & Winter, G. (1981). Computerized axial tomograms and dementia in elderly patients. *Journal of Gerontology, 36,* 164–169.

Ford, C. V. (1983). *The somatizing disorders: Illness as a way of life.* New York: Elsevier.

Ford, D. E. (1994). Recognition and under-recognition of mental disorders in adult primary care. In J. Miranda, A. Hohmann, C. C. Attkisson, & D. P. Larson (Eds.), *Mental disorders in primary care* (pp. 186–205). San Francisco: Jossey-Bass.

Fordyce, W. E. (1976). *Behavioral methods for chronic pain and illness.* St. Louis: C. V. Mosby.

Forstein, M. (1990). HIV testing. In American Psychiatric Association AIDS Education Project (Eds.), *AIDS primer* (pp. 57–61). Washington, DC: American Psychiatric Association.

Francis, J., & Kapoor, W. N. (1990). Delirium in the hospitalized elderly. *Journal of General Internal Medicine, 5,* 65–79.

Frank, R. G., & Johnstone, B. (1996). Changes in the health work force: Implications for psychologists. In R. L. Glueckauf, R. G. Frank, G. R. Bond, & J. H. McGrew (Eds.), *Psychological practice in a changing health care system* (pp. 39–51). New York: Springer.

Franz, N. J. (1990). Commentary. *Diabetes Spectrum, 3,* 369–370.

Frasure-Smith, N., Lesperance, F., & Talajic, M. (1993). Depression following myocardial infarction. *Journal of the American Medical Association, 270,* 1819–1825.

Frasure-Smith, N., Lesperance, F., & Talajic, M. (1995). The impact of negative emotions on prognosis following myocardial infarction: Is it more than depression? *Health Psychology, 14,* 388–398.

Freund, K. M., Graham, S. N., Lesky, L. G., & Moskowitz, M. A. (1993). Detection of bulimia in a primary care setting. *General Internal Medicine, 8,* 236–242.

Friedman, N., Fleischmann, N., & Price, V. A. (1996). Diagnosis of type a behavior pattern. In R. Allen & S. Scheidt (Eds.), *Heart and mind: The practice of cardiac psychology* (pp. 179–196). Washington, DC: American Psychological Association.

Friedman, N., & Rosenman, R. F. (1974). *Type a behavior and your heart.* New York: Knopf.

Friedman, N., & Rosenman, R. H. (1959). Association of specific overt behavior pattern with blood and cardiovascular findings: Blood cholesterol level, blood clotting time, incidence of arcus senilis, and clinical coronary artery disease. *Journal of the American Heart Association, 169,* 1286–1296.

Friedman, N., Thoresen, C. E., Gill, J. J., Ulner, D., Powell, L. A., Price, P. A., Brown, B., Thompson, L., Rabin, D. D., Breall, W. S., Bourg, E., Levy, R., & Dixon, T. (1996). Alteration of type A behavior and its effect on cardiac recurrences in post myocardial infarction patients: Summary results of the recurrent coronary prevention project. *American Heart Journal, 112,* 653–665.

Friedson, R. L., Wey, J. J., & Tabler, J. B. (1991). Psycho-stimulants for depression in the medically ill. *American Family Physician, 43,* 163–170.

Frymoyer, J. W., & Cats-Varil, L. (1991). An overview of the incidence and cost of low back pain. *Orthopedic Clinics of North America, 22,* 263–271.

Ganzini, L., Lee, M. A., Heintz, R. T., Bloom, J. D., & Fenn, P. S. (1994). The effect of depression treatment on elderly patient's preferences for life sustaining medical therapy. *American Journal of Psychiatry, 151,* 1631–1636.

Gatchel, R. J., Polatin, P. B., Mayer, T. G., & Garcy, P. D. (1994). Psychopathology in the rehabilitation of patients with chronic low back pain disability. *Archives of Physical Medicine and Rehabilitation, 75*, 666–670.

Gatchel, R. J., Polatin, P. B., Mayer, T. G., & Garcy, P. D. (1995). The dominant role of psycho-social risk factors in development of chronic low back pain disability. *Spine, 20*, 2702–2709.

Gates, J. R., Luciano, D., & Devinsky, N. O. (1991). Classification and treatment of non-epileptic events. In N. O. Devinsky & W. H. Theodore (Eds.), *Epilepsy and behavior* (pp. 251–263). New York: Wiley.

Gauthier, J., Cote, G., & French, D. (1994). The role of home practice in the thermal biofeedback treatment of migraine headache. *Journal of Consulting and Clinical Psychology, 62*, 180–184.

Geller, G., Tambor, E. S., Chaese, G. A., Hofman, K. J., Faden, R. R., & Holtzman, N. A. (1993). Incorporation of genetics in primary care practice: Will physicians do the counseling and will they be directive?. *Archives of Family Medicine, 2*, 1119–1125.

Gillette, R. B. (1996). Behavioral factors in the management of back pain. *American Family Physician, 53*, 1313–1318.

Gilligan, C. (1982). *In a different voice: Psychological theory and women's development.* Cambridge, MA: Harvard University Press.

Glassman, A. H., Helzer, J. E., Covey, L. S., Cottler, L. B., Stetner, F., Tipp, J. E., & Johnson, J. (1990). Smoking, smoking cessation, and major depression. *Journal of the American Medical Association, 264*, 1546–1549.

Godard, S. L., & Bloom, J. (1990). Driving, mental illness, and the duty to protect. In J. C. Beck (Ed.), *Confidentiality versus the duty to protect.* (pp. 191–204). Washington DC: American Psychiatric Press.

Gold, J. P. (1996). Psychological issues in coronary artery bypass surgery. In R. Allan & Schedit (Eds.), *Heart and mind: The practice of cardiac psychology* (pp. 219–232). Washington, DC: American Psychological Association.

Goldberg, D., & Tomlanovich, M. C. (1984). Domestic violence victims in the emergency department. *Journal of the American Medical Association, 251*, 3259–3264.

Goldberg, R. J., & Posner, D. A. (1994). Anxiety in the medically ill. In A. Stoudemire & B. S. Fogel (Eds.), *Psychiatric care for the medical patient* (pp. 87–104). Washington DC: American Psychiatric Association.

Goldstein, E. G. (1990). *Borderline disorders: Clinical models and techniques.* New York: Guilford Press.

Gradman, A. H., Bell, P. A., & De Busk, R. F. (1977). Sudden death during ambulatory monitoring: Clinical and electrocardiographic considerations. Report of a case. *Circulation, 55*, 210–211.

Gray, K. F., & Cummings, J. L. (1996). Dementia. In J. R. Rundell & M. G. Will (Eds.), *Textbook of consultation—Liaison psychiatry* (pp. 276–309). Washington DC: American Psychiatric Press.

Greene, C. S., Olson, R. E., & Laskin, D. M. (1982). Psychological factors in the etiology, progression, and treatment of MPD syndrome. *Journal of the American Dental Association, 105*, 443–448.

Greist, J. H. (1995). Apparent depression, hidden obsession: Uncovering obsessive compulsive disorder. *Primary Care Psychiatry*, 2-A.

Greist, J., Chouinard, G., Duboff, E., Halaris, A., Won Kim, S., Koran, L., Liebowitz, M., Lydiard, R. B., Rasmussen, S., White, K., & Sikes, C. (1995). Double-blind parallel comparison of three dosages of Sertraline and placebo in outpatients with obsessive compulsive disorder. *Archives of General Psychiatry, 52*, 289–295.

Grisso, T. (1994). Clinical assessments for legal competence for older adults. In M. Storandt & G. R. VandenBose (Eds.), *Neuropsychological assessment of dementia and depression in older adults: A clinician's guide* (pp. 119–140). Washington, DC: American Psychological Association.

Grossman, D. C., Putsch, R. W., & Inui, T. S. (1993). The meaning of death to adolescents in an American Indian community. *Family Medicine, 25*, 593–597.

Groves, J. E. (1975). Management of the borderline patient on a medical or surgical ward: The psychiatric consultant's role. *International Journal of Psychiatry in Medicine, 32*, 178–183.

Gurland, B. J. (1994). The range of quality of life: Relevance to the treatment of depression in elderly patients. In L. S. Schnedier, C. F. Reynolds, B. D. Lebowitz, & A. J. Friedhoff (Eds.), *Diagnosis and treatment of depression in late life: Results of the NIH Consensus Development Conference* (pp. 61–80). Washington, DC: American Psychiatric Press.

Gustafson, Y., Berggrenn, D., Brannstrom, B. Bucht, G., Norberg, A., Hansson, L. & Winblad, B. (1988). Acute confusional states in elderly patients treated for femoral neck fracture. *Journal of the American Geriatric Society, 36*, 525–530.

Hadjistavropoulos, H. D., & Craig, A. D. (1994). Acute and chronic low back pain: Cognitive affective and behavioral dimensions. *Journal of Consulting and Clinical Psychology, 62*, 341–349.

Haley, J. (1976). *Problem solving therapy*. San Francisco: Jossey-Bass.

Haley, J. (1980). *Leaving home: The therapy of disturbed young people*. New York: McGraw-Hill.

Haley, J. (1996). *Learning and teaching therapy*. New York: Guilford Press.

Hall, R. C. W. (1996). Eating disorders. In J. R. Rundell & M. T. Wise (Eds.), *Textbook of consultation-liaison psychiatry* (pp. 486–505). Washington, DC: American Psychiatric Press.

Hansel, N. K. (1990). Measures for early detection of alcohol abuse for the primary care setting. *Proceedings of the 1990 Primary Care Research Methods and Statistics Conference*. San Antonio: University of Texas Health Science Center.

Hanson, R. W., & Gerber, K. E. (1990). *Coping with chronic pain: A guide to self management*. New York: Guilford Press.

Harrison, A. E. (1996). Primary care of lesbian and gay patients: Educating ourselves and our students. *Family Medicine, 28*, 10–23.

Hathaway, S. R., & McKinley, J. C. (1951). *Minnesota Multiphasic Personality Inventory: Manual*. New York: Psychological Corporation.

Havassy, B. E., & Schmidt, C. J. (1994). Alcohol and other drug abuse disorders in primary medical settings: Current and future research. In J. Miranda, A. A. Hohmann, C. C. Attkison, & D. B. Larson (Eds.), *Mental disorders in primary care* (pp. 34–63). San Francisco: Jossey-Bass.

Hayden, P. W., & Gallagher, T. A. (1992). Child abuse intervention in the emergency room. *Pediatric Emergency Medicine, 39*, 1053–1081.

Heyman, A., Wilkinson, W. E., Hurwitz, B. J., Schmechel, D., Sigmon, A. H., Weinberg, T., Helms, M. J., & Swift, M. (1983). Alzheimer's disease: Genetic aspects and associated clinical disorders. *Annals of Neurology, 14*, 507–515.

Health & Public Policy Committee, American College of Physicians. (1986). Methods for stopping cigarette smoking. *Annals of Internal Medicine, 105*, 281–291.

Heinzelman, F., & Bagley, R. W. (1970). Response to physical activity programs and their effects on health behavior. *Public Health Reports, 85*, 905–911.

Hepburn, K., & Reed, R. (1995). Ethical and clinical issues with Native-American elders: End of life decision making. *Clinics and Geriatric Medicine, 11*, 97–111.

Herman, J. L., Perry, J. C., & Vander Kolk, P. A. (1989). Childhood trauma in borderline personality disorder. *American Journal of Psychiatry, 146*, 490–495.

Herzog, D. B., & Copeland, P. M. (1985). Eating disorders. *New England Journal of Medicine, 313*, 295–303.

Hillman, E., Kripke, D. F., & Gillin, J. C. (1990). Sleep restriction, exercise, and bright lights: Alternative therapies for depression. In A. Tasman, S. M. Goldfinger, & C. A. Kaufmann (Eds.), *Review of psychiatry: Vol. 9* (pp. 132–144). Washington, DC: American Psychiatric Press.

Hodgman, C., Kaplan, S., Kazdin, A., & VanDalen, A. (1993). Managing depression in children. *Patient Care, 27*, 51–60.

Holmes, G. P., Kaplan, J. E., & Gantz, N. M. (1988). Chronic fatigue syndrome: A working case definition. *Annals of Internal Medicine, 108*, 387–389.

Holroyd, K. A., France, J. L., Cordingley, G. E., Rokicki, L. A., Kvaal, S. A., Lipchik, G. L., & McCool, H. R. (1995). Enhancing the effectiveness of relaxation—Thermal biofeedback training with propranolol hydrochloride. *Journal of Consulting and Clinical Psychology, 63*, 327–330.

Holt, S., Skinner, H. A., & Israel, Y. (1981). Early detection of alcohol abuse, I: Clinical and laboratory indicators. *Canadian Medical Association Journal, 124*, 1279–1295.

Horwath, B., & Weissman, M. M. (1997). Epidemiology of the anxiety disorders in cross cultural groups. In S. Friedman (Ed.), *Cultural issues in the treatment of anxiety* (pp. 21–39). New York: Guilford Press.

Howard, K. I., Kopta, S. M., Krause, M. S., & Orlinsky, T. E. (1986). The dose response effect relationship in psychotherapy. *American Psychologist, 41*, 159–164.

Hughes, J. R. (1988). Clonidine, depression and smoking cessation. *Journal of the American Medical Association, 259*, 2901–2902.

Husten, C. G., & Manley, M. W. (1990). How to help your patient stop smoking. *American Family Physician, 42*, 1017–1026.

Huygens, F. J. A. (1978). *Family medicine: The medical life history of families.* New York: Brunner-Mazel.

Institute of Medicine (1995). *Weighing the options: Criteria for evaluating weight management programs.* Washington, DC: National Academy Press.

Jacobson, A. N., Adler, A. G., Wolsdorf, J. I., Anderson, B. J., & Derby, O. (1990). Psychological characteristics of adults with IDDM: Comparison to patients in poor and good glycemic control. *Diabetes Care, 13*, 375–381.

Jacobson, G. R. (1983). Detection, assessment, and diagnosis of alcoholism: Current techniques and recent developments. *Alcoholism, 1*, 377–413.

Jansen, M. C., Brant-Zawadzki, M. N., Obuchowski, N., Modic, M. T., Malkasian, D., & Ross, J. S. (1994). Magnetic resonance imaging of the lumbar spine in people without back pain, *New England Journal of Medicine, 331*, 69–73.

Jenkins, C. D., Rosenman, R. H., & Zyzanski, S. J. (1974). Prediction of clinical coronary heart disease by a test for the coronary-prone behavior pattern. *New England Journal of Medicine, 23*, 1271–1275.

Johnson, J. G., Williams, J. P., Rabkin, J. G., Goetz, R. R., & Remien, R. H. (1995). Axis I psychiatric symptoms associated with HIV infection in personality disorder. *American Journal of Psychiatry, 152*, 551–554.

Jones, B., Teng, E., Folstein, M., & Harrison, J. S. (1993). A new bedside test of cognition for patients with HIV infection. *Annals of Internal Medicine, 119*, 1001–1004.

Kalichman, S. C. (1993). *Mandated reporting of suspected child abuse: Ethics, law, and policy.* Washington, DC: American Psychological Association.

Kandel, D. B., & Davies, M. (1986). Adult sequelae of adolescent depressive symptoms. *Archives of General Psychiatry, 43*, 255–262.

Kannel, W. B., & Thom, T. J. (1990). Incidence, prevalence and comorbidity of cardiovascular diseases. In J. W. Hurst, R. C. Schland, & C. E. Rackley (Eds.), *The Heart, Arteries and Veins* (pp. 627–638). New York: McGraw–Hill.

Kaplan, R. N., & Hartwell, S. L. (1987). Differential effects of social support and social network on physiological and social outcomes in men and women with type II diabetes mellitus. *Health Psychology, 6*, 387–398.

Karoly, P., & Jensen, M. P. (1987). *Multi-method assessment method of chronic pain.* New York: Pergamon Press.

Kashani, J. H., Husain, A., Shekim, W. O., Hodges, K. K., Cytryn, L., & McNew, D. H. (1981). Current perspectives in childhood depression: An overview. *American Journal of Psychiatry, 138*, 143–153.

Kassler, W. J., & Wu, A. W. (1992). Addressing HIV infection in office practice. Assessing risk, counselling, and testing. *Primary Care, 19*, 19–33.

Kathol, R. G., Mutgi, A., & William, S. J. (1990). Major depression diagnosed by DSM–III, DSM–III–R, RDC and Endicott criteria in patients with cancer. *American Journal of Psychiatry, 147*, 1021–1024.

Katon, W. J. (1990). Chest pain, cardiac disease, and panic disorder. *Journal of Clinical Psychiatry, 51*, 27–30.

Katon, W., Von Korff, M., Lin, E., Lipscomb, P., Wagner, E., & Polik, E. (1990). Distressed high utilizers of medical care: DSM–III–R diagnosis and treatment needs. *General Hospital Psychiatry, 12*, 355–362.

Katz, M. R., Abbey, S., Rydall, A., & Lowy, F. (1995). Psychiatric consultation for competency to refuse medical treatment: A retrospective study of patient characteristic outcome. *Psychosomatics, 36*, 33–41.

Katzman, R., Lasker, B., & Bernstein, N. (1988). Advances in the diagnosis of dementia: Accuracy of diagnosis and consequences of misdiagnosis of disorders causing dementia. In R. D. Terry (Ed.), *Aging and the brain* (pp. 17–62). New York: Raven Press.

Kavan, M. G., Pace, T. M., Ponterotto, J. G., & Barone, E. J. (1990). Screening for depression: Use of patient questionnaires. *American Family Physician, 41*, 897–904.

Kazniak, A., & Christenson, G. D. (1994). Differential diagnosis of dementia and depression. In M. Storandt & G. R. Vandenbos (Eds.), *Neuropsychological assessment of dementia and depression in older adults: A clinician's guide* (pp. 81–118). Washington, DC: American Psychological Association.

Kelly, J., Murphy, D., Bahr, G., Brasfield, T. L., Davis, D. R., Hauth, A.C., Morgan, M. G., Stevenson, L. Y., & Eilers, M. K. (1992). AIDS/HIV risk behavior among the chronically mentally ill. *American Journal of Psychiatry, 149*, 886–889.

Kenford, S. L., Fiore, N. C., Jorenby, D. E., Smith, S. S., Wetter, D., & Baker, T. B. (1994). Predicting smoking cessation: Who will quit with and without the nicotine patch. *Journal of the American Medical Association, 271*, 589–594.

Kessler, O., Cleary, P., & Burke, J. (1987). Psychiatric diagnoses of medical service users: Evidence from the epidemiologic catchment area program. *American Journal of Public Health, 77*, 18–24.

Kick, S. D., & Cooley, D. B. (1997). Depressive, not anxiety, symptoms are associated with current cigarette smoking among university internal medicine patients. *Psychosomatics, 38*, 132–139.

Kim, K. Y., McCartney, J. R., Kaye, W., & Boland, R. J. (1996). The effect of cimetidine and ranitidine on cognitive function in postoperative cardiac surgical patients. *International Journal of Psychiatry in Medicine, 26*, 295–307.

King, M. (1986). At risk drinking among general practice attenders: Validation of the C.A.G.E. Questionnaire. *Psychological Medicine, 16*, 213–217.

Kirmayer, L. J., Robbins, J. M., Dworkind, M., & Yaffe, M. J. (1993). Somatization and the recognition of depression in primary care. *American Journal of Psychiatry, 150*, 734–741.

Kleinman, A. (1980). *Patients and healers in the context of culture: An exploration of the borderland between anthropology, medicine, and psychiatry*. Berkeley: University of California Press.

Kleinman, A. (1988). *The illness narratives*. New York: Basic Books.

Klesges, R. T., Winders, S. E., Meyers, A. W., Eck, L. H., Ward, K. D., Hultquist, C. M., Ray, J. W., & Sadish, W. R. (1997). How much weight gain occurs following smoking cessation? A comparison of weight gain using both continuous and point prevalence abstinence. *Journal of Consulting and Clinical Psychology, 65*, 286–291.

Knight, R. G., & Longmore, B. E. (1994). *Clinical neuropsychology of alcoholism*. New York: Erlbaum.

Koenigsberg, H. W., Kaplan, R. D., Gilmore, M. M., & Cooper, A. M. (1985). The relationship between syndrome and personality disorder in DSM–III: Experience with 2,462 patients. *American Journal of Psychiatry, 142*, 207–212.

Kohut, N., & Singer, P. (1993). Advance directives in family practice. *Canadian Family Physician, 39*, 1087–1093.

Kornstein, S. G., & Gardner, D. F. (1993). Endocrine disorders. In A. Stoudemire & B. S. Fogel (Eds.), *Psychiatric care of the medical patient* (pp. 657–680). New York: Oxford University Press.

Kovacs, M. (1991). Rating scales to assess depression in schoolage children. *Acta Paedopsychiatrica, 46*, 305–315.

Kroenke, K., Wood, D. R., Mangelsdorff, A. D., Meier, N. J., & Powell, J. B. (1988). Chronic fatigue in primary care—Prevalence, patient characteristics, and outcome. *Journal of the American Medical Association, 260*, 929–934.

Kroger, W. S., & Fezler, W. D. (1976). *Hypnosis and behavior modification: Imagery conditioning*. Philadelphia: J. B. Lippincott.

Krosnick, J. A., & Judd, C. M. (1982). Transitions and social influence at adolescence: Who induces cigarette smoking? *Developmental Psychology, 18*, 359–368.

Kurtz, S. N. S. (1990). Adherence to diabetes regimens: Empirical status and clinical applications. *Diabetes Educator, 16*, 50–56.

Kushner, K., Meyer, D., & Hansen, M. (n. d.). *The family conference: What do patients want?* Madison: Department of Family Medicine and Practice, University of Wisconsin.

Lam, W., Sze, P. C., Sacks, H. S., & Chalmers, T. C. (1987, July). Meta-analysis of randomized controlled trials of nicotine chewing gum. *Lancet*, 27–29.

Langosch, W. (1988). Psychological effects of training in coronary patients: A critical review of the literature. *European Heart Journal, 9*, 37–42.

Latham, J., & Davis, B. D. (1994). The socioeconomic impact of chronic pain. *Disability and Rehabilitation, 16*, 39–44.

Leaf, P. J. (1994). Psychiatric disorders and the use of health services. In J. Miranda, A. Hohmann, C. C. Attkisson, & D. P. Larson (Eds.), *Mental disorders in primary care* (pp. 377–401). San Francisco: Jossey-Bass.

Leavitt, F., Garron, D. C., Whisler, W. W., & D'Angelo, C. M. (1980). A comparison of patients treated by chymopapain and laminectomy for low back pain using a multi-dimensional pain scale. *Clinical Orthopedics and Related Research, 146*, 136–143.

Lee, P. (1994). The economic impact of musculoskeletal disorders. *Quality of Life Research, 3*, S85–S91.

Lerman, C. (1997). Psychological aspects of genetic testing: Introduction to the special issue. *Health Psychology, 16*, 3–7.

Lerman, C., & Croyle, R. T. (1994). Psychological issues in genetic testing for breast cancer susceptibility. *Archives of Internal Medicine, 154*, 609–616.

Levenson, J. L. (1993). Cardiovascular disease. In A. Stoudemire & B. S. Fogel (Eds.), *Psychiatric care of the medical patient* (pp. 539–564). New York: Oxford University Press.

Leviton, A. (1978). Epidemiology of headache. In B. S. Schoenberg (Ed.), *Advances in neurology* (Vol. 19, pp. 341–352). New York: Raven Press.

Lewis, M. I., & Butler, R. N. (1974). Life review therapy: Putting memories to work in individual and group psychotherapy. *Geriatrics, 29*, 165–173.

Lichtenstein, E., & Brown, R. A. (1982). Current trends in the modification of cigarette dependence. In A. S. Beilack, M. Hersen, & A. E. Kazdin (Eds.), *International handbook of behavior modification therapy* (pp. 575–611). New York: Plenum Press.

Linn, E. H., VonKorff N., Katon, W., Bush, T., Simon, T. E., Walker, E., & Robinson, P. (1995). The role of the primary care physician in patients' adherence to antidepressant therapy. *Medical Care, 33*, 67–74.

Lishman, W. A. (1987). *Organic psychiatry: The psychological consequences of cerebral disorder* (2nd ed.). Oxford: Blackwell Scientific Publications.

Littman, A., Fava, M., McKool, K., Lamon-Fava, S., & Pegg, E. (1993). Buspirone therapy for type A behavior, hostility, and perceived stress in cardiac patients. *Psychotherapy & Psychosomatics, 59*, 107–110.

Loue, S. (1995). Living wills, durable powers of attorney for health care, and HIV infection: The need for statutory reform. *The Journal of Legal Medicine, 15*, 461–480.

Lown, B., DeSilva, R. A., Reich, P., & Murawski, B. J. (1980). Psychologic factors in sudden cardiac death. *American Journal of Psychiatry, 137*, 1325–1335.

Ludwig, K. H., Roll, G., Breithardt, G., Buedde, T., & Borggrefe, N. (1994). Post infarction depression and incomplete recovery six months after acute myocardial infarction. *Lancet, 343*, 20–23.

Lum, O. N. (1995). Health status of Asians and Pacific Islanders. *Clinics in Geriatric Medicine, 11*, 53–67.

Macklin, R. (1991). HIV infected psychiatric patients: Beyond confidentiality. *Ethics and Behaviors, 1*, 3–20.

MacLean, W. E., Perrin, J. N., Gottmaker, S., & Pierre, C. B. (1992). Psychological adjustment of children with asthma: Effects of illness severity and recent stressful life events. *Journal of Pediatric Psychology, 17*, 159–171.

MacQueen, K. M. (1994). The epidemiology of HIV transmission: Trends, structure, and dynamics. *Annual Review of Anthropology, 23*, 509–526.

Madanes, C. (1981). *Strategic family therapy*. San Francisco: Jossey-Bass.

Magruder-Habib, K., Durand, A. N., & Frey, K. A. (1991). Alcohol abuse and alcoholism in primary health care settings. *Journal of Family Practice, 32*, 406–413.

Malla, A., & Merskey, H. (1987). Screening for alcoholism in family practice. *Family Practice Research Journal, 6,* 138–147.

Manley, A. F., & DeLeon, P. H. (1997). Expanding psychology's vision—bridges to the 21st century. *Professional Psychology: Research and Practice, 28,* 99–100.

Mann, J. M., Tarantola, D., & Netter, T. W. (Eds.). (1992). *AIDS in the world.* Cambridge MA: Harvard University Press.

Mann, T. (1996). Why do we need a health psychology of gender or sexual orientation? In P. N. Kato & T. Mann (Eds.), *Handbook of diversity issues in health psychology* (pp. 187–198). New York: Plenum press.

Marcus, M. D., & Wing, R. R. (1990). Introduction. *Diabetes Spectrum, 3,* 362–364.

Marin, B. V. O., & Gomez, C. A. (1994). Latinos, HIV disease, and culture: Strategies for HIV prevention. In P. T. Cohen, M. A. Sande, & P. A. Volberding (Eds.), *The AIDS Knowledge Base* (2nd ed., pp. 10.81–10.83). Boston: Little, Brown & Company.

Marlatt, G. A., & Gordon, J. R. (Eds.). (1985). *Relapse prevention: Maintenance strategies and the treatment of addictive behavior.* New York: Guilford Press.

Marmot, N. G., Syme, S. L., Kagan, A., Kato, H., Cohen, J. B., & Belsky, J. (1975). Epidemiological studies of coronary heart disease and stroke in Japanese men living in Japan, Hawaii, and California: Prevalence of coronary and hypertensive heart disease and associated risk factors. *American Journal of Epidemiology, 102,* 514–525.

Marzuk, P. M., Tierney, H., Tardiff, K., Gross, E. M., Morgan, E. B., Hsu, M. A. (1988). Increased risk of suicide in persons with AIDS. *Journal of the American Medical Association, 259,* 1333–1337.

Masand, P., Pickett, P., & Murray, G. B. (1991). Psychostimulants for secondary depression in medical illness. *Psychosomatics, 32,* 203–208.

Mason, H. R. C., Marks, G., Simoni, J. N., Ruiz, M. S., & Richardson, J. L. (1995). Culturally sanctioned secrets? Latino men's nondisclosure of HIV infection to family, friends, and lovers. *Health Psychology, 14,* 6–12.

Matthews, K. A., & Angulo, J. (1980). Measurement of the type A behavior pattern in children: Competitiveness, impatience-anger, and aggression. *Child Development, 51,* 466–475.

Matthews, K. A., & Jennings, J. R. (1994). Cardiovascular responses of boys exhibiting the type A behavior pattern. *Psychosomatic Medicine, 46,* 44–497.

Matthews, W. C., Booth, M. W., Turner, J. D., & Kessler, T. P. (1986). Physicians attitudes towards homosexuality: A survey of the California Medical Society. *Western Journal of Medicine, 144,* 106–110.

McAllister, T. W. (1985). Recognition of pseudodementia, *American Family Physician, 32,* 175–180.

McCord, W., & McCord, J. (1964). *The Psychopath: An essay on the criminal mind.* New York: VanNostrand-Reinholdt.

McCullough, P., & Rutenberg, S. (1989). Launching children and moving on. In B. Carter & M. McGoldrick (Eds.), *The changing family life cycle: A framework for family therapy* (2nd ed., pp. 285–310). Boston: Allyn & Bacon.

McDaniel, S., Campbell, T. L., & Seaburn, D. P. (1990). *Family oriented primary care: A manual for medical providers.* New York: Springer-Verlag.

McGoldrick, M. (1989). The joining of families through marriage: The new couple. In B. Carter & M. McGoldrick (Eds.), *The changing family life cycle: A framework for family therapy* (2nd ed., pp. 209–234). Boston: Allyn & Bacon.

McGoldrick, N., & Gerson, R. (1985). *Genograms in family assessment.* New York: Norton.

McKenna, P. J., Kane, J. M., & Parrish, K. (1985). Psychotic syndromes in epilepsy. *American Journal of Psychiatry, 142*, 895–904.

McLachlan, R. S. (1993). Managing the first seizure. *Canadian Family Physician, 39*, 858–893.

McNamara, M. E. (1993). Clinical neurology. In A. Stoudemire & B. S. Fogel (Eds.), *Psychiatric care of the medical patient* (pp. 455–484). New York: Oxford University Press.

Melamed, B. G., & Williamson, D. J. (1991). Programs for the treatment of dental disorder: Dental anxiety and temporomandibular disorders. In J. J. Sweet, R. H. Rozensky, & S. M. Tovian (Eds.), *Handbook of clinical psychology in medical settings* (pp. 539–566). New York: Plenum Press.

Melzack, R. (1975). The McGill Pain Questionnaire: Major properties and scoring methods. *Pain, 1*, 277–299.

Melzack, R., & Wall, P. D. (1965). Pain mechanisms: A new theory. *Science, 150*, 971–979.

Mendez, M. F., Cummings, J. L., & Benson, D. F. (1996). Depression and epilepsy— Significance and phenomenology. *Archives of Neurology, 43*, 766–770.

Merikangas, A. R., & Weissman, M. N. (1986). Epidemiology of DSM–III Axis II Personality Disorders. In A. J. Frances & R. E. Hales (Eds.), *American Psychiatric Association Annual Review* (Vol. 5, pp. 258–278). Washington, DC: American Psychiatric Press.

Meyer, R. J., & Haggerty, R. J. (1962). Streptococcal infections in families: Factors affecting individual susceptibility. *Pediatrics, 29*, 539–549.

Milgrom, H., Bender, B., Sarlin, N., & Leung, D. Y. N. (1994). Difficult to control asthma: The challenge posed by noncompliance. *American Journal of Asthma and Allergy for Pediatricians, 7*, 141–146.

Milhorn, H. T. (1989). Nicotine dependence. *American Family Physician, 39*, 214–224.

Miller, C. K., & Searight, H. R. (in press). Informed consent for research in drug trials as viewed by the private practitioner. In A. Cato (Ed.), *Clinical drug trials and tribulations* (2nd ed.). New York: Marcel Dekker.

Miller, G. E., & Prinz, R. J. (1990). Enhancement of social learning family interventions for childhood conduct disorder. *Psychological Bulletin, 108*, 291–307.

Miller, G. H., Golish, J. A., & Cox, C. E. (1992). The physician's guide to smoking cessation. *Journal of Family Practice, 34*, 759–766.

Millon, T. (1981). *Disorders of personality*. New York: Wiley.

Minuchin, S. (1974). *Families and family therapy*. Cambridge, MA: Harvard University Press.

Minuchin, S., Rosman, B., & Baker, A. (1978). *Psychosomatic families*. Boston: Harvard Press.

Miranda, J., Hohmann, A. A., & Attkisson, C. C. (1994). Epidemiology of mental disorders in primary care. In J. Miranda, A. A. Hohmann, C. C. Attkisson, & D. P. Larson (Eds.), *Mental disorders in primary care* (pp. 3–15). San Francisco: Jossey-Bass.

Mitchell, W. G., Gorrell, R. W., & Greenberg, R. A. (1980). Failure to thrive: A study in a primary care setting: Epidemiology and follow-up. *Pediatrics, 65*, 971–977.

Montauk, S. L., & Gebhardt, B. (1997). Opportunistic infections and psychosocial stress in HIV. *American Family Physician, 56*, 87–96.

Moriksy, D. E., Levine, D. M., Green, L. W., Shapiro, S., Russell, R. P., & Smith, C. R. (1983). Five year blood pressure control and mortality following health education for hypertensive patients. *American Journal of Public Health, 73*, 153–162.

Mossey, J. N., Knott, K., & Craik, R. (1990). The effects of persistent depressive symptoms on hip fracture recovery. *Journal of Gerontology, 45*, M163–M168.

Mullins, L. L., & Olson, R. A. (1990). Familial factors in the etiology, maintenance and treatment of somatoform disorders in children. *Family Systems Medicine, 8*, 159–176.

Mumford, E., Schlesinger, H., Glass, G., Patrick, C., & Cuerdon, T. (1984). A new look at evidence about reduced cost about medical utilization following mental health treatment. *American Journal of Psychiatry, 141*, 1145–1158.

Murphy, B. C. (1991). Educating mental health professionals. *Journal of Homosexuality, 22*, 229–246.

Murphy, E. (1994). The course and outcome of depression in late life. In L. Schneider, C. F. Reynolds, B. D. Lebowitz, & A. J. Friedhoff (Eds.), *Diagnosis and treatment of depression in late life: Results of the NIH Consensus Development Conference* (pp. 81–98). Washington, DC: American Psychiatric Press.

Muscari, M. E. (1996). Primary care of adolescents with anorexia nervosa. *Journal of Pediatric Health Care, 10*, 17–25.

Nahlik, J. E., & Searight, H. R. (1996). Diagnosis and treatment of attention deficit/ hyperactivity disorder. *Primary Care Reports, 2*, 65–74.

Nahlik, J. E., & Searight, H. R. (1998). Behavioral problems of children. In R. Taylor (Ed.), *Family medicine: Principles and practice* (pp. 173–182). New York: Springer-Verlag.

Neal, A. M., Nagle-Rich, L., & Smucker, W. D. (1994). The presence of panic disorder among African American hypertensives: A pilot study. *Journal of Black Psychology, 20*, 29–35.

Nieslen, A. C., & Williams, T. A. (1980). Depression in ambulatory medical patients: Prevalence by self-report questionnaire and recognition by non-psychiatric physicians. *Archives of General Psychiatry, 37*, 999–1004.

Nouwen, A., Gingras, J., Talbot, F., & Bouchard, S. (1997). The development of an empirical psychosocial taxonomy for patients with diabetes. *Health Psychology, 16*, 263–271.

Novak, L. L. (1996). Childhood behavior problems. *American Family Physician, 53*, 257–262.

Noyes, R., Reich, J., Christansen, J., Suelzer, M., Pfohl, B., & Corye II, W. A. (1990). Outcome of panic disorder: Relationship to diagnostic subtypes in comorbidity. *Archives of General Psychiatry, 47*, 809–818.

Nymberg, J. H., & Van Noppen, B. (1994). Obsessive compulsive disorder: A concealed diagnosis. *American Family Physician, 49*, 1129–1137.

O'Brien, M. E. (1994). The dementia syndromes: Distinguishing their clinical differences. *Post Graduate Medicine, 9*, 91–101.

O'Connell, C. B. (1993). Risk assessment interviewing for HIV. *Physician Assistant*, 35–43.

O'Hanlan, K. A. (1996). Homophobia in the health psychology of lesbians. In P. M. Kato & T. Mann (Eds.), *Handbook of diversity issues in health psychology* (pp. 261–284). New York: Plenum Press.

Oken, D. (1961). What to tell cancer patients. *Journal of the American Medical Association, 175*, 86–94.

Openlander, P., & Searight, H. R. (1983). Family therapy perspectives in a college counseling center. *Journal of College Student Personnel, 24*, 423–427.

Oper, K., Devinsky, O., Perrine, K., Vazquez, B., & Luciano, D. (1993). Nonepileptic seizures in childhood sexual and physical abuse. *Neurology, 43*, 1950–1953.

Oppel, W. C., Harper, P. A., & Rider, R. V. (1968). The age of attaining bladder control. *Pediatrics, 42*, 614–626.

Osler, W. (1910). The Lumleian lectures on angina pectoris. *Lancet, 1*, 839–844.

Osmond, D. H. (1994). Prevalence of infection and projections for the future. In P. T. Cohen, M. A. Sande, & P. A. Volberding (Eds.), *The AIDS knowledge base* (2nd ed., pp. 1.4–1.11). Boston: Little, Brown.

Othmer, E., & DeSouza, C. (1985). A screening test for somatization disorder (hysteria). *American Journal of Psychiatry, 142,* 1146–1149.

Otto, M., & Gould, R. A. (1996). Maximizing treatment outcome for panic disorder, cognitive behavioral strategies. In M. H. Pollack, M. W. Otto, & J. F. Rosenbaum (Eds.), *Challenges in clinical practice: Pharmacologic and psychosocial strategies* (pp. 113–140). New York: Guilford Press.

Paradis, C. N., Friedman, S., & Hatch, M. (1997). Isolated sleep paralysis in African Americans with panic disorder. *Cultural Diversity and Mental Health, 3,* 69–76.

Patterson, C. J. (1992). Children of lesbian and gay parents. *Child Development, 63,* 1025–1042.

Patterson, G. R. (1971). *Families: Application of social learning theory to family life.* Champaign, IL: Research Press.

Perez-Stable, E., Miranda, J., Munoz, R. F., & Ying, Y. W. (1990). Depression in medical outpatients: Under recognition and misdiagnosis. *Archives of Internal Medicine, 150,* 1083–1088.

Perkins, D. O., Davidson, E. J., Leserman, J., Liao, B., & Evans, B. L. (1993). Personality disorder in patients infected with HIV: A controlled study with implications for clinical care. *American Journal of Psychiatry, 150,* 309–315.

Perry, S., Jacobsberg, L., Card, C., Ashman, T., Frances, A., & Fishman, B. (1993). Severity of psychiatric symptoms after HIV testing. *American Journal of Psychiatry, 150,* 775–779.

Perry, S., Jacobsberg, L., & Fishman, B. (1990). Suicidal ideation and HIV testing. *Journal of the American Medical Association, 263,* 679–682.

Pfeffer, C. R. (1986). *The suicidal child.* New York: Guilford Press.

Pizzi, M. (1992). Women, HIV infection and AIDS: Tapestries of life, death and empowerment. *American Journal of Occupational Therapy, 46,* 1021–1027.

Pliszka, S. R. (1987). Tricyclic antidepressants in the treatment of children with attention deficit disorder. *Journal of the American Academy of Child and Adolescent Psychiatry, 26,* 127–132.

Pliszka, S. R. (1991). Attention deficit hyperactivity disorder: A clinical review. *American Family Physician, 43,* 267–275.

Polonsky, W. H. (1993). Psychosocial issues in diabetes mellitus. In R. J. Gatchel & E. B. Blanchard (Eds.), *Psychophysiological disorders: Research and clinical applications* (pp. 357–382). Washington, DC: American Psychological Association.

Portenoy, R. K. (1993). Chronic pain management. In A. Stoudemire & B. S. Fogel (Eds.), *Psychiatric care of the medical patient* (pp. 341–366). New York: Oxford University Press.

Powell, L. H. (1996). The hook: A metaphor for gaining control of emotional reactivity. In R. A. Allan & S. Scheidt (Eds.), *Heart and mind: The practice of cardiac psychology* (pp. 313–328). Washington, DC: American Psychological Association.

Price, B. A., Friedman, N., & Ghandour, G. (1995). Relation between insecurity and type A behavior. *American Heart Journal, 129,* 488–491.

Prochaska, J. O., & DiClemente, C. C. (1983). Stages and processes of self change in smoking: Toward an integrative model of change. *Journal of Consulting and Clinical Psychology, 51,* 390–395.

Pugsley, W., Klinger, L., Paschalis, C., Treasure, T., Harrison, M., & Newman, S. (1994). The impact of microemboli during cardiopulmonary bypass on neuropsychological functioning. *Stroke, 25,* 1393–1399.

Rakel, R. E. (1996). A primary care provider sees anxiety and depression in the medically ill. *Medical Psychiatry Forum,* (June) 2–5.

Rankin, E. J., Adams, R. L., & Jones, H. E. (1996). Epilepsy and nonepileptic attack disorder. In R. L. Adams, O. A. Parsons, J. L. Culbertson, & S. J. Nixon (Eds.) *Neuropsychology for clinical practice* (pp. 131–174). Washington, DC: American Psychological Association.

Rankow, E. J. (1995). Lesbian health issues for the primary care provider. *Journal of Family Practice, 40,* 486–493.

Rapoport, J. L. (1990). The waking nightmare: An overview of obsessive-compulsive disorder. *Journal of Clinical Psychiatry, 51*(Suppl.), 25–28.

Rasmussen, N. H., & Avant, R. S. (1989). Somatization disorder in family practice. *American Family Physician, 40,* 206–214.

Rauch, S. L., Baer, L., & Jenike, N. A. (1996). Treatment resistant obsessive compulsive disorder: Practical strategies for management. In M. H. Pollack, M. W. Otto, & J. F. Rosenbaum (Eds.), *Challenges in clinical practice: Pharmacologic and psychosocial strategies* (pp. 201–218). New York: Guilford Press.

Reconciliation Act of 1990, Title IV, Section 4206 Oct. 26, Cong. Rec. 12638.

Reid, W. (1989). *DSM–III–R training program: Videotaped clinical vignettes.* New York: Brunner/Mazel.

Richards, J. (1992). Words as therapy: Smoking cessation. *Journal of Family Practice, 34,* 687–692.

Ridsdale, L., Robins, D., Fitzgerald, A., Jeffrey, S., & McGee, L. (1996). Epilepsy in general practice: Patient psychological symptoms and the perception of stigma. *British Journal of General Practice, 46,* 365–366.

Robins, L. N. (1966). *Deviant children grown up.* Baltimore: Williams & Wilkins.

Robins, L. N., Helzer, J. E., & Weissman, M. M. (1994). Lifetime prevalence of specific psychiatric disorders in three sites. *Archives of General Psychiatry, 41,* 949–958.

Robinson, J. R. (1989). The natural history of mental disorder in old age. *British Journal of Psychiatry, 154,* 783–789.

Rohling, M. L., Binder, L. M., & Langhinrichsen-Rohling, J. (1995). Money matters: A meta-analytic review of the association between financial compensation and the experience and treatment of chronic pain. *Health Psychology, 14,* 537–547.

Rome, E. S. (1996). Eating disorders in adolescents and young adults: What is a primary clinician to do? *Cleveland Clinic Journal of Medicine, 63,* 387–420.

Rosen, R. C., Brondolo, E., & Kostis, J. B. (1993). Nonpharmacological treatment of essential hypertension: Research and clinical applications. In R. J. Gatchel & E. B. Blanchard (Eds.), *Psychophysiological disorders: Research and clinical applications* (pp. 63–110). Washington, DC: American Psychological Association.

Roskies, E. (1987). *Stress management for the healthy type A: Theory and practice.* New York: Guilford Press.

Rost, K., Smith, G. R., Matthews, B. P., & Guise, B. B. (1994). The deliberate misdiagnosis of major depression. *Archives of Family Medicine, 3,* 333–337.

Roth, M. E. (1993). Advances in Alzheimer's disease: A review for the family physician. *The Journal of Family Practice, 37,* 593–607.

Rouchell, A. M., Pounds, R., & Tierney, J. G. (1996). Depression. In J. R. Rundell & M. G. Wise (Eds.), *Textbook of Consultation—Liaison Psychiatry* (pp. 310–345). Washington, DC: American Psychiatric Press.

Rousseau, P. (1995). Native American elders: Health care status. *Clinics and Geriatric Medicine, 11*, 83–95.

Rovner, B. W., German, P. S., Brant, L. J., Clark, R., Brown, L., & Folstein, M. F. (1991). Depression and mortality in nursing homes. *Journal of American Medical Association, 265*, 993–996.

Rovner, B. W., German, P. S., Broadhead, J., Moriss, R. K., Brunt, L. J., Blaustein, J., & Folstein, M. F. (1990). Prevalence and management of dementia and other psychiatric disorders in nursing homes. *International Psychogeriatrics, 2*, 13–24.

Rubin, R. H. (1988). Acquired immune deficiency syndrome. *Scientific American—Medicine, 7*, 1–19.

Ruffin, M. T., & Cohen, N. (1994). Evaluation and management of fatigue. *American Family Physician, 50*, 625–632.

Rugh, J. D., & Solberg, W. K. (1976). Psychological implications in temporomandibular pain and dysfunction. *Oral Sciences Review, 7*, 3–30.

Rutter, M. (1986). The developmental psychopathology of depression: Issues and perspectives. In M. Rutter, C. Izard, & P. Read (Eds.), *Depression in Young People: Developmental and Clinical Perspectives* (pp. 3–32). New York: Guilford.

Sachs, D. P. L., Sawe, U., & Leischow, S. J. (1993). Effectiveness of a 16 hour transdermal nicotine patch in a medical practice setting, without intensive group counseling. *Archives of Internal Medicine, 153*, 1881–1890.

Salmon, P., & May, C. R. (1995). Patients' influence on doctor's behavior: A case study of patient strategies in somatization. *International Journal of Psychiatry in Medicine, 25*, 319–329.

Sandhu, H. S. (1986). Psychological issues in chronic obstructive pulmonary disease. *Clinics in Chest Medicine, 7*, 629–642.

Sanderson, P. L., Todd, B. D., Holt, G. R., & Getty, C. J. M. (1995). Compensation, work status and disability in low bask pain patients. *Spine, 20*, 554–556.

Sansone, R. A., & Sansone, L. A. (1996). Dysthymic disorder: The chronic depression, *American Family Physician, 53*, 2588–2544.

Sarason, I. G., & Sarason, B. R. (1993). *Abnormal psychology* (7th ed.). Englewood Cliffs, NJ: Prentice-Hall.

Scheidt, S. (1996). A whirlwind tour of cardiology for the mental health professional. In R. Allen & S. Scheidt (Eds.), *Heart and mind: The practice of cardiac psychology* (pp. 15–62). Washington, DC: American Psychological Association.

Scherger, J. E. (1998). Managed care. In R. B. Taylor (Ed.), *Family medicine: Principles and Practice* (5th ed., pp. 1139–1143). New York: Springer-Verlag.

Schmeller-Berger, L., Handal, P. J., Searight, H. R., & Katz, B. (1998). A survey of psychologists' education, knowledge, and experience treating clients with HIV/AIDS. *Professional Psychology: Research and Practice, 29*, 160–162.

Schmidt, D. D. (1983). When is it helpful to convene the family? *The Journal of Family Practice, 16*, 967–973.

Schmitt, P. (1985). Rehabilitation of chronic pain: A multi-disciplinary approach. *Journal of Rehabilitation, 51*, 72–75.

Schurman, M, Kramer, P., & Mitchell, J. (1985). The hidden mental health network. Treatment of mental illness by non-psychiatric physicians. *Archives of General Psychiatry, 42*, 84–94.

Schvehla, T. J., Mandoki, M. W., & Sumner, G. S. (1994). Clonidine therapy for co-morbid attention deficit hyperactivity disorder and conduct disorder: Preliminary findings in a children's inpatient unit. *Southern Medical Journal, 87,* 692–695.

Schwartz, J. L. (1987). *Review and evaluation of smoking cessation methods: The United States and Canada, 1978–1985.* Bethesda: National Institute of Health.

Seaburn, P. B., Lorenz, A. D., Gunn, W. B., Gawinski, B. A., & Mauksch, O. B. (1996). *Models of collaboration: A guide For mental health professionals working with healthcare practitioners.* New York: Basic Books.

Searight, H. R. (1992a). Assessing patient competence for medical decision making. *American Family Physician, 45,* 751–759.

Searight, H. R. (1992b). Borderline personality disorder: Diagnosis and management in primary care. *Journal of Family Practice, 34,* 605–612.

Searight, H. R. (1992c). Screening for alcohol abuse in primary care: Current status and future directions. *Family Practice Research Journal, 12,* 193–204.

Searight, H. R. (1994). Psychosocial knowledge and allopathic medicine: Points of convergence and departure. *The Journal of Medical Humanities, 15,* 221–232.

Searight, H. R. (1997a). Childhood sexual abuse: Psychosocial assessment in primary care. In L. K. Hamberger & S. Burge (Eds.), *Violence education for health care professionals* (pp. 207–222). Binghamton, NY: Haworth Press.

Searight, H. R. (1997b). The Tarasoff warning and the duty to protect: Implications for family medicine. In K. Hamberger & S. Burge (Eds.), *Violence education for healthcare professionals* (pp. 153–168). Binghamton, NY: Haworth Press.

Searight, H. R. (1997c). *Family of origin therapy and diversity.* Washington, DC: Taylor and Francis.

Searight, H. R., & Barbarash, R. A. (1994). Informed consent: Clinical and legal issues in family practice. *Family Medicine, 26,* 244–249.

Searight, H. R., Bennett, S., Clansy, C., Heine, B., Horn, G., Klocek, J., Rankin, C., Richardson, P., Tschannen, T., Williams, L., & Williams, T. (1997). Therapy with unmarried heterosexual couples: Clinical and ethical issues. *The Family Journal, 5,* 295–302.

Searight, H. R., Nahlik, J. E., & Campbell, D. C. (1995). Attention-deficit/hyperactivity disorder: Assessment, diagnosis and management. *Journal of Family Practice, 40,* 270–279.

Searight, H. R., & Noce, J. J. (1988). Towards a systemic model of healthcare compliance: Rationale and interview protocol. *Journal of Strategic and Systemic Therapies, 7,* 45–53.

Searight, H. R., & Pound, P. (1994). The HIV-positive psychiatric patient and the duty to protect: Ethical and legal issues. *International Journal of Psychiatry in Medicine, 24,* 259–270.

Searight, H. R., & McLaren, L. (1997). Behavioral and psychiatric aspects of HIV infection. *American Family Physician, 55,* 1227–1237.

Searight, H. R., & McLaren, L. (1999). Attention deficit/hyperactivity disorder: The medicalization of misbehavior. *Journal of Clinical Psychology in Medical Settings.*

Seidman, S. N., & Rieder, R. O. (1995). Sexual behavior through the life cycle: An empirical approach. In J. Oldham & N. Riba (Eds.), *Review of psychiatry* (Vol. 14, pp. 639–676). Washington, DC: American Psychiatric Press.

Selzer, N. L. (1971). Michigan Alcoholism Screening Test: The quest for a new diagnostic instrument. *American Journal of Psychiatry, 127,* 1653–1658.

Shapiro, D. (1965). *Neurotic styles.* New York: Basic Books.

Shearer, S. L., & Adams, G. K. (1993). Non-pharmacologic aids in the treatment of depression. *American Family Physician, 47,* 435–441.

Shiloh, S. (1996). Genetic counseling: A developing area of interest for psychologists. *Professional Psychology: Research and Practice, 27*, 475–486.

Shiloh, S., & Saxe, L. (1989). Perception of recurrence risks by genetic counselees. *Psychology and Health, 3*, 45–61.

Simon, R. I. (1992). *Clinical psychiatry and the law* (2nd ed.). Washington, DC: American Psychiatric Association.

Sleek, S. (1994, June). Psychologists, physicians piece together patient care. *APA monitor*, p. 22.

Smith, G. R., Monson, R. A., & Ray, D. C. (1986). Psychiatric consultation in somatization disorder: A randomized controlled study. *New England Journal of Medicine, 314*, 1407–1413.

Smith, L. W., & Dimsdale, J. E. (1989). Postcardiotomy delirium: Conclusions after 25 years? *American Journal of Psychiatry, 146*, 452–458.

Smoller, J. W., & Pollack, M. H. (1996). Pharmacologic approaches to treatmeant resistant social phobia are generalized anxicty disorder. In M. Pollack, M. Otto, & J. Rosenbaum (Eds.) *Challenges in Clinical Practice* (pp. 141–170). New York: Guilford.

Snow, L. F. (1993). *Walkin over medicine*. Boulder, CO: Westview Press.

Spira, J. L., & Spiegel, D. (1993). Group psychotherapy of the medically ill. In A. Stoudemire & B. S. Fogel (Eds.), *Psychiatric care of the medical patient.* (pp. 31–50). New York: Oxford University Press.

Starr, P. (1982). *The social transformation of American medicine*. New York: Basic.

Steel, J. N., Young, R. J., Lloyd, G. G., & MacIntyre, C. C. A. (1989). Abnormal eating attitudes in young insulin dependent diabetics. *British Journal of Psychiatry, 155*, 515–521.

Stern, R. G., & Davis, K. L. (1991). Treatment approaches in Alzheimers disease: Past, present and future. In M. F. Weiner (Ed.), *The dementias: Diagnosis and management* (pp. 227–248). Washington, DC: American Psychiatric Press.

Stern, Y., Tang, M., Albert, M., Brandt, J., Jacobs, D. M., Bell, K., Marder, M., Sano, M., Devanand, D., Albert, S., Bylsma, F., & Tsai, W. (1997). Predicting time to nursing home care and death in individuals with Alzheimer disease. *Journal of the American Medical Association, 277*, 806–812.

Stevens, J. R. (1988). Psychiatric aspects of epilepsy. *Journal of Clinical Psychiatry, 49*, 49–57.

Straus, N. A., Gelles, R. J., & Steinmetz, S. K. (1980). *Behind closed doors*. Garden City, NY: Anchor Books.

Strub, R. L., & Black, F. W. (1993). *The mental status examination in neurology* (3rd ed.). Philadelphia: F. A. Davis.

Stuart, M. R., & Lieberman, J. A. (1993). *The 15 minute hour: Applied psychotherapy for the primary care physician* (2nd ed.). Westport, CT: Praeger.

Stuart, R. R. (1980). *Helping couples change: A social learning approach to marital therapy*. New York: Guilford Press.

Suhl, J., Simons, P., Reedy, P., & Garrick, T. (1994). Myth of substituted judgment: Surrogate decision making regarding life support is unreliable. *Archives of Internal Medicine, 154*, 90–96.

Summergrad, P., Rauch, M. S., & Neal, R. R. (1993). Human immunodeficiency virus and other infectious disorders affecting the central nervous system. In A. Stoudemire & B. S. Fogel (Eds.), *Psychiatric care of the medical patient* (pp. 713–738). New York: Oxford University Press.

Swanson, J., Holzer, C., Ganju, V., & Jono, R. (1990). Violence and psychiatric disorder in the community: Evidence from the epidemiological catchment area surveys. *Hospital and Community Psychiatry*, *41*, 761–770.

Syme, S. L., Marmot, M. T., Kagan, A., Kato, H., & Rhoads, G. (1975). Epidemiologic studies of coronary heart disease and stroke in Japanese men living in Japan, Hawaii, and California: Introduction. *American Journal of Epidemiology*, *102*, 477–480.

Tabrizi, K., Littman, L. A., Williams, R. B., & Schedit, S. (1996). Psychopharmacology and cardiac disease. In R. Allan & S. Scheidt (Eds.), *Heart and mind: The practice of cardiac psychology* (pp. 397–420). Washington, DC: American Psychological Association.

Talley, J. H. (1986). Masks of major depression. *Medical Aspects of Human Sexuality*, *16*, 20–22.

Taylor, C. P., Baundra, A., Ewart, C. K., Miller, N. H., & DeBusk, F. F. (1985). Exercise testing to enhance wive's confidence in their husband's cardiac capacity soon after clinically uncomplicated acute myocardial infarction. *American Journal of Cardiology*, *55*, 635–638.

Taylor, G. J., Ryan, D., & Bagby, R. M. (1985). Toward the development of a new self-report alexithymia scale. *Psychotherapy and Psychosomatics*, *44*, 191–199.

Taylor, R. O. (1990). *Distinguishing psychological from organic disorders: Screening for psychological masquerade*. New York: Springer.

Taylor, S. E. (1983). Adjustment to threatening events: A theory of cognitive adaptation. *American Psychologist*, *41*, 1161–1173.

Taylor, S. E. (1991). *Health psychology* (2nd ed.). New York: McGraw-Hill.

Thelen, N. H., Mann, L. N., Pruitt, J., & Smith, M. (1987). Bulimia: Prevalence and component factors in college women. *General Psychosomatic Research*, *31*, 73–78.

Thompson, W. L., & Thompson, T. L. (1993). Pulmonary disease. In A. Stoudemire & B. S. Fogel (Eds.), *Psychiatric care of the medical patient* (pp. 591–610). New York: Oxford University Press.

Tong, K. L., & Spicer, B. J. (1994). Chinese palliative patients and family in North America: A cultural perspective. *Journal of Palliative Care*, *10*, 26–28.

Transdermal Nicotine Study Group (1991). Transdermal nicotine for smoking cessation. *Journal of the American Medical Association*, *266*, 3133–3138.

Turk, D. C., Meichenbaum, D., & Genest, M. (1983). *Pain and behavioral medicine: A cognitive behavioral perspective*. New York: Guilford Press.

Uhlman, R. F., Pearlman, R. A., & Cain, K. C. (1988). Physicians and spouses predictions of elderly patients resuscitation preferences. *Journal of Gerontology*, *43*, 115–121.

United States Department of Health and Human Services. (1998). *Health consequences of smoking: nicotine addiction: A report of the surgeon general*. Rothfield, MD: U.S. Department of Health and Human Services, Public Health Service, Office on Smoking and Health.

Vasquez, N. J. T. (1994). *Latinos*. In L. Comas-Diaz & B. Greene (Eds.), *Women of color: Integrating ethnic and gender identities in psychotherapy* (pp. 114–138). New York: Guilford Press.

Venters, M. H. Jacobs, P. R., Luepkekr, R. B., Maiman, L. A., & Gillum, R. F. (1984). Spouses concordance of smoking patterns: The Minnesota heart survey. *American Journal of Epidemiology*, *120*, 608–616.

Verbrugge, L. (1989). The twain meet: Empirical explanations of sex differences in health and mortality. *Journal of Health and Social Behavior*, *30*, 282–304.

Visintainer, P. F., & Matthews, K. A. (1987). Stability of overt type A behaviors in children: Results from two- and five-year longitudinal study. *Child Development, 58,* 1586–1591.

Vogel, W., Young, M., & Primack, W. (1996). A survey of physician use of treatment methods for functional enuresis. *Developmental and Behavioral Pediatrics, 17,* 90–93.

vonKorff, M., & Myers, L. (1987). The primary care physician and psychiatric services. *General Hospital Psychiatry, 9,* 235–240.

Waddell, G., Main, C. J., Morris, E. W., DiPaolo, N., & Gray, I. (1984). Chronic low back pain, psychologic distress, and illness behavior. *Spine, 9,* 209–213.

Walker, C. E. (1978). Toilet training, enuresis and encopresis, In P. Magrub (Ed.), *Psychological management of pediatric problems (Vol. I),* (pp. 129–189). Baltimore MD: University Park press.

Walker, C. E. (1995). Elimination disorders: Enuresis and encopresis. In M. C. Roberts (Ed.), *Handbook of pediatric psychology* (2nd ed., pp. 537–557). New York: Guilford Press.

Waller, D., Fairburn, C. G., McPherson, A., Kay, R., Lee, A., & Nowell, T. (1996). Treating bulimia nervosa in primary care: A pilot study. *International Journal of Eating Disorders, 19,* 99–103.

Walsh, F. (1989). The family in later life. In B. Carter and M. McGoldrick (Eds.), *The changing family life cycle: A framework for family therapy* (2nd ed., pp. 311–333). Boston: Allyn & Bacon.

Waters, W. E. (1970), Community studies of the prevalence of headache. *Headache, 9,* 178–186.

Waters, W. E. (1974). *Epidemiology of migraine.* Bracknell, Berkshire, United Kingdom: Boehringer Ingelheim.

Weiss, S. N., Anderson, R. T., & Weiss, S. N. (1991). Cardiovascular disorders: Hypertension and coronary heart disease. In J. J. Sweet, R. H. Rozensky, & S. N. Tovian (Eds.), *Handbook of clinical psychology in medical settings* (pp. 353–374). New York: Plenum Press.

Weiten, W. (1983). *Psychology applied to modern life: Adjustment in the 80s.* Monteray, CA: Brooks/Cole Publishing.

Welkowitz, L. A., & Gorman, J. M. (1997). An overview of the treatment of anxiety disorders: Focusing on panic disorders as a model. In S. Friedman (Ed.), *Cultural issues in the treatment of anxiety* (pp. 40–55). New York: Guilford Press.

Wells, K. B., Stewart, A., Hayes, R. D., Burnam, M. A., Rogers, W., Daniels, M., Berry S., Greenfield, S., & Ware J. (1989). The functioning and well being of depressed patients: Results from the medical outcome study. *Journal of the American Medical Association, 262,* 914–919.

Wender, P. H. (1995). *Attention deficit hyperactivity disorder in adults.* New York: Oxford University Press.

Westman, E. C., Levin, E. D., & Rose, J. E. (1993). The nicotine patch and smoking cessation: A randomized trial with telephone counseling. *Archives of Internal Medicine, 153,* 1917–1923.

White, N. (1984). Pseudo-Encopresis: From avalanche to victory, from vicious to virtuous cycles. *Family Systems Medicine, 2,* 150–160.

Whitehead, D., & Doherty, J. W. (1989). Systems dynamics in cigarette smoking: An exploratory study. *Family Systems Medicine, 7,* 264–273.

Wickline v. State, 228 Cal. Rptr. 661 (Cal. App. 2 Dist., 1986).

Williams, S. J. (1989). Chronic respiratory illness and disabilities: A critical review of the psychosocial literature. *Social Science and Medicine, 28,* 791–803.

Williams, S. J., & Bury, M. R. (1989). "Breathtaking": The consequences of chronic respiratory disorder. *International Disability Studies, 11*, 104–112.

Williamson, P. S., & Yates, W. R. (1989). The initial presentation of depression in family practice in psychiatric outpatients. *General Hospital Psychiatry, 11*, 188–193.

Wilson, M., & Daly, N. (1993). Spousal homicide risk and estrangement. *Violence and Victims, 8*, 3–16.

Wolraich, M., Lindgren, S. M., Stromquist, A., Melich, R., Davis, C., & Watson, D. (1990). Stimulant medication used by primary care physicians in the treatment of attention deficit hyperactivity disorder. *Pediatrics, 86*, 95–101.

Wyszynski, A. A., & Wyszynski, B. (1996). *A Case Approach to Medical-Psychiatric Practice.* Washington, DC: American Psychiatric Press.

Yesavage, J. A., Brink, T. L., & Rose, T. L. (1983). The geriatric depression rating scale: Comparison with other self reported psychiatric rating scales. In T. Cook, S. Ferris, & R. Bartus (Eds.), *Assessment in geriatric psychopharmacology* (pp. 37–49). New Cannan, CT: Mark Powley.

Zborowski, M. (1969). *People in pain.* San Francisco: Jossey-Bass.

Zung, W. K. (1965). A self rating depression scale. *Archives of General Psychiatry, 12*, 63–70.

Zybenko, G. S., George, A. W., Soloff, P. H., & Schulz, P. (1987). Sexual practices among patients with borderline personality disorder. *American Journal of Psychiatry, 144*, 748–752.

Index